Kellogg
on China

Dearest Jenny

With warmest wishes!

Kellogg on China

Strategies for Success

EDITED BY

Anuradha Dayal-Gulati
and
Angela Y. Lee

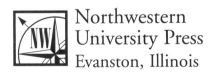
Northwestern
University Press
Evanston, Illinois

Kellogg
School of Management

Northwestern University Press
Evanston, Illinois 60208-4170

Printed in Canada

10 9 8 7 6 5 4 3 2 1

ISBN 0-8101-2225-1

Library of Congress Cataloging-in-Publication Data

Kellogg on China : strategies for success / edited by Anuradha
Dayal-Gulati and Angela Y. Lee.
    p. cm.
  Includes bibliographical references and index.
  ISBN 0-8101-2225-1 (trade paper : alk. paper)
  1. China—Foreign economic relations. 2. Business enterprises,
Foreign—China. I. Dayal-Gulati, Anuradha. II. Lee, Angela Y.
III. J.L. Kellogg School of Management.
HF1604.K45 2004
382'.0951—dc22
                                   2004011800

CONTENTS

TABLES AND FIGURES

TABLES

FIGURES

FOREWORD

I have been teaching business strategy for more than twenty years, so very few comments from my students really surprise me anymore. But a few years ago I was shocked by one of my graduate students, a young American executive who had just returned from Asia. This gentleman had earned a master's degree in business administration from one of the most prestigious business schools in the United States. I asked him how well he felt his business education had prepared him for the "real world" of international business. He proceeded, very bluntly, to tell me that everything he had learned in his top-rated M.B.A. program was utterly irrelevant in Asia—and especially, in China.

Perhaps I should not have been so surprised. His professors no doubt did their best to provide their students with the most effective business education grounded in a curriculum based on the most successful system they knew: the western, or American, system. In retrospect, both the school and its faculty can be excused for a bit of cultural and institutional tunnel vision. After all, the system of enterprise they took as their blueprint, that is, the American model, had created by far the most powerful economic engine in history.

We must remember, too, that only a few short years ago every western politician, business executive, and economist believed, quite firmly, that an unleashing of the merciful powers of capitalism would be the salvation of eastern Europe. It was widely held that once the political obstacles were removed, an American-style, market-based, profit-driven system of business and economic growth would simply replace the centrally planned economic systems behind the Iron Curtain. Unfortunately, when these countries did adopt capitalism, what occurred was not so much an ascent into a paradise of western-style consumerism, but rather a descent into a chaotic, Wild West kleptocracy (to borrow a term from Thomas Friedman) that very nearly brought the former Soviet states to their knees.

The Russian experience has been instructive: it signaled to business interests everywhere that the American model, at least in its purest form, might not be an appropriate socioeconomic model for all areas of the globe. China presents perhaps the most complex dilemma for western business interests, because it has so incredibly little in common with western Europe, the United States, or even Japan. The Chinese ethos—and Chinese business methods—present an entirely new set of challenges for western business managers and investors because the fundamental mismatch between West and East is not economic but cultural. More, the issue of China can no longer be avoided; China is already well on the road to economic superpowerhood. As one western businessman put it: "China is too complex to solve—but too big to ignore."

Indeed, it would be foolhardy to underestimate the potential economic impact of so vast a nation. Currently the world's fifth-largest trading power, China has averaged better than 7 percent real economic growth for each of the last twenty years. The country has become a veritable factory to the world, with a 50 percent share (as producer or consumer) in such industries as steel, textiles, and consumer electronics; it will soon occupy a commanding position in many more. Its 2003 agreement with the Association of Southeast Asian Nations (ASEAN) members creates a new economic entity that could develop into the world's largest free-trade zone, encompassing some two billion consumers and more than a trillion dollars in trade.

It is not surprising, therefore, that China has become a magnet for business interests worldwide. However, these investors and managers—including some of the most sophisticated and forward-thinking multinational corporations in the world—must prepare themselves to modify significantly their current definitions of business success. Indeed, China may be able to avoid many of the bumps and bruises suffered by Russia on the road to the free-market system. China, unlike Russia, will not adjust *to* western capitalism; rather, it will actually adjust western capitalism.

Consider the many ways in which China has already begun to influence capitalism as we know it. Currently, western investors are not confronted with pure socialism in China, but with a hybrid socialist-capitalist system: "a socialist market economy." This system is one shaped by institutional concerns rooted in thousands of years of Chinese history. It is, for instance, influenced by the country's personal and business connections and by an extensive network of overseas "business families" (which, incidentally, constitute a formidable economic power in their own right).

For the most part, western businesspeople have been raised to believe, almost unquestioningly, in the supremacy of their business culture and its practices. As financiers, investors, and managers, many have never worked outside the system into which they were born. Consequently, westerners tend to view China and the Chinese market not only as an alien system but also as one riddled with wrong-headed inconsistencies and contradictions.

In sharp contrast, the Chinese were raised in one economic system, were revolutionized into another, and watched as yet a third evolved. Their original business system derived from their care for relationship and respect for family, the fundamental social and economic unit. With the advent of socialism, the basic hierarchic structure remained intact, but patriarchal authority was ceded to the government. Some twenty-five years ago, China began its economic liberalization campaign, and modern western-style business ideas began to take root in the form of market socialism, a form of government-sanctioned entrepreneurialism. Now, having gained entry to the World Trade Organization (WTO), China seems to be gingerly approaching the adoption of a western-style economic system.

From the West, we see a fundamental contradiction in the Chinese "socialist market economy." For the Chinese, however, there is no contradiction. The traditional Chinese business yardstick (reinforced by more than fifty years of socialism) fully embraces multiple "bottom lines"—creating jobs, contributing to community well-being, maintaining good relationships with government at all levels and with customers of all kinds, and working to achieve long-term stability.

Undeniably, the American enterprise system has fueled the global economic engine, but to China (and most of the East), the system is too narrowly confined to economic spheres, with investors and financial interests dominating corporate, cultural, social, and governmental decisions. The effects of such a system are at times bizarre by Chinese standards: How can a company's value increase when it eliminates ten thousand jobs? The Chinese believe that development of their country must strive for economic efficiency—but not at the cost of social-political stability. Instead of overnight reform or immediate liberalization, they prefer patience, gradualism, and conservatism. The Chinese agree with Thomas Jefferson: Delay is preferable to error.

Perhaps the most challenging problem facing expatriate investors in China is not "market socialism" or even the fact that the underlying culture is foreign to their way of thinking. It is that, today, Chinese society and business seem to be in constant flux, a situation that presents tremendous uncertainties for business planners.

China's hybrid industrial system, for instance, is in constant tension, pulled one way by private enterprise, which employs 30 percent of the workforce and produces 70 percent of the goods, and another way by state-owned enterprises, which employ 70 percent of the workers to produce the other 30 percent of goods. As the economy continues its transition toward a market orientation, both enterprise types will undergo major changes as native Chinese managers are forced to focus less on production quotas and guaranteed employment levels and more on industrial efficiency and market development. Meanwhile, overall industrial planning in China (which until a few years ago aimed mainly at encouraging labor-intensive industries to maximize the country's labor cost advantages) has begun to concentrate on developing industries that demand highly skilled and educated workers.

Another challenging issue is China's entrance into the WTO, which western observers hailed as a great victory for the world economy. However, the issue of China's full engagement in the world economy brings with it a host of complex consequences, far beyond the merely economic. It must not be forgotten, either, that while China has become a formidable economic power in a short time, it is still hampered by inadequate infrastructure and vast differences in regional economic development. In addition, at this stage of its development, it remains heavily dependent on foreign investment.

As an example, this volume invites us to consider the special economic incentive zones developed throughout the country by the Chinese government. These zones, designed to attract investors, offer subsidies and special tax treatments for multinational corporations that choose to locate in the designated areas. But these zones had the effect of creating a dual tax system. As tariffs decline with WTO membership, this presents the government—and foreign investors—with a dilemma. Should the playing field be leveled and the incentives eliminated (thereby endangering future investment), or should all taxes be lowered to the rates in the incentive zones?

Furthermore, as more multinational corporations choose to locate in China, the overall competitive pressure will intensify, and the effectiveness of existing regulations and commercial laws will increasingly be called into question. In one example cited in this volume, a multinational corporation now complains that it is allowed to keep its young workers for only a few years, since Chinese law requires them to return to their native towns in the interior of the country. Such cross-currents present new and complex challenges to any company interested in participating in the Chinese economy.

Fortunately, there are encouraging signs that the Chinese system is incorporating new initiatives to make things easier for expatriate investment. As pointed out in the following chapters, Pudong, in response to the burgeoning software industry in the city, has become the first Chinese city to create an intellectual property division in its court system. In addition, the Chinese government is training provincial-level officials in WTO rules and regulations as they relate to foreign investment—a clear sign that we can expect increased transparency in bureaucratic decision making. Another signal to note is that China is opening wider its import doors, with its reduction of tariffs on Hong Kong imports and its ASEAN agreements. And there is a strong movement at the management level to meet the future needs of the country. As expatriate managers learn to work within the Chinese business culture, Chinese professionals, in record numbers, have begun to enroll in western-style and western university–affiliated M.B.A. programs.

Finally, one of the more encouraging signs is the publication of this volume—a clear demonstration that U.S. business schools not only recognize but celebrate the global opportunities and challenges China presents. (China is now among the leading countries hosting international study tours for many western M.B.A. programs.)

In what most people recognize as the typical "American" style, this book identifies the problems—but emphasizes solutions. This book is not an academic treatise but a close examination of the economy and a guide to its business practices. It is, in effect, "a how-to" manual based on practical, effective procedures of some of the multinational corporations that have proven successful in their Chinese business ventures. The material presented in these chapters includes strategic approaches to start-up situations as well as lists of simple but experience-proven "dos" and "don'ts" across a variety of industries. It should be noted that the book's survey of expatriate investors is designed to be useful not only for other foreign investment sources but also for Chinese officials who wish to find out what attracts and sustains western investment.

Without doubt, this book will be helpful to both sides of the cross-cultural business exchange. China's entrance into the WTO has exposed the gaps between eastern and western business practices and has demonstrated the need for a new, refined enterprise system to bridge the gulf and enable both Chinese and U.S. interests to conduct business on a truly global basis.

The Chinese way of doing business and China's "socialist market" economy will continue to challenge—and frustrate—many western businesspeople. It may also provide an opportunity for the development of a new sort of business model, one that could make "globalization" a reality instead of a bumper-sticker slogan. U.S. businesses can be justifiably proud of the accomplishments of capitalism. The system has worked wonders for two hundred years.

However, it must not be forgotten that Chinese business enterprises have also worked rather well—for almost five thousand years. Therefore, when we talk about China's emergence as an economic power, we should remember that from their point of view, the Chinese are thinking about their *re*-emergence.

To achieve genuine globalization, as well as strong relationships and an enduring presence in China and other emerging economies, business enterprises will need, ultimately, to develop programs able to balance the needs of a diverse array of interests and parties. As in diplomacy, so in business: While the two ways of doing business come into closer contact, the United States and China can accommodate and learn from each other and perhaps develop a common platform at the enterprise level—a platform that fully recognizes western and eastern institutions and differences and draws on their respective strengths.

As we view the world economy, it is clear that the two giants, China and the United States, must either become strategic partners or strategic competitors—or perhaps a combination of both. When will we know the outcome? As we remind ourselves that that the Chinese economic system is five thousand years old, going on twenty-five, we must give the same answer the Chinese ambassador gave to the French ambassador. At a state dinner, the Frenchman asked his Chinese guest, "What do you think about the impact of the French revolution?" The Chinese ambassador replied: "It's too early to tell."

Ming-Jer Chen

E. Thayer Bigelow Research
Professor of Business Administration

The Darden School,
University of Virginia

PREFACE

Since 1979, when China[1] emerged from its long isolation and launched the first of its economic reforms, the nation has changed dramatically. The country has gone from producing low-quality exports to manufacturing sophisticated high-technology goods and is now a major player in the world economy. China's share of global trade, just 1 percent in 1980, was around 6 percent in 2003. Its electronic exports account for nearly 30 percent of Asia's total exports in that sector, and China, including Hong Kong, is now the leading producer of several consumer electronic products. It is also the world's fifth-largest recipient of foreign direct investment, with an estimated US$450 billion that has flowed into the economy since the start of reforms in 1979.

With the Chinese economy experiencing annual average growth rates in excess of 7 percent over the last twenty years, China's transformation into a major economic power has far-reaching implications for the world and for global corporations. With its admission to the World Trade Organization (WTO), China is joining Japan, the United States, and the European Union in shaping the pattern of world trade and economic policy. Since the country's accession to the WTO, China's economy has continued to grow despite the recent global economic downturn, and its growth is sustaining prices for a wide range of industrial commodities and benefiting trading partners. Some observers have commented that China has become the new engine of global economic growth.

As China continues to implement the commitments agreed on as conditions of membership in the WTO, the environment for multinational corporations (MNCs) in China is changing rapidly.

Opportunities are opening up for multinationals, which are being allowed to operate on the same footing as domestic firms. Companies need to understand the implications of the changes that the WTO has wrought and the effects on their competitive advantage. China's manufacturing advantage can have a profound impact on the competitive capabilities of global corporations. Companies need to reassess their strategy in China and their China operations in the context of their global opportunities. The challenge for firms is to use China's manufacturing base not just to compete regionally and globally but also to compete successfully in its burgeoning domestic market. China is one of the world's largest potential markets in a wide range of consumer goods. As incomes of Chinese consumers rise, this potential is being transformed into market reality. China has high penetration rates for a wide range of consumer goods, although parts of the country, especially in the remote rural regions, are still preindustrial. The domestic market promises huge opportunities, and with WTO accession, key service sectors of the economy are being opened to foreign businesses. This change implies that foreign companies can now operate in areas such as banking, insurance, distribution, and other services from which they were previously barred. Competition for domestic market share is likely to be fierce, however. Although there is a move toward greater transparency and a dismantling of trade and investment barriers, there are still challenges to doing business in China, such as intellectual property violations, management constraints, and governmental interference, to name a few.

This book examines some of the changes China's accession to the WTO is bringing to different sectors of the Chinese economy, highlighting the changes in the market environment and the resulting challenges and opportunities that arise for companies doing business in China. A unique feature of this book is that it draws on extensive field research by graduate students at the Kellogg School of Management who visited China as part of Kellogg's Global Initiatives in Management (GIM) program. Established in 1989, the GIM program provides opportunities for students to pursue business-related research in emerging overseas economies. Working in conjunction with a Kellogg faculty adviser, these students conducted a wide range of interviews with Chinese corporate executives, government officials, and representatives of nongovernment organizations. Drawing on this research, the authors are able to provide insights into the current operating environment in China and suggest strategies for companies seeking to establish a sustainable competitive advantage in the country's evolving marketplace.

The book consists of four parts. The first part, "WTO Entry and a Changing China," examines the ramifications of China's entry into the World Trade Organization in 2001 in some key areas. Chapter 1, "China's Global Integration and the Impact of WTO Accession," provides an overview of the changes that China's entry into the WTO has brought to China as well as to the Asia-Pacific region as a whole. It discusses how the surge in foreign investment and the increase in imports and exports have redefined China's evolving relationship with the region. Chapter 2, "The Changing Nature of China's Economic Zones," discusses how the special economic zones are altering their value propositions to attract firms in key industries, such as information technology and pharmaceuticals. As Chinese tariffs are declining, in keeping with WTO commitments, the advantages of operating in the special economic zones are decreasing. Through an online survey, the authors document how foreign investors and the zones themselves are responding to these changes. Chapter 3, "Chinese Trading Companies: Creating New Value Propositions," discusses how trading companies can stay ahead by being innovative and maintaining a strong focus on their customers' needs. With China's accession to the WTO, foreign companies can establish their own trading operations, and buyers can bypass middlemen by establishing their own sourcing operations to improve their margins. This chapter shows how trading companies can take advantage of the rapidly changing environment to establish a viable and sustainable long-term advantage with the right strategy.

The second part of the book, "Managing and Maneuvering in the New Chinese Economy," suggests how western businesses should navigate in the new waters of the Chinese economy. As competition in the marketplace intensifies, corporations are prompted to adopt management styles that reflect western values and practices. Yet the cultural context in which these firms operate and the importance of *guanxi* ("relationships") cannot be ignored. Chapter 4, "Franchising as an Expansion Strategy in China," outlines the opportunities and challenges related to franchising. The authors offer strategic recommendations for companies contemplating entry as a franchisor on such important issues as choice of local partners, distribution networks, and financing. Chapter 5, "Overcoming the Leadership Gap," highlights the growing demand for leadership talent in multinational corporations as well as in Chinese corporations. This chapter discusses how businesses in China need to move away from a paternalistic style of leadership and identify managers with western management skills to compete in the evolving business environment. However, it is also critical that multinational companies adapt to various aspects of local management practices in order to be effective. Weak management is a major constraint that multinational corporations face, and this chapter provides recommendations on how companies can successfully meet the challenge. Chapter 6, "Combating Piracy through *Guanxi*," looks at the use of relationship building as a strategy to protect intellectual property rights and combat counterfeiting. Such tactics as frequent product releases, packaging changes, and raids all help combat counterfeiting in the short term. However, as counterfeiters become increasingly sophisticated, corporations need a long-term strategy to combat this trend. This chapter examines how multinationals are working to combat piracy through the Quality Brands Protection Committee (QBPC), a trade association formed by multinational corporations, and provides recommendations for developing an effective long-term strategy.

The third part, "Understanding Marketing in China," offers a fresh perspective to understanding marketing in China and provides insights into how foreign firms can overcome the cultural divide between their home base and their overseas market. The focus is on adapting western marketing strategies to the cultural and social preferences of the Chinese market. Chapter 7, "Sports Marketing in China," examines important cultural and socioeconomic dynamics and emerging trends in formulating and implementing a sports marketing strategy in China. In a country where consumers do not grow up playing sports and domestic professional leagues are still in a nascent stage of development, marketing campaigns and grassroots initiatives aimed to develop sports awareness and participation can be risky. This chapter analyzes the winning strategies of corporations such as Nike and Mild Seven and offers guidelines for companies to leverage sports as a promotional tool. Chapter 8, "Taking Global Brands to Local Success: Marketing Western Snack Foods in China," examines how market research that takes into account cultural considerations has enabled MNCs, such as General Mills and Frito-Lay, to successfully launch products that satisfy the local tastes and preferences regarding shape and size, flavor, product names, and packaging. Chapter 9, "The Challenge of Winning Local Clients for Multinational Advertising Agencies," outlines the current advertising and marketing landscape and analyzes key operating strategies to gain local clients and maintain sustainable growth. With a population of 1.2 billion, a liberalizing economy, and a rising middle class, China has emerged as the most exciting media market in the world. Although most aspects of the Chinese media industry remain closed to foreign investment, the advertising agency business in China stands as the stark exception, and multinational advertising agencies have been allowed to operate in China since 1986. However, the key to a viable practice is the ability to win local clients. This chapter first looks at the myths versus reality of a rapidly changing environment, then draws upon interviews with industry experts to develop a strategy for attracting local clients.

The fourth part, "Looking to the Future," examines two events that are shaping public perception of China. Chapter 10, "Delivering on the Dream: 2008 Olympics in Beijing," documents how China is preparing to host the important event through massive investments in infrastructure, specialized sporting facilities, and environmental initiatives. The chapter examines the potential legacy of these initiatives by drawing comparisons with the impact of past Olympics. The book concludes with chapter 11, "China: Coping with SARS." This chapter focuses on the impact of Severe Acute Respiratory Syndrome (SARS) on the Chinese economy. While the service industries in China were hard hit, the economy of China as a whole remained buoyant throughout the ordeal. Some even say that a stronger China emerged from the crisis because SARS has encouraged a higher degree of transparency in the Chinese government and hastened much needed public health and social reforms. More importantly, by prompting China to cooperate with other nations, SARS helped bring China closer to the rest of the world.

This is an exciting time for the world community. As China grows from strength to strength, the investment and involvement of western businesses will continue to help China define its role in the world community. This book is recommended to the next generation of managers whose job it is to stay abreast as the world realizes the China dream.

We would like to thank a number of people who have been instrumental in making this book a reality. First and foremost, we would like to thank the authors for their time and effort in making revisions and meeting deadlines. We would also like to thank Mark Finn, the director of the Global Initiatives in Management Program, for his unflagging support and encouragement for this book. We would also like to thank Sapna Gupta, Tom Truesdell, Regina Mckie, Alisha Fund, Maureen Vaught, Jean Hsu, Vanessa Del Campo, and Lisa Parikh, who assisted in preparing and editing these chapters for publication. We would also like to thank Donna Shear, director of Northwestern University Press, who guided us through this process. And, finally, we would like to thank Dean Dipak Jain, who provided the vision and support for this book.

NOTES

1. In the press and academic literature, the People's Republic of China may be referred to as the PRC, mainland China, or simply China. Taiwan may also be referred to in several different ways: Taiwan; Republic of China; or Taipei, China; or by some international organizations, such as the International Monetary Fund, as Taiwan, Province of China. Hong Kong after the handover to China in 1997, is referred to as Hong Kong, Special Administrative Region (SAR). In the interests of readability and consistency, throughout the book, we refer to the three economies as China, Taiwan, and Hong Kong, respectively

Kellogg
on China

PART 1

WTO ENTRY AND A CHANGING CHINA

Chapter 1

CHINA'S GLOBAL INTEGRATION AND THE IMPACT OF WTO ACCESSION

*Anuradha Dayal-Gulati and
Thomas Rumbaugh*

On December 11, 2001, China joined the World Trade Organization (WTO), marking the culmination of a fifteen-year quest for membership. Its accession is not an isolated event but rather is part of an ongoing process of integration into the global economy that China initiated in the late 1970s. Nevertheless, WTO membership does signify the beginning of a new stage in China's economic restructuring. It is also a political statement on the part of the Chinese leadership that the current policy of reform and opening up of the economy will continue and deepen. Membership indicates a broadening of trade reform from a policy that has been focused on special economic zones to a more comprehensive approach under which China will need to adhere to agreed timetables on further reform and market opening. Moreover, by joining the WTO, China has agreed to change its laws, institutions, and policies so that they conform with the norms of international trade. Reforms will increasingly be based on the rule of law, transparency, national treatment for foreign firms, and a closer adherence to international business practices.

What implications does this accession have for China and for the regional and global economy? This chapter provides an overview of the commitments China made as part of its entry into the WTO and the resulting changes membership has wrought in global and regional trade and production patterns. Since accession, China has seen rapid economic growth despite the unfavorable global economic environment. Rising profitability for foreign affiliates operating in China, increasing export and import growth, and growing domestic consumer demand have positively affected regional growth rates, sustained prices for a wide range of industrial commodities, and benefited trading partners. These trends suggest that China's sustained growth will continue to have a significant impact on the global economy.

We begin this chapter with an overview of China's commitments under the WTO and an assessment of its compliance so far; we will then discuss some of the challenges China faces as it tries to comply with the commitments made as a WTO member. Finally, we evaluate the regional and global impact of accession in terms of shifts in the patterns of production and trade.

China's WTO Commitments and Compliance

The changes in trade and investment policies that China has agreed to with its accession to the WTO will have far-reaching implications for China's economic structure and social outlook. The terms of accession include tariff reductions, elimination of nontariff barriers in industrial sectors, agricultural trade liberalization, and the opening up of major service sectors of the economy to foreign investment. The WTO agreement will also ensure greater access for China to the markets of industrialized countries, in part through the scheduled phasing out of import quotas on Chinese textiles and clothing by North American and European countries. The proportion of the state-owned economy, in terms of industrial output, dropped from more than three-fourths at the start of the reforms in the late 1970s to currently about one-third, and the proportion is likely to drop further as WTO accession brings a greater level of competition from foreign players to the domestic market.

China's commitment on trade in services represents a milestone; in fact, some observers have concluded that it represents the most radical services program negotiated to date as part of a WTO accession. The plans include the opening up of key service sectors where foreign participation was previously nonexistent or marginal, notably in telecommunications, financial services, and insurance. In those sectors, full access will eventually be guaranteed to foreign providers through transparent and automatic licensing procedures. The reforms encompass state monopoly sectors of the economy, such as power, civil airlines, and the railways. In these sectors, the government plans to increase competition and establish modern regulatory systems. China has also agreed to remove restrictions on trading and domestic distribution for most products. The overall breadth of trade reforms and market opening to which China has agreed stands in sharp contrast to the more limited reforms previously implemented by other East Asian countries.

In contrast to the path-breaking commitments in the services sector, China's commitments on tariff reductions under the WTO agreement are the continuation of a long-standing trend. For instance, in the 1990s, there were substantial trade reforms, which included tariff reductions and the dismantling of most nontariff barriers. As part of the accession process, this trend accelerated sharply after 2000. Consequently, the average tariff level has fallen from 43 percent in 1992 to 12 percent in 2002. By 2005, it is expected to fall further, to around 10 percent. China will also reduce and abolish nontariff measures such as licenses and quotas for imported products and other trading barriers.

As part of the conditions of membership, China has also made significant concessions in the agricultural sector. It has agreed to limit domestic agricultural subsidies to 8.5 percent of the value of production, which is less than the 10 percent limit allowed for developing countries under the WTO *Agreement on Agriculture*. In striking contrast with past commitments by other WTO members, it also agreed to eliminate all export subsidies upon WTO entry. The average tariff on imports will fall from 22 percent to 15 percent in trade-weighted terms, and this change is expected to lead to a major increase in imports in such areas as rice, wheat, corn, and cotton.

The government has also agreed to establish intellectual property (IP) laws and enforcement procedures that would comply with the WTO's Trade-Related Aspects of Intellectual Property Rights (TRIPS) agreement. This agreement entailed a commitment from the Chinese government to rewrite, add, or delete hundreds of IP laws and create a domestic IP regime that would live up to its WTO commitments. In addition, China has also established a chamber of specialized IP courts throughout the country.

INCREASED MARKET ACCESS FOR CHINA

The most immediate benefit of WTO accession for China is increased market access overseas. China is permanently granted most-favored-nation (MFN) treatment by other WTO members, which is a significant step in normalizing its trade relations. Although the impact of this change might appear to be limited because most countries had already granted China MFN access before its WTO accession, this status will no longer be subject to annual review in the United States, which is a significant step in improving investor confidence. Also, upon China's accession, several of its trading partners eliminated many of their restrictions on imports from China. In general, easier access to foreign markets is likely to boost China's labor-intensive exports in a number of sectors, including low- and medium-tech electronics.

Additionally, although China's clothing and textile exports have remained subject to sharp restrictions by countries in North America and Europe, the removal of these restrictions will most likely allow China to significantly increase its world export market share in these areas. However, the timing of such a benefit remains uncertain owing to safeguards that can be imposed by importing countries as part of China's accession protocol.

CHINA'S COMPLIANCE AND INITIAL WTO IMPACT

In the two years following entry, China made significant progress on its WTO commitments: it reduced import tariffs on schedule and even lowered tariffs ahead of schedule for certain products.

China also issued and revised legislation to meet its yearly commitments. In 2002, the government expanded the number of sectors open for foreign investment from 186 to 262 and increased the proportion of foreign shares in such service areas as banking, insurance, foreign trade, tourism, telecommunications, transportation, accounting, auditing, and legal affairs. It also granted foreign securities and fund-management firms permission to enter once off-limit markets through joint ventures.

When China entered the WTO, press reports and analysis were highly positive about the expected economic impact on China and the world. With annual economic growth rates of over 7 percent, China has been transforming a market potential of 1.3 billion consumers into market reality. It has one of the world's largest potential markets for a wide range of goods. Multinational companies were buoyed by China's entry and the market prospects resulting from proposed liberalization measures. Since China's accession, trade with China has expanded rapidly, largely because of the reduction in tariffs and the high rate of Chinese economic growth. While China's exports are growing, its imports from virtually every country in the world at all levels of development are also increasing rapidly. China is now the world's third largest importer of developing country exports after the United States and the European Union. Strong demand from China is also supporting prices for a wide range of industrial commodities. Table 1.1 shows how the United States, the European Union, Japan, and other Asian countries have significantly increased their share of exports to China since WTO accession. Exports to China from the United States rose by 22 percent in the first seven months of 2003 over the same period in 2002, and China is now the second largest trading partner of the United States after Canada. Agricultural exports from the United States to China increased by 139 percent in 2003 over the previous year. In contrast, exports from the United States to the rest of the world increased by only 3 percent in the same period.

The legal reforms China has implemented in conformity with WTO requirements have made it possible for foreign firms to set up wholly owned subsidiaries in China. In 2000, the total number

Table 1.1
Exports of Selected Countries to China (in percent of their total exports)

	1980	1985	1990	1995	2000	2002	2003*
Japan	3.9	7.1	2.1	5	6.3	9.3	11.1
Korea	0	0	0	7	10.7	12.8	16.2
European Union†	0.8	1.8	1.2	2	2.4	3.2	3.5
United States	1.7	1.8	1.2	2	2.1	3.2	3.6
Philippines	0.8	1.8	0.8	1.2	1.7	3.7	3.9
Thailand	1.9	3.8	1.2	2.9	4.1	5.2	6.9
Singapore	1.6	1.5	1.5	2.3	3.9	5.5	6.4
Indonesia	0	0.5	3.2	3.8	4.5	5.6	5.4
India	0.3	0.3	0.1	0.9	1.8	3.5	4.5

Source: Data from International Monetary Fund, Direction of Trade Statistics.
* Data for 2003 are for the first half of the year (January–June).
† Adjusted for intra-E.U. trade.

of companies wholly owned by foreign investors in China overtook the number of companies jointly owned by Chinese and foreign investors, and these firms accounted for 45 percent of the total capitalization of all companies with foreign investment. As China increasingly opens up sectors of the economy and lowers trade barriers, capital inflows have been surging, particularly into the manufacturing sector, with the services sector also beginning to increase. In keeping with increased investor confidence, net foreign direct investment (FDI) inflows rose to US$47 billion in 2002, an increase of 25 percent over the previous year. In 2003, net FDI inflows were estimated to be US$48 billion, Severe Acute Respiratory Syndrome (SARS) notwithstanding—about the same as recorded in 2002. Investment growth was estimated to be 28 percent higher in 2003 than in 2002, one of the highest in the world, although some analysts argue that some of the investment is inefficient and that the investment statistics may be inflated.

A survey of member companies released by the American Chamber of Commerce in Beijing in September 2003 noted that business conditions had improved significantly over the past five years and companies planned to expand their China operations. Growing confidence in the Chinese market also reflects the strength of the current leadership, its commitment to weed out corruption, and its willingness to create a level playing field over time.

IS THE WTO HONEYMOON OVER?

Despite these developments, some foreign investors who were China's biggest defenders before accession are turning into critics, complaining that the country is not fulfilling commitments it made under its historic entry in 2001. This criticism is coupled with a growing perception that the "honeymoon" period of adapting to WTO membership is ending as China struggles to implement reforms that are fundamentally altering the nature of its economic system.

Part of this altered view is driven by concerns that China has become a "sink for cheap labor" and is leading to a loss of jobs in the United States and other developed countries. Lost manufacturing jobs in the United States are being attributed to the country's soaring bilateral trade deficit with China, which increased from US$75 billion in 1999 to US$103 billion in 2002 and was US$124 billion in 2003. Although this number is substantial, it may well misrepresent the degree to which China is a threat. The way the U.S. trade deficit is calculated can be misleading: for example, sales made to U.S. customers by China-based affiliates of U.S. firms are counted as U.S. imports from China, whereas sales made to Chinese customers by China-based affiliates of U.S. firms are *not* counted as U.S. exports. The U.S. trade deficit with China also reflects a reorientation of production and trade within Asia (as discussed in a later section). In fact, China's overall trade surplus declined in 2003, as China recorded growing deficits with other Asian countries. Conversely, the U.S. overall trade balance with Asia has not changed much in recent years. In other words, U.S. imports from China have largely substituted for imports from other Asian countries, and therefore, rising trade with China cannot be viewed as responsible for job losses in U.S. manufacturing.

Other criticisms stem from the lack of progress in some areas of reform. Although China successfully completed its second annual implementation review by the WTO in December 2003, there are concerns about delays in the implementation of commitments on transparency (a term which denotes government consultation with affected parties in making new laws and regulations and publicizing them thereafter) and about enforcement issues in specific areas, such as agriculture, the financial sector, or intellectual property rights. Critics have accused China of raising new market barriers even as it lowers others. They argue that although China is reducing agricultural tariffs, it is imposing "unreasonable" quarantine inspections on some farm imports. In particular, U.S. and European business groups have argued that barriers to agricultural imports are more prevalent in China now than they were before its WTO entry. Other complaints relate to high capital requirements for setting up bank branches, even though foreign-owned banks and insurance companies are now permitted to operate in China. Another contentious area is trading and distribution rights. China is supposed to permit majority foreign ownership in trade and distribution ventures and to widen the number of products foreign companies can sell in the country. Full trading and distribution rights are to be implemented by December 11, 2004, but a key unresolved issue is just how imported products will be distributed in China.

THE CHALLENGES OF WTO ACCESSION

Chinese compliance with WTO commitments is likely to be tested continually in the future as China faces the challenges of accession. Analysts have argued that the reforms may not be sustainable owing to growing unemployment and resulting social unrest. In the context of the concessions China made as part of entry, we look at three specific issues China faces as it tries to balance increasing global integration with domestic constraints. First, we examine the challenges China faces with regard to implementation and enforcement—challenges that stem from the strength of vested interests. Second, we look at the implications for the agricultural sector from WTO accession, given the extensive opening of the agricultural sector and contentious trade relations in agriculture. Finally, we look at potential constraints on export growth resulting from the concessions to trading partners that China made in its accession agreement that go beyond the standard practices contained in the WTO *Agreement on Safeguards*. China faces many other challenges, including the fragility of its banking system, potential fiscal constraints, industrial restructuring, and risks of social unrest caused by increased unemployment and industrial and agricultural policies, but we do not focus on these in this chapter.

THE ROLE OF VESTED INTERESTS

Some observers believe that the delays in implementing China's WTO commitments in certain areas reflect, in part, technical difficulties arising from the change in national government administration in the spring of 2003 and from the SARS epidemic. However, the vested interests at various levels of provincial and municipal government, of government bureaucracies at every level, and of state-run monopolies and industries also play a role. Chinese leaders hope that admission to the WTO will provide momentum to the reform process. Their expectation is that the requirements imposed by membership will strengthen the hand of the central government in dealing with vested interests and other constraints at the local and provincial levels.

Although the regulatory and legal framework at the level of the central government has been extensively upgraded, progress is much more difficult at the provincial levels because local governments exercise a great deal of control. Administrative and judicial capacity constraints at various levels of government also hamper implementation and enforcement. There also appears to be growing protectionism on the part of government bureaucracies as they try to protect their powers and their own interests. One instance of conflicts between the national and provincial levels can be seen in the ineffective enforcement of intellectual property rights. To help overcome this, the Chinese government has been focusing on institutional "capacity building" by running courses for government officials at various levels to educate them about WTO requirements and commitments.

There has also been considerable resistance from such entrenched interests as state-owned enterprises and quasi-governmental associations, particularly with respect to banking, insurance, telecommunications, and the steel and auto industries. The strength of these entrenched interests can be seen where there are inconsistencies between the WTO accession agreement and China's national and provincial laws and regulations. For instance, when China joined the WTO, it agreed to increase ownership by foreign companies in express-delivery joint ventures over three years and to allow wholly foreign-owned subsidiaries within four years of accession. Yet, shortly after becoming a member, China unexpectedly introduced regulations that were designed to protect its postal monopoly, China Post, against competition, which adversely affected foreign express carriers operating in China. After intensive negotiations over several months by U.S., Japanese, and European authorities and WTO officials, the restrictions were lifted and a compromise was achieved.

These inconsistencies suggest that changes in key sectors are likely to occur incrementally and not dramatically. As ministries and local governments fight to retain their power and prerogatives, the introduction and enforcement of regulations are likely to become more difficult. Although foreign investors may have placed great expectations on China's WTO accession—whose impact certainly cannot be underestimated—it is nevertheless unlikely to solve the challenges of doing business in China in the near future.

RETHINKING AGRICULTURAL POLICY

Increasing openness in the agricultural sector as a result of WTO entry is expected to have a significant negative impact on rural workers. In the near-term, the Chinese government estimates that 13 million people are likely to lose their agriculture-related jobs— the majority of them in rural China. According to the European-based Organization for Economic Cooperation and Development, total agricultural employment is expected to fall by an estimated 75 million between 1997 and 2010. This loss may be offset to some extent by increased access to foreign markets for fruit, vegetable, and meat producers, creating, according to official estimates, two million jobs. However, the decline in agricultural employment creates the prospect for increased labor migration to urban areas, as well as the potential for rural unrest and political instability.

These overall potentially destabilizing changes require a shift in government strategy. For nearly a half-century, the government has favored industry over agriculture, and Chinese peasants have typically been forced to pay heavier taxes and grow grain crops for food security in the event of a western food embargo. They are also subject to a number of taxes, fees, and other charges that are locally and often illegally imposed. Consequently, there have been recurrent, though isolated, outbreaks of social unrest, particularly in the middle provinces that are further inland than the richer coastal areas. Of China's 328 million farmers, about 10 percent are officially considered poor, but independent observers believe this to be a drastic underestimate. Moreover, the rural-urban income gap has also been widening, with rural incomes only a third of urban incomes in 2001. From 1998 to 2002, the annual rate of growth of urban incomes—17 percent—far outpaced that of rural incomes, which grew by only 6 percent over the same period.

With huge rural-urban income disparities, rural residents have been flocking to urban areas over the past twenty years in search of higher incomes. This outflow of labor from agriculture will need to continue in order to improve rural incomes in a post-WTO environment. To make these pools of rural labor even more accessible to factories, ongoing investment in roads, power, and rural infrastructure is necessary. At the same time, restrictions on labor mobility, which have been an important part of labor markets in China, will have to be removed. In a move toward integrating the rural and urban labor markets, the State Council issued a directive in early January 2003 that eliminated regulations that discriminated against rural residents who had moved to urban areas. This directive gives legal migrants the right to work in cities and makes it easier for them to obtain residency permits.

In addition to increasing labor mobility and improving rural infrastructure, liberalizing crop distribution by phasing out state distribution companies and allowing farmers to switch from grain to more profitable crops may reduce some of the negative impact of WTO changes in the agricultural sector. Although some of these changes are already in evidence, there are also proposals in the pipeline to turn land use into a tradable asset. Land will still ultimately remain the property of the state, however.

Clearly, the road to agricultural prosperity is going to be far from smooth. China's farm exports, although increasing, still account for only a small amount of the country's exports. For instance, in the first half of 2003, farm products accounted for just over 5 percent of China's exports (with a value roughly equivalent to that of agricultural imports). In this context, China's attempt to balance increasing global integration against difficult domestic constraints is becoming a cause of contention in agricultural trade relations. In 2002, the United States and China argued over China's import regulations on genetically altered soybeans, a key U.S. export, and in the fall of 2003, China halted soybean imports from several countries, claiming that they were contaminated by a fungus. Observers noted, however, that the latter decision was timed to coincide with China's domestic soybean harvest. On the other side, Chinese officials have argued that technical trade barriers imposed by other countries affected 71 percent of Chinese exporters and caused US$17 billion worth of losses in 2002 alone. China has indeed been the recipient of such measures. For instance, Japan and the European Union recently banned several Chinese foods.

Despite these disagreements, agricultural imports into China have been increasing. For instance, U.S. soybean exports to China more than doubled in the first eight months of 2003. Of course, technical trade disputes between nations are not new, and with China's entry into the WTO, these conflicts can now be brought under the aegis of multilateral dispute settlement procedures. It remains to be seen, however, whether agricultural policy measures introduced by the Chinese government can raise rural incomes and head off political destabilization in the countryside while simultaneously facilitating the inevitable outflow of rural labor. Whereas farming groups in other parts of the world, including southeast Asia, have a strong influence on trade policies, the interests of China's 328 million farmers have generally been given lower priority than the national urban-dominated trade agenda. But, with WTO entry, this may yet change.

WTO Agreement on Safeguards

China's integration with the global economy is not unprecedented in its scope and speed. Japan and the Asian newly industrialized economies (NIEs) had rapid export growth and increased their share of world exports over an extended period. As Table 1.2 shows in some detail, Japan, some countries of the Association of Southeast Asian Nations (ASEAN), and the Asian NIEs maintained double-digit export growth on average for about a thirty-year period.[1] So far, China's exports, though increasing rapidly, have grown at a slightly slower rate than the earlier experience of these countries.

With its WTO accession, China may be well situated to continue its export growth. However, under the WTO *Agreement on Safeguards,* China's accession protocol incorporates highly discriminatory provisions that could constrain its export market gains in the coming years. The terms of the mechanisms under which these provisions or "safeguards" can be invoked are exceptionally favorable to China's partners. Therefore, potential actions by China's trading partners through invoking these provisions represent a downside risk that could both slow the future growth of China's exports and lead to retaliation by China (e.g., in the form of antidumping claims). A cycle of increasing protectionism that would lower trade volumes is thus possible even within the framework and procedures of the WTO.

One of the benefits for China of WTO accession is the phased removal of quotas against China's textiles and clothing exports. The phasing out of quotas on textile and clothing exports from developing countries is based on the Uruguay Round *Agreement on Textiles and Clothing* (ATC), which took effect in 1995. Although

Table 1.2
Average Annual Export Growth Rates
(percent change in export values in constant US$)

	*Period**	*Number of Years*	*Growth Rate*
Japan	1954–1981	27	14.2
Korea	1960–1995	35	21.5
Malaysia	1968–1996	28	10.2
China	1978–2002	24	11.9
NIEs	1966–1997	31	13.1

Source: Data from International Monetary Fund, Direction of Trade Statistics.
*Selected periods begin when sustained export expansion started and end when the three-year moving average export growth rate declined below 10 percent.

China was not part of the Uruguay Round, China has been included formally in the ATC as a consequence of its WTO accession. These quotas are bilateral, and the extent of their restrictiveness varies from country to country. Most of the restrictive quotas are likely to be removed only at the end of the ten-year transition period (1995–2005).

One of the WTO safeguards protecting China's trading partners includes a mechanism that allows countries to maintain quotas on textile and clothing imports from China until the end of 2008, even though under the Uruguay Round *Agreement,* such restrictions should be removed by the end of 2004. In fact, the United States proposed to impose quotas on some (relatively minor) categories of Chinese clothing exports in November 2003.

In addition to continuing quotas on textiles and clothing imports for some time, under the WTO *Agreement on Safeguards* a country may impose restrictions on imports if it can demonstrate that the imports clearly cause or threaten to cause "serious injury" to domestic firms producing similar products. In China's case, interpretation of "serious injury" has been replaced with the concept of "market disruption," which is a much lower threshold for imposing quotas within the context of the WTO agreement. Moreover, as part of China's accession agreement, these safeguard provisions can be invoked for a period of twelve years after entry instead of the usual eight and do not come with a requirement that they be removed gradually over time, as is required by standard WTO safeguards. In addition, instead of being implemented on a most-favored-nation basis (i.e., uniformly against all exporting countries), these safeguards can be implemented specifically against China. These product-specific safeguards can also be used in the case of textiles and clothing. Thus, if an importing WTO member (such as the United States) has experienced an increased share of imports for particular products coming from China, it could potentially impose quotas for twelve years (until 2013) without any obligation to gradually reduce the quotas in that twelve-year period.

With regard to antidumping safeguards, the mechanisms are again highly discriminatory against China. Under WTO rules, a product can be considered "dumped" if its export price is less than its "normal value" (generally defined as the comparable price for the product when it is destined for consumption in the exporting country) and if it creates a threat of material injury for the domestic industry. China, however, has agreed that WTO members could invoke the "non-market economy" provision to determine dumping cases for fifteen years following accession. The "non-market economy" provision states that in the case of imports from countries with state trading monopolies or domestic prices fixed by the state, a strict comparison with domestic prices may not be appropriate. Many experts contend, however, that price liberalization has proceeded so far in China that markets now set the price of almost all commodities. In practice, the "non-market economy" criterion may exempt countries from having to show that China is exporting goods at less than their "normal value." The investigating government is permitted to calculate what the price of Chinese goods "should be" based on manufacturing costs in a "surrogate" market economy country. In China's case, this surrogate is almost always India.

The Chinese Ministry of Foreign Trade and Economic Cooperation has estimated that Chinese exports have been the subject of nearly four hundred antidumping investigations in recent years. China hoped that WTO accession would protect it against such acts by developed countries, but in its first year as a member, Chinese exports were subject to more antidumping investigations around the world than any other country. In that year alone, there were forty-seven investigations of Chinese exports, and antidumping duties were levied in thirty-six cases. In response, China has begun exercising its own WTO rights. For instance, in March 2002, the country responded to the safeguard measures the United States took on steel exports by imposing its own tariff quotas on U.S. steel products. It also formally challenged the U.S. measures before a WTO dispute panel in Geneva.

As Chinese producers face increasing competition from foreign imports, Chinese industries are beginning to strike back through the country's own antidumping provisions. Of the twenty antidumping cases that China initiated against foreign imports since 1997, fourteen were initiated in 2001–2002 and nine in 2002 alone, that is, since China's WTO entry. Most of these cases against foreign firms involved steel and chemical imports and targeted neighboring countries, such as Taiwan, Japan, and South Korea. Dumping cases against foreign goods in China are now often initiated by state-owned enterprises struggling to survive in China's new market-oriented and competitive environment. These measures are typically not imposed on imports that are reprocessed and then turned into Chinese exports, which is in accordance with the WTO Antidumping Agreement that excludes reprocessed goods. On the whole, however, the Chinese government has encouraged Chinese exporters to defend trade investigations more aggressively since China's WTO entry.

China-"centric" Trade: The Global Impact of Accession

Prior to its entry, China was the largest economy outside of the WTO; in fact, its imports and exports have grown faster than world trade since the late 1970s. Increasing global integration initiated over the past two decades is reflected in China's rising share in global trade, which increased from 1 percent in 1980 to over 5 percent in 2002 (Table 1.3) and was approaching 6 percent in 2003. It has been estimated that China's accession to the WTO and the resulting increase in foreign direct investment would add approximately half a percentage point to the annual growth of the Chinese gross domestic product (GDP) in the first five years following accession. In addition, a World Bank study estimates that China's share of world trade may increase to nearly 10 percent by 2020, which would make it the world's second largest trading nation after the United States.

Studies on the impact of China's WTO accession have generally concurred that it would benefit the world as a whole. In the short to medium term, advanced economies and the most advanced developing countries would benefit most, mainly due to improved access to China's agricultural markets, increased exports to China of capital and technology-intensive manufactures, and increased trade and investment opportunities in China's service sectors. The countries most adversely affected by China's WTO accession are those

Table 1.3
Shares of Selected Countries in World Exports (in percent)

	1980	1990	2000	2002	2003*
China	1.0	1.9	3.9	5.1	5.8
Germany	10.5	12.1	8.6	9.4	9.2
Japan	7.1	8.5	7.5	6.5	6.4
Korea	1.0	2.0	2.7	2.5	2.5
NIEs	3.2	8.1	10.4	9.7	8.8
United States	12.0	11.6	12.1	10.8	10.4

Source: Data from International Monetary Fund, Direction of Trade Statistics, and CEIC Database, Inc.
* Data for 2003 are for the first half of the year (January–June).

that are direct competitors with China, such as those in the clothing sector.

As noted earlier, WTO-related trade liberalization has led to an increase in imports from virtually every country in the world. For instance, energy and mineral imports have increased rapidly and are expected to continue to do so, providing benefits to resource-rich countries. Within Asia, most of the countries are benefiting from rapidly increasing exports of intermediate products and components to China for processing. In addition, China's imports for domestic use have been increasing rapidly, and the country is now a leading international importer for both industrial and consumer goods. Thus, sustaining China's growth momentum should benefit all of its trading partners, especially countries with export patterns that closely match China's import demands.

Increased access to foreign markets has boosted China's labor-intensive exports in a number of sectors, particularly low- and medium-tech electronics. Once all restrictions on its clothing and textile exports have been removed, China could significantly increase its world export market share in these industries as well. The rapid increase in China's footwear exports, which are not subject to quota restrictions, provides an indication of the potential impact of China's inclusion in the Uruguay Round ATC. Whereas China's world export market shares in textile and clothing products remained at about 15 percent from 1990 to 2002, its market share in footwear increased from 7 percent to 28 percent.

Several other indicators already point to the potential for a substantial increase in China's exports when quota restrictions are lifted. For instance, quotas that accounted for just 15 percent of restrictive quotas and an even smaller percentage of China's total exports of textile and clothing were eliminated at the beginning of 2002. Since then, China has increased its exports to the United States in these categories by over US$1 billion, while the rest of the world collectively experienced a decrease of an equivalent amount. Economies that have shared in this decrease include such mature exporters as Hong Kong, Korea, and Colombia, as well as such emerging exporters as Cambodia and Bangladesh. So far, the effects have been small as a proportion of total global trade in textiles and clothing, but they could be considerably larger if the remaining textile and clothing quotas are removed at the beginning of 2005.

The Regional Impact of WTO Membership

With an annual average rate of growth of more than 7 percent over the last twenty years, the Chinese economy has outpaced every other economy in the region. Low wages, fueled by an abundant labor supply and increasing amounts of investment, have led to rapid export growth. As China's trade with the rest of the world has risen, its export market shares to industrial economies have increased, and exports to these markets have become more diversified. Exports from China to Japan, the European Union, and the United States have shown particularly sharp increases since the early 1990s (Table 1.4). China's growing global export share, however, has in most cases displaced the exports of other countries in the region to the advanced economies. The impact of China has been felt as far away as Mexico, where Royal Philips Electronics closed two-thirds of its television product lines in the summer of 2002 and relocated them to China.

China's growth has imposed broad structural changes across Asian economies, changes that are likely to continue after its WTO accession. Many of these changes began in the decade prior to accession, as manufacturing shifted from parts of southeast Asia to China. For instance, soon after China opened its doors in the

Table 1.4
China's Market Share in Major Export Markets (imports from China divided by total imports, in percent)

	1980	1990	1995	2000	2001	2002	2003*
Japan	3.1	5.1	10.7	14.5	16.6	18.3	18.8
United States	0.5	3.2	6.3	8.6	9.3	11.1	11.3
European Union	0.7	2.1	3.8	6.2	6.7	7.4	6.9

Source: Data from International Monetary Fund, Direction of Trade Statistics.
* Data for 2003 are for the first half of the year (January–June).

1980s, there was a mass influx of manufacturers, first from Hong Kong and then from Taiwan, to the southern China coast.

Mainland China has also replaced both Taiwan and Korea as the major U.S. footwear supplier and Taiwan, Korea, and Hong Kong as the major U.S. supplier of toys, games, and sporting goods. Increased U.S. imports of information technology products from China have also replaced imports from other Asian countries. Specifically, while the share of U.S. computer imports from China increased from almost nothing in the 1990s to 15 percent in 2003, the share for Japan, Singapore, and Taiwan decreased from 70 percent to 40 percent. In 2002, China overtook the United States as Taiwan's biggest export market and has passed Taiwan in the production of information technology products, desktop personal computers (PCs), optical drives, and liquid crystal displays.

Much of this rapid manufacturing growth in textiles, toys, and electronics in China was driven by the relocation of production facilities from Hong Kong and Taiwan; as a result many of the benefits flow to the Taiwanese companies that control 70 percent of the output. Talent from Taiwan and Hong Kong has also been instrumental in China's ability to maintain high rates of growth and plays an important role at multinational plants and research labs, such as Cisco Systems, Ford, Nokia, Sony, and Motorola.

With WTO accession, the economic integration of Taiwan, Hong Kong, and mainland China is creating a boom that is attracting huge amounts of technology, capital, and skilled immigrant labor from all over the world. In addition, Taiwan is establishing high-tech companies on the mainland, while companies from Hong Kong are moving into the inner provinces. As these developments continue, the share of world trade accounted for by mainland China, Taiwan, and Hong Kong (excluding trade between them) is expected to expand significantly; in five years, the combined share of world exports for these countries is expected to overtake Japan's, and their combined economic size is expected to nearly match that of the European Union.

China has become an important export destination, especially for regional economies. Reflecting the importance of the reprocessing trade, for every dollar of processed exports, China imports 92 cents. These imports represent a growing trend of intra-Asian trade that is reshaping the region into a China-centric economic zone (Table 1.5). In the decade prior to the Asian economic crisis in 1997, trade within Asia grew faster than any other component of Asian exports, and by 2001, intraregional exports accounted for 34 percent of the region's total exports. WTO accession has opened up the huge Chinese market to Asian imports (among others), and it has also opened up previously closed sectors of the economy. Consequently, the change in the regional economic landscape that began prior to China's WTO accession has quickened, reflecting increased vertical specialization of production in Asia as well as increased domestic demand in China.

Although China could be a direct competitor to Asian regional economies in the future, the threat posed by China is likely to be superseded by the benefits to the region from increasing vertical specialization. The growth of vertical specialization can be seen from several indicators: (1) strong FDI inflows from industrial

Table 1.5
China—Imports by Region and Country
(imports by China as a percent of total imports)

	1980	1990	1995	2000	2001	2002
Asia	15.7	41	47.1	50.6	49.1	58.1
ASEAN	3.4	5.6	7.4	9.8	9.4	9.0
Taiwan	—*	—	11.2	11.3	11.2	12.9
Korea	—	0.4	7.8	10.3	9.6	8.7
Japan	26.5	14.2	21.9	18.4	17.6	16.1
United States	19.6	12.2	12.2	9.9	10.8	8.8
European Union	15.8	17	16.1	13.7	14.7	12.9

Source: Data from International Monetary Fund, Direction of Trade Statistics, and CEIC Database, Inc.
*Dashes indicate data not available.

economies and the NIEs of Asia, (2) a high share of imports for processing embodied in China's exports, (3) a rapid increase in imports of electronic integrated circuits and microassemblies—key components used in the assembly of electronic products, and (4) changes in the pattern of trade, with imports from Asia increasing and exports going more and more to the United States and the European Union. Following China's entry into the WTO, the ASEAN countries have scored steady surpluses in trade with China. Furthermore, imports for processing (and reexport) increased from about 35 percent of all imports in the early 1990s to about 50 percent in 1997 and have remained at about that level since.

Instead of manufacturing products at a single location and shipping the finished product to end markets, manufacturers in Asia increasingly divide production processes among themselves. This shift in production patterns is reflected in the huge increase in the volume of Chinese trade in 2002 and 2003, which is straining the capacity of China's ports but has also been instrumental in reviving the flagging global shipping industry. The growth in trade appears to run well above apparent rates of consumption around the world and above the increases in China's market share that had been expected. Increased levels of specialization boost trade and aggregate exports because raw materials and product components may cross borders several times before they find their way to the end market.

As China continues to implement changes in keeping with its WTO commitments, both its attractiveness to international investors and its growing role as an export base are likely to increase. Although China's development could potentially hurt the economies of such countries as Thailand, Indonesia, the Philippines, and other exporters of labor-intensive products at similar stages of development as China, fewer restrictions on trading and more efficient and specialized production lines should positively impact the Asian region overall. For instance, most of China's increased information technology production requires high-value-added parts and components that are mainly produced in other Asian countries. So, although China is replacing some of its neighbors as the major technology products exporter, it is simultaneously creating a greater high-value-added parts economy in those countries as well.

Countries in this region will therefore have to take steps to ensure that they continue to move up the value chain from low-tech manufacturing to higher value-added products.

Growing benefits to the Asian region will also be driven by increased domestic demand in China. The expanding middle class of China is expected to be a major source of revenue for ASEAN states. For instance, outbound Chinese tourism increased by 37 percent in 2002, providing an economic boost to regional economies. Although the Asian region remains dependent on exports to the G-7 markets, increased trade with China has contributed to the ability of the region to maintain strong growth despite low growth in the rest of the world.

CONCLUSION

Despite an unfavorable global economic environment, WTO accession has provided further impetus to China's rapid growth. China's progress in reducing tariffs and opening up sectors of the economy has been remarkable. Rising profitability for foreign affiliates, increasing export and import growth, and strong domestic consumer demand indicate the growing importance of China's sustained growth for the global economy as well.

For China, the perpetuation of this growth is critical to managing the problems of both economic restructuring and agricultural and urban unemployment. Despite China's high global rank in terms of GDP and trade, Chinese annual per capita income is still below US$900. According to the World Bank, China has an estimated 16 to 18 million unemployed urban workers, while total surplus labor in the rural sector is estimated to be about 140 million.

Structural obstacles potentially restricting the sustainability of China's economic growth need to be addressed. For instance, the auto, aluminum, petrochemical, cement, light industry, and steel industries are plagued by excess capacity and inefficiency. The ability of the industrial sector to restructure successfully will be critical in ensuring continued growth in a stable environment. Moreover, as the strategic adjustment of the state sector continues and state-owned enterprises are edged out of their markets, rising unemployment could lead to social disruption and the possibility of policy reversals. Opening up of the Chinese economy, however, should generate employment in labor-intensive industries.

To tackle these problems, further efforts must be made to deepen reforms and improve China's socialist market system. Trading partners should encourage China's implementation of its WTO commitments and monitor its compliance closely rather than resorting to the extensive WTO safeguard provisions and antidumping measures that risk generating rising protectionism on the part of all parties.

NOTES

Thomas Rumbaugh is currently deputy chief of the China Division at the International Monetary Fund's Asia and Pacific Department. He has worked extensively on a wide variety of countries throughout Asia over the last fifteen years, including Indonesia, Malaysia, Thailand, Singapore, Sri Lanka, Nepal, Cambodia, and China. He received his Ph.D. from the University of Maryland. The views expressed in this chapter are those of the authors and do not necessarily represent those of the International Monetary Fund.

1. The NIEs of Asia are Taiwan, Singapore, Korea, and Hong Kong. The Association of Southeast Asian Nations was established in August 1967 in Bangkok by the five original member countries, namely, Indonesia, Malaysia, Philippines, Singapore, and Thailand. Brunei Darussalam joined on January 8, 1984; Vietnam on July 28, 1995; Laos and Myanmar on July 23, 1997; and Cambodia on April 30, 1999.

BIBLIOGRAPHY

Brahm, Laurence J. 2001. *China's Century: The Awakening of the Next Economic Powerhouse.* Singapore: John Wiley and Sons.
Cheng, Joseph Y. S. 2003. "Regional Impacts of China's WTO Membership." *Asian Affairs: An American Review,* 29 (4):217–37.

"China: Forgotten Farmers Given Chance to Catch Up." 2003. *Oxford Analytica Daily Brief,* January 24.

Crampton, Thomas. 2003. "A Strong China May Give Boost to Its Neighbors." *International Herald Tribune,* January 23.

Gilley, Bruce. 2001. "Farmers Need Freedom to Grow." *Far Eastern Economic Review,* 164 (47):36–38.

Gooley, Toby B. 2002. "China: Reforms May Take Awhile." *Logistics Management,* 42 (2):47–51.

Hsuing, James C. 2003. "The Aftermath of China's Succession to the WTO." *Independent Review,* 8 (1):87–113.

Lardy, Nicolas. 2002. *Integrating China into the Global Economy.* The Brookings Institution.

Mar, C. M. Pamela, and Frank-Jurgen Richter. 2003. *Enabling a New Era of Changes.* Singapore: John Wiley and Sons (Asia).

Murphy, David, Murray Hiebert, and Margot Cohen. 2003. "The Fine Art of Failure." *Far Eastern Economic Review* (Hong Kong), (Sept. 25), 166 (38):24.

Roberts, Dexter, Mark L. Clifford, Bruce Einhorn, and Pete Engardio. 2002. "Greater China." *Businessweek,* December 9.

Rumbaugh, Thomas, and Nicholas Blancher. 2004. "China: International Trade and WTO Accession." IMF Working Paper 04/36.

Tseng, Wanda, and Markus Rodlauer, eds. 2003. *China: Competing in the Global Economy.* Washington, D.C.: International Monetary Fund.

The US-China Business Council. 2003. "China's WTO Implementation: A Mid-Year Assessment." http://www.uschina.org/.

Wonacott, Peter. 2002. "China's Consumer Is Starting to Feel the Impact of WTO." *Wall Street Journal,* August 6.

———. 2003. "U.S. Pursues a Trade Ally in Beijing." *Wall Street Journal,* February 18.

Wonacott, Peter, and Phelim Kyne. 2003. "In Shift, US Investors Intensify Criticisms of China's Trade Policies." *Wall Street Journal,* October 6.

The World Bank. 1997. *China 2020: China Engaged.* Washington, D.C.: The World Bank.

Yang, Yongzheng. 2003. "China's Integration into the World Economy: Implications for Developing Countries." IMF Working Paper 03/245.

Yi, Kei-Mu. 2003. "Can Vertical Specialization Explain the Growth of World Trade?" *Journal of Political Economy,* 3 (1).

Zebregs, Harm. 2004. "Intraregional Trade in Emerging Asia." IMF Policy Discussion Paper.

Chapter 2

THE CHANGING NATURE
OF CHINA'S ECONOMIC
ZONES

*Rodrigo Cejas Goyanes, Luciane
Gallucci, Dean Lindo, Timothy
Riitters, and Attila Toth*

In the early 1980s, leaders in the Chinese Communist Party realized that international trade and commerce had the potential for improving the overall economic situation of China. They also recognized that by inviting investors into the country, they could learn about their technologies and business practices. Perhaps the single most important step these leaders took in fostering a more open economy was the creation of special economic zones (SEZs). The zones allowed the government to try out unconventional market-oriented techniques to promote economic development in limited geographical areas. If the measures were successful, they could be extended to other areas of the country and ultimately throughout the entire country. Conversely, if specific measures proved disastrous, the overall effect on China could be minimized. This gradual approach would enable the country to become more open and efficient while avoiding unnecessary economic and social instability.

China initially promoted these economic zones to attract foreign firms; however, with its accession to the World Trade Organization (WTO), the value propositions of the special economic zones are being altered. Through an online survey and interviews with corporations doing business in China, we look at how the zones can remain relevant in a post-accession environment.

In the late 1970s, the first four SEZs were developed, all located along the southeastern coast of the country (Figure 2.1). The first, Shenzhen, remains the largest today. The SEZs were structured to include a wide range of activities, such as agricultural and industrial projects, financial and banking services, real estate developments, tourist facilities, research and development establishments, educational institutions, and housing. However, the primary focus of SEZ development was building the country's industrial sector. Initial SEZ goals were to (1) attract and utilize foreign capital in a wide range of projects (not only trade-oriented projects); (2) acquire advanced foreign production and managerial technologies; (3) develop an ample economic structure to support general urbanization; (4) encourage foreign trade by promoting the advantages of the region; and (5) gain experience in economic reforms.

The focus of the SEZs was to attract both local and foreign investment. The areas showed a great degree of flexibility in attracting businesses and allowing different types of arrangements for foreign investors, such as joint ventures (JVs), wholly owned foreign enterprises (WOFEs), and coproduction with local partners. This experiment was the first time that China had allowed such flexible arrangements for foreign entities. More significantly, the zones provided investors with specific benefits that were not generally available in other parts of the country. Some of these policy incentives included duty-free privileges, tax concessions, preferential fees for land and facility use, and flexible treatment in employment and wage schemes. For instance, foreign investors were often offered tax breaks of up to 50 percent off the official national rate and multiyear tax holidays as an incentive to locate in an SEZ. Within a short period of time, these incentives along with infrastructure improvements and a legal and administrative system favoring the establishment of private and JV enterprises led to a flood of foreign investment. In Shenzhen, foreign capital investment grew from US$27 million in 1980 to over US$1 billion by 1993.

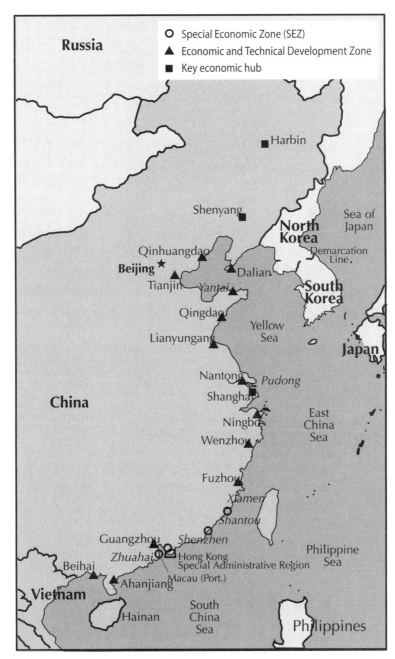

Figure 2.1: Economic Zones in China

Source: Modified from illustration in "Atlas of Understanding," found at Eastwest-Global.com. Used with permission.

CHINA'S ECONOMIC ZONES

China has experienced significant success with its SEZs—real gross domestic product (GDP) grew at an annual rate of 39 percent in Shenzhen from 1980 to 1993. However, the zones have not been without problems. Congestion has been a significant issue and has added to the cost of operating there. For instance, the population density in Shenzhen was 3,600 inhabitants per square mile in 1993—two to four times the population density of the country's fourteen other major coastal cities.

In addition, wages also increased exponentially during this time (Figure 2.2). Although these increases are beneficial from a social welfare standpoint, wages have increased so substantially and rapidly that they may be a concern for foreign investors who are considering a move to the SEZs. Other costs of operating in the zones have also risen sharply, most notably lease costs for commercial office and manufacturing space.

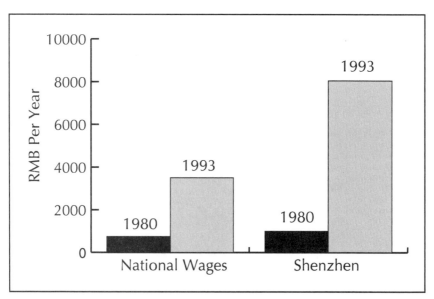

Figure 2.2:   Comparison of National Wages and Wages in Shenzhen SEZ: 1980 and 1993

Source: Data from Ge 1999.

Nevertheless, the success of these zones, particularly Shenzhen, led to the creation of a whole host of smaller, more focused SEZs in the 1980s and 1990s. For instance, China created economic and technological development zones (ETDZs) to focus on developing the country's high-technology capacity. There also was a proliferation of industrial parks, industrial zones, and development zones that granted local authorities the ability to approve foreign investment and provide special benefits and incentives. In the early 1990s, China also launched the Pudong New Area, which was established near Shanghai. The central government specially designated this area as the primary location to continue the impressive economic transition that started in Shenzhen. The scale of the proposed expansion was enormous. Establishing the Pudong New Area was a grand, bold strategic policy initiative to push ahead with China's economic transition, and it was conducted on a massive scale. In comparison, the four SEZs set up in the late 1970s and the early 1980s were small, experimental steps toward opening the economy.

With the experiences of the other SEZs in mind, the Chinese government created a massive ten-year plan to develop an entirely new suburb to the east of the old city of Shanghai. For nearly three years beginning in 1992, the government focused on completing several key infrastructure initiatives, including the construction of major river crossings, new roads, and updated utilities. With the infrastructure in place, the city then focused on developing the office building and manufacturing facilities necessary to propel Pudong forward.

Although widely regarded as the "sixth SEZ," Pudong is technically not an SEZ. Nevertheless, the area enjoys many of the incentives and benefits offered by the other SEZs, such as tax holidays and exemptions, land use incentives, customs duty privileges, streamlined application and registration procedures, and a high-quality business infrastructure. As most people we talked to in China indicated, the only difference between Pudong and the SEZs is the SEZ label.

To minimize confusion, we use the term economic zones (EZs) to refer to all special preferential zones in the Chinese economy, including SEZs, new areas, ETDZs, and all other zones. Our discussions, however, focus mainly on the five SEZs and Pudong, where the bulk of economic activities within China's economic zones takes place.

WTO IMPACT ON ECONOMIC ZONES

Real estate prices, substantial congestion, and significant wage pressures relative to other parts of China have increased the cost of operating in an EZ. China's membership in the WTO is compounding the zones' challenges and is likely to have a significant impact on the current operations of China's EZs. With China's accession to the WTO, the Chinese government is trying to unify income tax rates for domestic and foreign companies. Since their inception, China's EZs have attracted significant amounts of foreign investment by offering tax incentives. Foreign enterprises enjoyed a 15 percent income tax rate versus the standard national rate of 33 percent, and tax holidays of two to three years were common throughout the 1980s and 1990s. These incentives have softened to some extent the rising costs of operating in the EZs. With the new policy, however, this dual tax scheme may no longer exist. China faces the option of reducing the tax rate outside the zones to 15 percent or raising the tax rate in the EZs.

It is unlikely that the country can afford to lose its attractiveness to foreign investors by raising their tax rates to the level domestic firms face. Peter Wonacott, economic correspondent for the Beijing bureau of *The Wall Street Journal,* believes that the Chinese government would rather offer some tax breaks to national companies than take them away in their entirety from foreign investors. At this stage of its economic development, China is very dependent on foreign investment and may be reluctant to jeopardize this investment by changing its tax policies. Thus, although a reduction in the overall tax rate would be very expensive to China, the government may take this course of action to ensure high levels of foreign investment in the country. A 2001 report by the accounting firm Andersen notes that in the near future the Chinese authorities are likely to set a common national tax rate of 25 to 30 percent and completely eliminate the preferential tax holidays and incentives for foreign investors.

How does the dismantling of these incentives affect China's EZs? Some argue the loss of various incentives will cause foreign firms to locate in other parts of the country or, even worse, in other parts of Asia. There are others, however, who believe that China's accession to the WTO will *not* be the end of the EZ concept but will instead require the government to rethink the value proposition the EZs offer to potential investors. Indeed, there are voices on both sides of the debate.

We now look at how large EZs, and specifically the Pudong New Area, are altering their value propositions to meet these potential challenges. Our reason for choosing Pudong is twofold: First, it is the second-most developed EZ in the country after Shenzhen, and second, it is the most recent large-scale EZ, developed almost twenty years after the first EZs. We set out to answer the question of whether China's accession to the WTO would sound the death knell for special economic zones. In the course of our research, we spoke with foreign investors as well as EZ officials to learn their opinions on this subject, conducted an online survey of over two hundred foreign investors regarding their past and future investment decisions in China, and interviewed government officials and multinational corporations (MNCs) currently operating in China to examine what factors will be important in their future decisions regarding expansion in China. The information presented in this chapter will give firms a better understanding of the implications of WTO accession on their investment decisions in China's EZs.

THE EXPERIENCE OF PUDONG

Wei Chang Ming, director of the Economic and Trade Bureau of Shanghai Pudong New Area, noted that during the past twelve years, Pudong has experienced incredible growth along virtually every economic dimension. The area is home to hundreds of multinational firms in a diverse set of key industries, such as financial services, high technology, and pharmaceuticals. Large Chinese firms, including Legend Computers and Shanghai Automotive Industry Corporation (SAIC), also have a significant presence in the city. One of the innovative approaches the area has taken is to develop four distinct EZs within its boundaries. Each one of these zones is responsible for focusing on the needs of a specific type of investor. The multizone concept provides for a focused working relationship with the government and peer companies within the zone. Table 2.1 describes the four zones in Pudong.

Figure 2.3 shows the incredible pace at which change has taken place in Pudong over the past decade. The GDP of Pudong New Area increased from RMB 6 billion to well over RMB 90 billion in just a decade.

ALTERING THE VALUE PROPOSITION

With the tremendous growth of Pudong as a backdrop, we set out to understand how EZs like Pudong are altering their value proposition in the wake of China's WTO accession.

Officials, including Pudong New Area's Wei and David Lee from the Chinese Ministry of Foreign Affairs, acknowledge that accession to the WTO poses some challenges. However, Wei and his counterparts do not seem troubled by the new WTO stipulations. They certainly do not view China's entry into the WTO as the "death knell" for Pudong and other economic zones; instead, they

Table 2.1
Pudong New Area's Four Subzones

Subzone Name	Subzone Focus and Comments
Lujiazui Financial and Trade Zone	The focus is on banking, investing, and related financial business services.
Jinqiao Export-Processing Zone	This is the new area's primary manufacturing zone. It is designed to attract companies in such key industries as autos, steel, chemical, and computer hardware. (This zone has evolved into a center for both domestic and export manufacturing.)
Waigaoqiao Free Trade Zone	The focus is on warehousing and international trade export processing.
Zhangjiag High Tech Park	The focus is on software, pharmaceuticals, and biotechnology companies. This is the newest of the areas and is not as developed as the other zones.

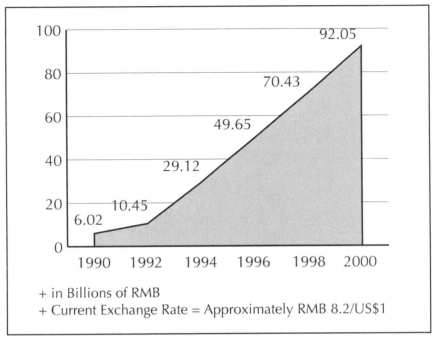

Figure 2.3: GDP of Pudong New Area over Time

Source: Data from Economic and Trade Bureau of Shanghai Pudong New Area 2001.

believe the relatively large and established EZs will continue to flourish. They point out that although the tax holidays and other related preferential policies will ultimately fade away, grandfather clauses and potential lengthy implementation periods will still make these incentives attractive to at least a portion of future investors in Pudong.

Nevertheless, these officials acknowledge that the loss of incentives will hurt some of the zone's business. They also recognize that land and labor costs in the region have risen dramatically, adding to the cost of doing business there. Wei believes that the areas in and around Pudong probably will not attract labor-intensive or low-value-added enterprises, but that Pudong will still be able to attract high technology, high-value-added, and capital-intensive foreign investment. "Over the next several years, we see the quality of corporate investment in Pudong continuing to improve," he has noted. This view is based on the belief that the zones possess attributes that will keep them vibrant in the future, such as a significant amount of physical infrastructure, efficient government and administrative structures, access to a skilled workforce, transparent laws and regulations, and experience in dealing with foreign investors. The area's focus on labor-intensive industries has lessened, and instead, Pudong is now keen to attract more financial and professional service firms, pharmaceutical companies, and advanced manufacturing organizations.

To enhance what Wei calls the quality of investment in the area, Pudong has crafted a two-pronged promotional strategy, consisting of both a "hardware" and a "software" component. The hardware portion of the strategy focuses on improving the zone's existing infrastructure. Although billions of dollars have already been invested in infrastructure throughout the city, the development of additional hardware is slated to continue with such projects as an international deep-water harbor and the high-speed magnetic levitation train connecting the new airport with downtown Pudong and Shanghai.

Wei believes the software portion of the plan is just as important in ensuring Pudong's future success. He outlines the software strategy into three broad categories:

- Ensuring an adequate supply of skilled labor
- Streamlining government bureaucracy and improving the rule of law
- Fostering an innovative technology development capacity

Wei notes that the area is taking a number of different steps to ensure the continued development of the software dimension. Pudong is the first city in China to create an intellectual property division in its court system. Another indication of the attention given to the software component of Pudong's strategy is the significant increase in the number of skilled workers in the city. By the end of 2000, the area was home to 230,000 "high-skilled professionals," up from just 66,000 people ten years before. Based on an analysis of recent developments and trends in Pudong and our conversations with Pudong officials, it is clear that the leading EZs are taking steps to address the value propositions of their regions. Government officials are proactively addressing the impending shift in policy brought about by WTO membership. For instance, the government has been offering training courses for provincial-level cadres on WTO rules, policies, laws, and regulations relating to foreign investment. This reflects the view that senior officials are expected to develop a new way of thinking to meet the challenges of globalization.

HISTORICAL AND CURRENT EXPECTATIONS OF FOREIGN INVESTORS—SURVEY RESULTS

In the course of our research, we sent out questionnaires to approximately two hundred foreign companies located in and outside of China's EZs to understand what has historically driven their location decisions in the country and what factors are likely to be important to these foreign investors in the future. Our online survey[1] sought to understand how investors' location criteria may be changing as a result of the economic and trade reforms that are taking place in China. We received a total of twenty-seven responses— a response rate of nearly 14 percent—from a broad variety of industries, including information and communication, agribusiness, apparel, and heavy manufacturing. Our survey sought to answer four major questions:

1. What were the most significant criteria affecting *prior* location decisions?
2. What are likely to be the most significant criteria affecting *future* location decisions?
3. What significant shifts in location selection criteria have occurred?
4. Given current information, would foreign companies choose to locate in or out of an economic zone?

The following presents our findings for each of these questions.

1. Important Criteria in Prior Location Decisions

To arrive at an appropriate baseline, we first sought to find out what factors were important to companies when they were considering investment in China. Our survey results indicate streamlined government regulations and adequate physical infrastructure top the list, followed by labor costs (Figure 2.4). These results show that even in the past, companies were very concerned about China's bureaucracy. Companies also wanted to ensure that there was an adequate amount of physical infrastructure (e.g., roads, ports, electric generating capacity) to allow easy transport of goods produced to their intended market (typically the export market).

Finally, the ability to secure relatively low-cost labor in the country was an important factor. Like other Asian countries, historically China has provided an abundant source of low-cost labor for multinational corporations looking to produce labor-intensive

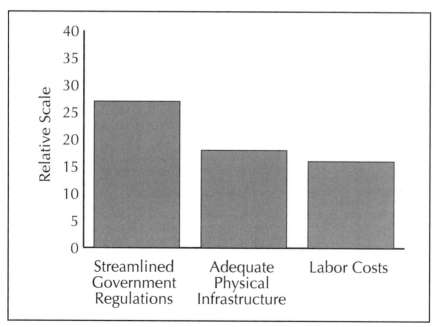

Figure 2.4: Three Most Important Criteria in Prior Decisions to Set Up Operations in China

goods. All of these results tend to support the export-oriented focus of most EZs in the 1980s and early 1990s. At that time, the majority of companies in the zones were labor-intensive operations and were interested primarily in minimizing labor costs.

2. CRITERIA LIKELY TO BE IMPORTANT IN FUTURE LOCATION DECISIONS

After identifying the key criteria that were important to companies in the past, we sought to understand how these criteria are changing with the maturing of the Chinese economy and the country's accession to the WTO. Streamlined government regulations continued to top the list in investment decisions, while access to skilled labor was now the second most important location factor mentioned in our survey. As more and more advanced manufacturing and high-technology companies enter China, securing skilled labor is taking on new prominence, as evidenced by its presence among the top three criteria. Adequate physical infrastructure continues to remain a high priority for foreign investors. Because the significant infrastructure improvements that have been made in areas like Pudong and Shenzhen have yet to be implemented in most other parts of the country, investors must continue to carefully analyze the quality of a location's infrastructure as part of their investment decision process (Figure 2.5).

3. SIGNIFICANT SHIFTS IN LOCATION SELECTION

We also sought to understand and explain any significant shifts in the location criteria between past and future investment decisions. In our survey results, we noted a significant change in the relative importance of both labor costs and access to skilled labor in the overall rankings (Figure 2.6). In fact, the importance of labor costs fell the most in absolute terms of any single criterion (eight weighting points[2]), while access to skilled labor increased more than any other single criterion (sixteen weighting points).

These survey results suggest that multinationals are viewing China as much more than just a place to conduct low-labor-cost

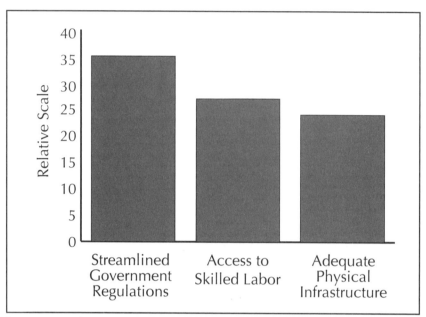

Figure 2.5: Three Most Important Criteria in Future Decisions to Set Up Operations in China

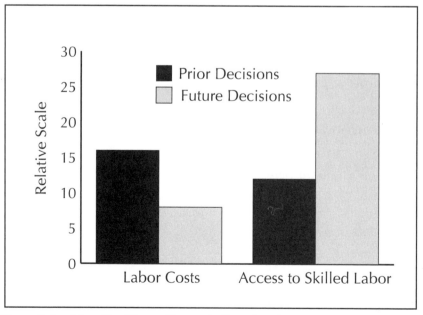

Figure 2.6: Most Significant Change in Location Decision Dimensions

manufacturing and provide support for Pudong's software strategy of ensuring an adequate supply of skilled labor. Companies that still employ a low-labor-cost model appear to be just as likely to locate production in parts of southeast Asia as they are in China, as the proliferation of apparel factories in parts of Indonesia and Vietnam indicates.

4. WOULD COMPANIES CHOOSE TO LOCATE IN OR OUTSIDE OF AN EZ?

To assess the attitudes of multinationals toward locating in an EZ, our final question in the survey asked whether a respondent, given all the current information at hand, would locate in or outside of an EZ. Figure 2.7 shows a high degree of uncertainty among

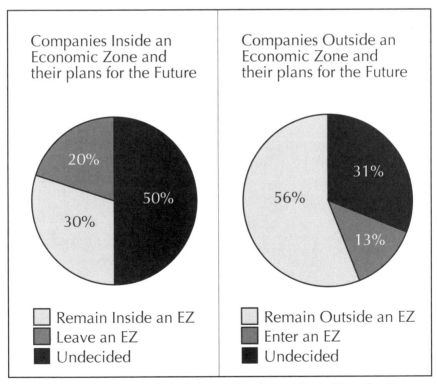

Figure 2.7:   Companies Inside and Outside EZs and Their Plans for the Future

both types of respondents, those whose companies are located in an EZ *and* those outside of EZs, regarding where their next investment might be. Only 30 percent of those located inside an EZ said they would remain in an EZ; 50% were undecided. As for those located outside an EZ, more than half of them said they would remain outside the EZ, with only a third indicating that they were undecided.

The majority of respondents currently outside of a zone indicated a desire to continue to locate new facilities outside of the zones (56 percent). Presumably, these companies have learned to do business without the hard and soft infrastructure benefits that an EZ provides. So while those outside of EZs appear, on average, to be ready to stay where they are, companies that are currently in an EZ have substantial doubt as to whether they will continue to locate future facilities where they are.

IMPLICATIONS OF THE SURVEY FOR ECONOMIC ZONES

The survey results offer important information for Chinese governmental units contemplating a strategy of how to continue to market their specific EZs as attractive places to do business. Based on these results and other economic data as well as interviews in China, we believe EZs need to focus on the following key items to remain viable entities in the coming years:

- Ensure that the level of governmental regulation is efficient and that the rule of law is followed.
- Provide an appropriate level of physical infrastructure.
- Ensure an adequate pool of skilled workers.

But the question remains, will the zones be successful in their change of strategy? This is a much more difficult question to answer. Obviously, the EZs have made great strides in building infrastructure, attracting quality labor, and even streamlining certain bureaucratic processes and structures. In fact, Pudong's hardware and software strategy appears to match almost perfectly with what potential investors are likely to look for in an EZ in the future.

However, there is still a fair amount of work to be done, especially in the area of streamlined administration.

LABOR, INFRASTRUCTURE, AND LOCATION DECISIONS OF COMPANIES OPERATING IN CHINA

Corporations locate in China for many reasons—to obtain access to the country's 1.2 billion potential consumers, to gain access to a large pool of researchers and scientists, and to take advantage of the country's relatively low cost of unskilled labor. With this variety in mind, we met with a cross section of companies to develop an understanding of the diverse needs and agendas of companies doing business in China today. We chose Nike, General Motors, and Motorola because the companies cover varied levels of capital investment requirements, with operations ranging from labor-intensive to medium- and high-tech manufacturing, and the companies have investments both inside and outside EZs.

NIKE

Nike is a classic example of a manufacturer looking for cost savings in the form of low labor rates. Although a portion of the company's output is sold within China, it is very hard to sell most of the company's models (which can retail for over US$100) in a country where the per capita GDP is less than US$900. So at least for now, an overwhelming majority of the company's Chinese output is destined for export markets in North America and Europe. Nike generally does not own its manufacturing facilities; rather it sources its goods from subcontractor facilities, and the company contracts with over 70 non-company-owned facilities throughout the country. We toured one of Nike's medium-sized manufacturing facilities in Suzhou, a small city about an hour outside of Shanghai that is not located in an EZ.

At the factory, we spoke with representatives of the company to learn what factors have been and likely will be important to the company in making decisions about location. As expected, access to low-cost labor was and remains a primary factor in Nike's location criteria. In fact, the manager indicated that the company typically recruits its workforce from the Chinese interior and houses the workers on site because the local wage rate in Suzhou is higher than what they have to pay for labor from the interior. In Nike's case, adequate physical infrastructure and the presence of a skilled workforce are not very important. The production process is decidedly low-tech and does not require a highly skilled workforce. The company can easily move truckloads of its shoes throughout the country, so physical infrastructure does not play a big part in its location decisions.

As for the future, the company sees many challenges in being located so close to coastal cities like Shanghai. Remaining near the coast would eventually push labor costs above the range that makes production in China an economically attractive proposition. As one manager put it, the company will need to continue to move westward in China over the next several decades to ensure it keeps its labor costs stable.

In fact, there are visible signs of rising costs that are affecting low-technology companies. As we toured the Nike facility, we noticed a large plot of land adjacent to the facility and asked about future development on the site. After informing us that the company used to own the land in question, a Nike representative said, "Recently we sold the unused land rather than expand—the wages are just too high in this part of the country now for our type of business." China's entry into the WTO will only accelerate this migration. In the past, tax and related incentives could at least "soften the blow" in terms of rising labor costs in the coastal areas, but as these incentives disappear, the labor cost issue in and around EZs will only become more acute for companies like Nike.

GENERAL MOTORS

Unlike export-focused Nike, General Motors has made a substantial bet on the local Chinese market. A testament to this commitment is its US$1.5 billion investment in a complete automobile production facility in the Pudong New Area. General Motors began construction of the facility in 1997 as a 50/50 joint venture with Shanghai Automotive Industry Corporation. The venture, known as GM-Shanghai, rolled its first car off the production line on December 17, 1998. There were a number of key reasons the company chose to locate its plant in Pudong. First and foremost, GM's Chinese joint venture partner was a Shanghai-based entity. As Mark Newman, chief financial officer of the joint venture, explained, the Chinese government controlled the selection of both the domestic and international partner for the new facility and picked SAIC and General Motors. With SAIC as the selected partner, it was almost certain that the plant would be built in Shanghai.

That said, Newman noted that even without the SAIC relationship, many of the benefits that Pudong offers would have made the location an attractive option for GM. Specifically, he pointed to a few key items:

- An assured level of steam, gas, and electricity to power the facility
- Access to a skilled workforce (50 percent of the facility's local workers are college graduates)
- Proximity to physical infrastructure to ship both raw materials and finished goods

Regarding tax incentives offered by EZs, Newman acknowledged that GM-Shanghai received some attractive short-term incentives for locating in Pudong. However, he added that the incentives were certainly not the driving factor for being in Pudong because they would eventually expire. The substantial up-front investment in property and equipment for the facility required GM to make a more strategic and long-term investment in the specific location chosen in China.

With the growing auto market in China, GM-Shanghai may expand using the "brownfield" approach by refurbishing a Chinese competitor's facility. There are twenty local auto competitors in China, all of which are struggling to gain an appreciable market share in the country. These circumstances may create an opportunity for foreign and joint ventures like GM-Shanghai to buy additional plant capacity relatively inexpensively.

However, Newman noted that the same key location items—appropriate level of infrastructure, access to a skilled workforce, and proximity to physical port infrastructure—would still be very important to the company. Given GM-Shanghai's investment considerations, it is unlikely that the elimination of preferences and tax incentives will have any appreciable impact on the company's future domestic location decisions. Although the company would seek out tax and related incentives, given the significant infrastructure investment required, it is unlikely that these incentives alone would be the determining factor in a location decision. Hence, the impact of China's post-WTO policies on the EZs would be less significant for companies like GM.

Motorola

Motorola was one of the first foreign companies to enter the China market and is the largest foreign direct investor in the country. Its outlook on investment location decisions differs from that of Nike and GM. For Motorola, access to a skilled workforce is probably the most important location decision. Research and development activities constitute a significant amount of the company's economic activity in China, and so it follows that the company would need top-quality researchers and scientists. Because the telecommunications sector is so regulated in China, frequent communication with the government is also important to the company. The dissemination of government information has historically been a problem in China. By being close to the government rule-making bodies, Motorola can ensure that it obtains the best-quality information as quickly as possible.

Motorola's need for skilled workers and close contact with the government led the company to establish its China headquarters in Beijing and its largest production facility in the nearby Tianjin EZ. Beijing is home to a large number of universities and other higher education institutions. In addition, the capital city is the location of a significant proportion of government offices and ministries.

Another factor influencing the location of Motorola's facilities is closeness to key consumer markets. Motorola wants to have a very visible presence in China and has chosen to locate many of its facilities in large Chinese cities, such as Shanghai and Hong Kong.

Top quality infrastructure does not appear to be as important for Motorola as it is for large-scale production facilities that produce durable goods like automobiles. The company does not produce large, hard-to-transport products, and therefore general infrastructure is not critical. In fact, many of the components that Motorola transports are shipped via air, making the quality of the road network almost a nonissue. When thinking about future location decisions for Motorola's China operations, Astra Lam and Steve Carroll of Motorola agreed that many of the factors that were critical in the past are also going to be important in the future:

- Access to skilled workers (including proximity to prominent universities)
- Closeness to the consumer markets
- Proximity to the government

To the extent that EZs can provide these items, the company would certainly consider locating in the EZs in the future. However, companies like Motorola are also likely to feel the effect of removing incentives that have softened the rising costs of operating in the EZs.

CONCLUSION

Clearly, the economic zone concept *is* undergoing a series of profound changes in China today. In fact, we believe that zone leadership is acutely aware of the challenges the EZs are facing. It is evident that the zones have expended a great deal of effort to alter the value proposition they offer to foreign investors. They appear willing to address the key concerns of foreign investors in China, namely, the need for a world-class physical infrastructure, an adequate pool of skilled labor, and improved administrative and legal structures.

The zones are now no longer interested in attracting low-technology, low-value-added industries. Instead, they are using their resources to target companies in high growth, high-value-added industries, such as high-tech, advanced manufacturing and biotechnology/pharmaceuticals.

What does this mean for the future of the zones? Low-technology companies will continue their migration to areas away from China's economic zones—primarily to areas in the Chinese interior and far west to take advantage of low-cost labor in these less developed parts of the country. As for companies in more advanced industries, the answer is more ambiguous. The EZs will increasingly compete amongst themselves for companies in key industries. As part of this competition, zones will begin specializing in certain sectors; or as Pudong's Wei Chang Ming notes, zones will begin branding themselves. This branding effort can already be seen in Pudong's significant focus on the financial and business services sector and in Shenzhen's recent development of a high-technology development park within its borders.

We believe the question still remains of whether the zones' new focus and value proposition will ultimately prove successful in continuing to attract foreign capital in key industries. Clearly, areas like Shenzhen and Pudong have an enormous head start in terms of infrastructure, workforce, and geographical advantages and are likely to continue to be viable economic areas in the future. However, whether these areas can sustain the impressive success they have experienced in the past remains to be determined.

The change in government policy will be even more challenging for the smaller, less-developed zones because they will have a difficult time keeping pace in a post-WTO China. With little in the way of systemic incentives (e.g., infrastructure and an educated workforce) to offer foreign investors, the principle of uniform national treatment will only add to the challenges for smaller EZs. Furthermore, larger EZs like Shenzhen and Pudong are likely now to compete much more often with these lesser zones for foreign capital than they have in the past. *The Wall Street Journal's* Wonacott noted that foreign investors are now beginning to set up their operations in close proximity to an EZ, but not within the zone's specific boundaries. With this strategy, the foreign investor is able to reap some of the systemic benefits of an EZ, such as an adequate road system, while reducing its exposure to the negative side effects of a zone. Wonacott pointed to Flextronics as a company that has recently employed this strategy when it established operations just outside of the Zhuhai SEZ.

The changes currently taking place in China's EZs will cause some zones to prosper and others to decline. Only time will tell who the winners and losers will be and just how much is at stake in the game. However, in the short term, EZs are likely to remain important areas in which to locate operations as China upgrades its infrastructure and business environment. Ultimately, the survival of EZs will depend on their ability to evolve to meet the changing demands of their foreign investors.

Notes

1. Further details of the survey methodology and a copy of the survey instrument are available on request by e-mailing gim@kellogg.northwestern.edu.

2. Weighting points are assigned to reflect importance on a scale from zero to thirty, with thirty being the most important.

Bibliography

Cheng, Joseph Y. S. 2003. "Regional Impacts of China's WTO Membership." *Asian Affairs: An American Review*, 29 (4):217–37.

Ching, L., and C. Chye. 2001. "Changes in China Tax Laws with Entry to WTO." Arthur Andersen LLP (Slide Show Presentation), December 7.

Eastwest-Global.com. 2003. "China Special Economic Zones." http://www.eastwest-global.com/atlast/maps.html. [Cited March 2003.]

Economic and Trade Bureau of Shanghai Pudong New Area. 2001. "Guide to the Investment in Pudong—2001/2002." Economic and Trade Bureau of Shanghai Pudong New Area.

Economist Intelligence Unit. 2001. "Country Profile—China 2001/2002."
Economist Intelligence Unit. http://db.eiu.com/reports.asp?valname=
CPBCNC&deliveryKey=CPCN&pubcode=. September 1, 2001.

Ge, W. 1999. *Special Economic Zones and the Economic Transition in China.*
Singapore: World Scientific Publishing Company.

"An Opening Door in China?" 2002. *McKinsey Quarterly,* March.

"Pudong New Area Shanghai 2001 Basic Facts." 2002. Beijing: China
Intercontinental Press.

"Special Economic Zones and the Opening of the Chinese Economy: Some
Lessons for Economic Liberalization." 1999. *World Development,*
November 7.

Chapter 3

CHINESE TRADING COMPANIES: CREATING NEW VALUE PROPOSITIONS

Karthik Krishnan, Paul Lee, Lewis Lin, Jason Ross, and Daniel Rosskamm

A trading company, by definition, matches buyers and sellers and assists in subsequent transaction negotiations—it adds value by reducing the costs of searching and bargaining. Chinese trading companies have been instrumental in facilitating China's explosive growth. China's Ministry of Foreign Trade and Economic Cooperation (MOFTEC) estimates that there are at least two thousand Chinese trading companies, ranging from family- and state-owned enterprises to large publicly traded companies. However, their value proposition of matching buyers with sellers is facing serious challenges. Increased use of the Internet, easier access to the Chinese market for foreign trading companies, the growing power of buyers, and the desire to cut costs are leading to disintermediation of Chinese trading companies.

The Internet has broken down the geographic, temporal, and informational barriers between buyers and sellers. As Victor Fung, chairman of Li and Fung, noted, "What the Internet and e-commerce could take away completely is the matching functions between buyer and seller, because that's very efficient on the Net." Mohanbir Sawhney, professor of e-commerce and technology at the Kellogg School of Management, has argued, "The world has become a dangerous place for intermediaries that add little value in building and enhancing relationships and merely serve as conduits for brokering information and transactions. The transactions and information can easily migrate to the Net, leaving intermediaries with little reason to exist. In these situations, the middlemen become corner solutions—adding no residual value once the information-intensive functions are migrated to the Net."

Alibaba.com, the world's largest web portal for foreign importers and exporters, is proof that the Internet is making middlemen trivial in today's networked world. Boasting over 1.6 million members from 216 countries, it "allows users to browse company information and trade leads by 27 industry categories and 700 product sub-categories, ranging from textiles to electronics." Any import-export company would be hard-pressed to match Alibaba's membership base or its depth of products.

In addition to the Internet, China's entry into the World Trade Organization (WTO) is also wreaking havoc on the Chinese trading company industry. Under the terms of agreement of China's accession to the WTO, foreign companies can establish their own trading operations. Restrictive requirements and licenses previously necessary for foreigners to open a sourcing office have been eliminated. Table 3.1 lists some of the pre- and post-WTO requirements

Table 3.1
Requirements for Chinese Trading Companies

	Pre-WTO	Post-WTO
Foreign Companies		
Organization form	Joint venture	Foreign-invested enterprise
Total sales	US$5 billion	US$10 million
Average trade volume prior to application	US$30 million annually	US$1 million annually
Registered capital	RMB 100 million	RMB 10 million
Domestic Companies		
Average import-export volume prior to application	US$200 million annually	US$2 million annually
Average export volume prior to application	US$100 million annually	US$1 million annually
Registered capital	RMB 5 million	RMB 1 million RMB

Source: Data from Zeng 2002.

imposed on trading companies and shows how requirements have been eased. Consequently, foreign companies that source from China no longer need Chinese trading companies to help meet import-export requirements.

The Chinese trading company industry is struggling, as can be seen in the falling share of these companies in Chinese trade (see Figure 3.1). However, a closer look indicates that this share has been declining steadily since 1998, even before China's WTO membership was ratified. As the power of large buyers increases, they are bypassing their trading company partners and setting up their own sourcing offices in Hong Kong. For instance, Sears, a large U.S. retailer, with over US$4 billion in annual sales, has numerous international buying offices (IBOs) around the world, with the largest in Hong Kong. According to Sharon Bringelson, director of import operations and customs for Sears, IBOs function as trading

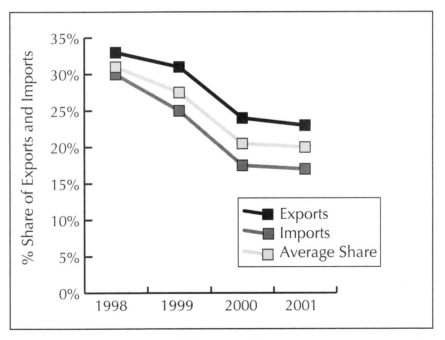

Figure 3.1: Declining Share of Chinese Trading Companies in Exports and Imports

Source: Analysis derived from Beijing MOFTEC figures and PRC Administration of Customs, China's Customs Statistics.

companies: "They identify factories, follow up on the orders, logistical details, and determine what and when customs documents need to be handled." When a U.S.-based Sears buyer makes the decision to source from one of the IBOs, the "IBO then becomes the liaison and is responsible for managing the entire supply chain process," Bringelson noted. "They do inspections, monitor factories, and get samples; they are the ones responsible for making sure that the products show up on the shelves."

Similarly, Charming Shoppes, a U.S. retailer that operates such stores as Fashion Bug and Lane Bryant with over US$2 billion in annual sales, has four sourcing offices in Asia, including a regional office in Hong Kong. The Hong Kong office acts as an import arm for the corporation—its functional responsibilities include maintaining ordering systems, management information systems, and human resources. Established in the early 1980s, the Hong Kong office currently employs 120 people and sources US$600 million in goods annually.

Sourcing products through their own buying offices is advantageous for large firms. First, as Stephen Yeung, Charming Shoppes's vice president of sourcing for Asia, stated, working directly with manufacturers gives companies more control over the sourcing process. Sourcing directly also makes it easier to have differentiated and unique products. Second, purchasing directly from the manufacturer allows companies to obtain better discounts and, hence, to improve profitability. Thus, the cost of internalizing the sourcing function for Sears and Charming Shoppes is less than the cost of sourcing via a trading company. Third, sourcing directly reduces principal-agency costs arising due to conflicts of interest with a trading company.

ANALYZING CHINESE TRADING COMPANIES

In this changing environment, will Chinese trading companies survive? Can they alter their value propositions and continue to be relevant? To help answer these questions, we look at three trading companies that are representative of the different kinds of trading companies doing business in China: (1) Sumec, a state-owned enterprise, (2) Chemind, a family-owned trading company; and (3) Li and Fung, a publicly owned Chinese trading company.

SUMEC: A STATE-OWNED ENTERPRISE

Sumec is a state-owned Chinese trading company headquartered in Nanjing, China. In 2002, it was ranked as China's thirty-third largest trading company with an import and export trading volume of US$600 million. It employs over 750 people and has several product lines that include marine equipment, textiles, heavy machinery, hardware and tools, and electrical products. Trading companies like Sumec have historically provided their services in a wide range of product categories.

Similar to the trend at other Chinese trading companies, some of Sumec's employees have recently left the company to start their own trading operations, attempting to take their customer accounts with them. Although Sumec is now facing this entrepreneurial competition (facilitated by decreased barriers to entry), it has been able to remain profitable (a profit margin of 1.5 percent) by adopting a differentiation strategy.

Sumec's strength, similar to that of other state-owned trading companies, is based on its ability to obtain large amounts of financing from Chinese banks, which it uses to facilitate trading between Chinese manufacturers and foreign companies. Foreign companies typically place large orders with Chinese manufacturers but do not pay until they take delivery of the goods. Sumec provides manufacturers with interim financing to purchase raw materials and pay workers until the final payment is made upon delivery. As a result, Sumec is able to develop strong, powerful relationships with manufacturers that allow the state-owned enterprises (SOEs) to be the trading company of choice for importers.

State-owned trading companies offer a valuable service because Chinese banks are extremely conservative about making loans to small, unproven firms. Given the sizable number of bad loans of the banking system, the Chinese government has mandated that Chinese banks revise their banking policies. Now, 70 percent of state-owned bank loans go to large SOEs that possess positive credit histories. Thus, due to the banking system, state-owned trading companies still enjoy a barrier to entry because smaller companies cannot replicate their financing strategy.

However, Sumec will likely have difficulty maintaining its success in the future, largely because foreign companies can now establish their own trading operations. These companies do not have to rely on the Chinese banking system for financing; they are usually well financed or can obtain financing from outside the Chinese banking system for their manufacturers. Indeed, Sumec's biggest concern is that its customers may set up their own trading operations, and some have already done so. In addition, some of Sumec's employees have left the company to start their own trading operations and have taken their customer accounts with them. We believe that this situation will only get worse as the impact of the Internet and WTO increases competition.

Furthermore, Sumec's strategy of financing customers may not work in the long term. Although Sumec may be able to assess the financial health of its clients and hence feel comfortable extending financing to its customers, this financing strategy has potential for grave misuse. Divisional managers may be willing to strike deals with customers that have a high risk of default. This strategy may no longer be sustainable as China begins to reform its banking system by tightening credit requirements and clamping down on providing liberal credit to SOEs.

Access to capital has also caused Sumec to focus on revenues instead of profits, because revenues determine its leverage with banks. Indeed, the size of the business is an important factor in gaining access to financing from the banking system. With a relatively low profit margin and faced with increasing competition, Sumec and other state-owned trading companies need to rethink their strategies.

CHEMIND: A FAMILY-OWNED TRADING COMPANY

Chemind is a family-owned Chinese trading company focused on the fine chemical segment of the chemical industry. Like many new entrepreneurs in China, Eric Suo, the founder of Chemind, formerly worked at Sinochem, a large Chinese trading company in the chemical industry. Suo used his position at Sinochem to learn about the trading company industry and to gain experience working with customers. In Chemind's first year, the company achieved sales of almost US$1 million and aimed to reach US$2 million by the end of 2003. Chemind enjoyed a profit margin of 10 percent in 2002, although a single company, Bayer AG, accounted for 100 percent of its sales that year.

Chemind's healthy margin can be traced to the company's focused strategy. By selecting just one target segment, Chemind can specialize to meet its needs and therefore better serve the market. As a start-up with few employees, the company has lower overheads than the large trading companies, which allows it to pursue a low-cost advantage that leads to higher margins.

As Chemind gains stability, Suo plans to backward integrate into manufacturing. This production base will allow Chemind to guarantee its customers delivery of the product in the agreed time frame. By expanding its offering while serving only a small niche segment of the chemical industry, Chemind will avoid competition from large firms. Meanwhile, it will be building a specialized product offering that will foster a high degree of customer loyalty, which will keep other small competitors from entering the market.

Chemind's extraordinary growth and performance in such a short period is impressive. As a family-owned business, Chemind has a lower overhead cost structure than the typical large trading company. However, with 100 percent of its sales going to a single customer, the company faces a near-term threat of disintermediation. Although the customer, which has a purchasing office in Shanghai, uses trading companies for its relationships with local suppliers, it could deal directly with the manufacturers once those supplier relationships are in place. Therefore, while targeting one product segment with specialized product offerings is an attractive strategy for a trading company, Chemind will still need to offer additional value to overcome the threat of disintermediation, or it must expand its client base to reduce its reliance on a single firm.

LI AND FUNG: A PUBLICLY OWNED TRADING COMPANY

The first Chinese-owned trading company, Li and Fung, was founded in 1906 and specialized in porcelain, antiques, silk, jade, and ivory. Today, Li and Fung employs over five thousand people and has an annual trading volume of nearly US$5 billion. As Victor Fung commented, "The Limited knows all the big factories; why do they want to work with Li and Fung?" His answer, "It's the way we orchestrate the production." Given the complexity of the production process and the product life cycle, many companies, including the Limited, have found it easier to outsource their supply chain "orchestration" to a third party. For instance, Avon Products has a product life cycle that includes product development, manufacturing, material sourcing, and distribution stages. From start to finish, that process may take as long as thirty-eight months (see Table 3.2). Furthermore, any company that deals with manufacturing and material sourcing has to consider many issues, including the selection of raw materials and the manufacturing site, the reliability of manufacturers, factory skill level, lead times and quota availability, product quality, packaging, and pricing. Soft factors, such as protectionist considerations (e.g., quotas and tariffs), and the financial integrity of factories also need to be taken into account.

For companies like the Limited, the cost of internalizing the sourcing function is greater than the cost of outsourcing to Li and Fung. In addition, Li and Fung also brings a lot more value to distribution than sourcing internally would. As one Li and Fung cus-

Table 3.2
Avon's Product Life Cycle Process

Life Cycle Step	Process	Time Frame
Product development	Develop product in line with marketing themes	9 months to 1 year prior to launch
Manufacturing	Determine what goes into the product and the cheapest way to make it	6–8 months prior to launch
Material sourcing	Select raw material suppliers and assembly points	3–5 months prior to launch
Distribution	Showcase product at trade shows; distribute product to shore shelves	1–3 months prior to launch

Source: Slater 1999. Reprinted with permission of *Far Eastern Economic Review.*

tomer mentioned, "[Li and Fung] allows us to focus on the product development without worrying about where to source it. . . . We're able to develop products smarter, faster, and with cost efficiencies."

Li and Fung's sourcing cost advantage over other trading houses (both Chinese trading companies and buying offices of foreign companies) is based on a series of innovative technologies developed in the area of supply chain management (SCM). Li and Fung developed the "production program" in the 1980s and the "virtual factory" in the 1990s to increase its SCM capabilities.

The production program, which specified a set of processes to manage a customer's order, allowed Li and Fung to evolve from a buyer-supplier matchmaker into a manager of manufacturing programs. In the first step of the program, with the product specifications in hand, appropriate product inputs are identified. Next, product concepts are converted into prototypes. These steps are the front end of the production program supply chain. Based on customer feedback, an entire manufacturing program is then conceived, along with the product mix and the schedule. Finally, all the resources, including factory capacities, are contracted. Particular attention is given to working closely with the manufacturer to ensure quality and on-time delivery.

In the early 1990s, Hong Kong's manufacturing costs increased dramatically, causing Li and Fung to move its labor-intensive manufacturing into southern China, while it retained in Hong Kong its skilled, high-end services, such as design, testing, transportation, and financing. Coined the "virtual factory," this physical separation of the supply chain dissected the manufacturing process at each stage of the process and outsourced the "best solution" to the appropriate part of the process. In the late 1990s, Li and Fung expanded its virtual factory model by forward integrating into the design phase and backward integrating into back-end services like sales support.

An example of Li and Fung's virtual factory is the production of a ski parka. First, Li and Fung's merchandising specialists in Hong Kong work closely with the client to design plans, working with the buyer to determine the fabrics, colors, and styles of the garment. Next, the company approaches four to five medium-sized manufacturers to reserve their capacity. Reserving capacity in advance shortens the manufacturing lead time—Li and Fung's relationships and virtual factory system reduce the normal three-month lead time to five weeks. The shorter production time gives the buyer flexibility to adjust product specifications and to adjust production volumes. Spreading manufacturing across several plants also reduces Li and Fung's reliance on a single manufacturer. To take advantage of manufacturing cost heterogeneities, the finished product may be composed of lining from Taiwan, filler from China, a zipper from Japan, labels from Hong Kong, and a shell from Korea. These sub-products are assembled in low-cost manufacturing plants in China with the process orchestrated by Li and Fung in Hong Kong.

Even after recent market shocks, Li and Fung is able to eke out significant profits in the trading company business, typically generating commissions of 7 percent to 12 percent on the value of each order it fills. After deducting operating expenses, Morgan Stanley estimates that the company's 2003 profit margin was about 3 percent. Li and Fung's customer list includes a number of large retailers, such as Abercrombie and Fitch, American Eagle Outfitters, and Gymboree.

Li and Fung's profitability was not achieved by squeezing manufacturer's margins but rather by consolidating manufacturing and shipping. As Victor Fung explained, "If the ex-factory price is around US$1, the final retail price might be between US$4 and US$5. A good product manager might be able to squeeze 15 cents off the margin from the manufacturer but we look to get the larger part of the margin from consolidating the rest of the process. There is a great deal of value to the customer in preventing stock outs, excess inventory, interest charges, ensuring equality, and the like. This is where we can gain more value from the supply chain."

STRATEGIES FOR SUCCESS

New channels and potential challenges of disintermediation do not necessarily signal the end of the world for trading companies but merely mean that they will have to carefully evaluate their business model, understand their competitive advantage, and focus on a unique set of activities that provide value to their customers. In the sections below, we discuss multiple strategies trading companies can use to successfully operate in China.

ONE SIZE DOESN'T FIT ALL

We can identify three generic business models for trading companies: functional diversification, product diversification, and geographic diversification. Trading companies face different cost-benefit trade-offs when making fundamentally different strategic choices.

- *Product Diversification:* Companies that adhere to a product diversification strategy choose to focus on offering either a narrow or a vast range of products. Trading companies often have diversified product lines to reduce risk and increase their market power, which they leverage to reduce the cost of capital. In *The General Trading Company: Concepts and Strategies,* researchers Ansoff, Salter, and Weinhold identify the benefits of such a diversification strategy and the growth in profits through cross subsidization.
- *Geographic Diversification:* A trading company may choose to either limit its activities to a certain region or expand its activities outside the region. It can leverage its regional expertise and information to secure more business opportunities and superior operating profits.
- *Functional Diversification:* Companies that adopt a functionally diversified strategy choose to integrate into front-end services (e.g., transportation and warehousing) and back-end services (e.g., product design and planning). An end-to-end solutions strategy for a focused market has its advantages in meeting the various needs of a target customer segment and increasing barriers to entry for potential competition. A company can also choose to limit its functional scope to a focused set of activities, such as product design or supply chain management.

The choice of specialization in products, geographies, or functional skill sets depends on the customers' needs and the firm's core competencies. Our interviews with company executives in China and the United States suggest that different market segments do look to trading companies but for fundamentally different reasons. Table 3.3 identifies several segments and what customers in these segments value most.

Table 3.3 also illustrates the limitations of a "one-size-fits-all" approach—different product groups have different sets of needs. After-sales support, for example, is critical for shipbuilding but is not of utmost importance for hand machine tool manufacturers. To service ship manufacturers, trading companies need to deliver the product but also help deploy it and ensure that repairs and maintenance are easily facilitated for smooth operations. Thus, trading companies that are shipbuilding intermediaries would offer extensive after-sales support to alleviate

Table 3.3
Customer Needs for Diverse Product Segments

| Product Diversification | *Functional Diversification Customer Needs* | | | |
	Front-End Design and Planning	*Manufacturing*	*Distribution*	*After-Sales Support*
Retail merchandise	Need very short turnaround due to fast-changing fashion trends and to reduce markdowns at end of selling season **Importance: High**	Low cost manufacturing essential for every manufacturer **Importance: High**	Distribution costs are often higher than manufacturing costs **Importance: High**	Not critical because of the low complexity **Importance: Medium**
Shipbuilding	Customers don't need fast turnaround **Importance: Low**	Low cost manufacturing essential for every manufacturer **Importance: High**	Delivery is a small portion of overall project costs **Importance: Low**	Critical for customers to receive after-sales support, including repair/maintenance **Importance: High**
Small machine tools	Customers don't need fast turnaround **Importance: Low**	Low cost manufacturing essential for every manufacturer **Importance: High**	Distribution costs are high **Importance: Medium**	Not critical because of low complexity **Importance: Low**

customers' concerns and gain their business. Trading companies serving retailers will have to optimize their systems and organization for lower distribution costs and quick turnaround times from design to manufacturing.

CREATING A SUSTAINABLE VALUE PROPOSITION

There are three broad areas that trading companies need to pay close attention to in order to develop a sustainable long-term value proposition:

- *A focused set of activities:* Trading companies must develop a unique value proposition for customers. This unique value proposition will need to be delivered to the customer through a focused set of activities that meets all of the needs of the target customer segment.
- *Infrastructure implementation:* Systems will have to be deployed to link the trading company with its buyers and sellers in a seamless fashion to maximize the value added and make the trading firm indispensable to its customers.
- *Organizational structure:* Trading companies will have to create an organizational structure that provides decision rights, sets incentive schemes, and establishes performance measures that help maximize profits for the firm.

A FOCUSED BUSINESS STRATEGY

Understanding customers and providing value-added services that meet most or all of their needs are critical to establishing a sustainable value proposition for customers. Trading is a vast industry, and Chinese imports and exports exceeded US$500 billion in 2001. In such a diverse industry, different market segments and customers are likely to have vastly diverging views on what is mission critical for their business. Consequently, trading companies must develop a clear positioning statement that defines what they stand for and for whom. Developing such a statement, by definition, means identifying customer segments that they will not target and services they will not provide.

Michael Porter, who is a professor of business administration at the Harvard Business School, has asserted that need-based positioning occurs when a firm targets a set of customers and serves most or all the needs of a particular subset or group. According to Phil Kotler, professor of marketing at the Kellogg School of Management, an attractive niche is "one where customers have a distinct set of needs and will pay a premium to a firm that best meets their needs. Niches are not likely to attract competitors and will most likely gain certain economies through specialization that has size, growth and profit potential." In this regard, trading companies need to pay close attention to the customers and develop a value proposition that occupies a distinct place in the mind of the target market.

We see two positioning strategies that deal with lower barriers to entry in the Chinese market. Chemind developed a focused strategy by targeting only the chemical market segment, while Li and Fung effectively developed a cost leadership strategy to gain scale and scope efficiencies that has allowed it to offer a more efficient product. Porter argues that companies that position themselves strategically within an industry will be able to return superior profits even though the industry may have below-average profitability. Hence, once a trading company has defined its positioning strategy, the next step is to develop a clearly defined set of activities that it will perform. The firm should focus on fulfilling its customers' unmet needs as opposed to focusing on the services it has been performing. A satisfied customer, one who finds a trading company proactively trying to meet its critical needs, is less likely to switch to competitors or backward integrate into the trading business.

We believe a functionally diversified but narrow product line would optimize organizational systems to meet customer needs. For instance, Li and Fung and Chemind have functional diversification in the product segments that they serve. By mobilizing the company's resources to serve a specific target segment, they have developed highly valued expertise and have acquired segment-specific assets that have become a source of competitive advantage. Sumec, conversely, has functional and product diversification. Its advantages are a well-diversified customer base and access to capital. Yet its diversified product base and, hence, lack of focus mean that delivering a superior value proposition to any one particular product segment is difficult. Each of its product segments is also prone to niche competitors capturing market share.

INFRASTRUCTURE IMPLEMENTATION

Trading companies have a critical advantage in being able to leverage their relationships with their suppliers and in having an indepth understanding of the local market. Pooling together customer orders and leveraging this power over suppliers is a crucial advantage that buyers will find hard to replicate. Nonetheless, trading companies will have to move fast to implement advanced supply chain management systems to coordinate orders, obtain timely responses from suppliers, and maximize turnaround of orders for buyers.

They will also have to invest in systems that provide the complex capabilities required to meet the needs of customers who are competing in the demanding global markets. For example, Li and Fung installed a PC-based intranet to link offices and facilitate access to pricing information. According to Rick Darling, senior vice president of merchandising for Li and Fung USA, the company's network connectivity allows its offices worldwide to communicate with one another. Whether it is to tap into its database to understand the capabilities of its three-thousand-strong supplier base or to inquire whether or not dyed-cotton shirts can be produced in Thailand or Indonesia, using such a system, as Darling has pointed out, increases Li and Fung's "competitive edge because we can get back to our customers in the shortest possible time."

Li and Fung invested significant capital to upgrade its supply chain management systems, which helped the company integrate its distribution logistics more closely with those of its customers. It facilitated the management of consignment deliveries not just to central docking stations but to different destinations as well. The company also developed the capabilities to eliminate consolidator middlemen by customizing its consignments for customers (compared with the traditional mass deliveries that were then unpacked and sorted to assemble the targeted consignment). All these services are offered to Li and Fung's customers as a bundle, thus allowing the company to recover the capital costs that were invested in installing these systems.

ORGANIZATIONAL STRUCTURE

The typical Chinese trading company rarely has the right management teams and incentive structures that allow it to compete in the market economy and build a sustainable business. Managers often do not have formal business management training, and financial, strategic, and marketing models and theories are not readily used. Consequently, decision making is opportunistic and reactive to customer need and desire. This lack of management and business acumen certainly hinders the ability of the firm to make strategic, long-term, sustainable business decisions. For example, Sumec retains numerous unprofitable businesses, such as machine tools, when it should have exited those businesses long ago.

Incentive structures such as compensation systems often focus on revenues, not profits. To be successful in the future, trading companies will have to focus their managerial efforts on profitability. Such a change will require a fundamental realignment of incentive structures as well as organizational training to focus efforts on activities that maximize shareholder value. Specific incentives will have to be provided to ensure that managers are continually thinking about providing value-added services to meet customer needs and reduce their total cost of ownership. Incentives for managers, infrastructure systems deployed, and tight integration with buyers and suppliers complement each other and create an organization that is hard to imitate and can deliver compelling value to its customer segments.

CONCLUSION

The trading industry is wrought with rapid change, a trend that is likely to accelerate during the next decade. China's WTO accession and the rapid expansion of the Internet will continue to integrate China more closely with world markets and provide alternative channels to bring buyers and suppliers together. Indeed, the era of protectionism and decades of state patronage of state-owned trading companies are coming to an end. Still, some trading companies are surviving the threat of cost-conscious buyers amid the new WTO regulations and Internet technology environment and have retained their relevance in China's new trade environment. Li and Fung, for instance, has developed a set of focused activities that fully meet its customers' needs, deployed information technology (IT) systems that help manage its customers' procurement and ordering process, and expanded its ability to source from countries outside of China. These activities have given Li and Fung a compelling customer value proposition that is responsible for the company's high profitability and market share relative to its competitors.

Unfortunately, Li and Fung is not representative of Chinese trading companies in general. Chinese trading companies must create a unique value proposition for each targeted customer segment and develop a set of focused activities that fully meet their customer needs. Considering the projected growth in China trade, with the right strategy and a strong focus, trading companies should be able to weather the storm and also take advantage of the changing environment to establish a viable and sustainable long-term advantage.

BIBLIOGRAPHY

Alibaba, Internet Based B2B Exchange Web Page. http://www.alibaba.com.

Chinese Ministry of Foreign Trade and Economic Cooperation Web Page. http://www1.moftec.gov.cn/moftec_en/.

Cho, Dong-Sung. 1987. *The General Trading Company: Concepts and Strategy.* Toronto, Canada: D. C. Heath and Company.

George, Anthony. 1998. *Li and Fung: Beyond "Filling in the Mosaic," 1995–1998.* Cambridge, Mass.: Harvard Business School Publishing.

Kotler, Philip. 2002. *Marketing Management.* 11th ed. Upper Saddle River, N.J.: Prentice Hall.

Kristof, Nicholas, and Sheryl Wudunn. 1998. *China Wakes.* New York: Vintage.

Li and Fung. 2002. "Annual Report." Hong Kong: Li and Fung.

Magretta, Joan. 1998. "Fast, Global, and Entrepreneurial: Supply Chain Management, Hong Kong Style: An Interview with Victor Fung." *Harvard Business Review,* 76 (5):103–114.

Morrison, Wayne. 2001. "China's Economic Conditions." Congressional Research Service Issue Brief for Congress, December 27.

Perry, Anne C. 1992. *The Evolution of U.S. Trade Intermediaries: The Changing International Environment.* Westport, Conn.: Quorum Books.

Porter, Michael E. 1996. "What Is Strategy?" *Harvard Business Review,* 74 (6):61–78.

Sawhney, Mohanbir S., and Jeff Zabin. 2001. *The Seven Steps to Nirvana: Strategic Insights into eBusiness Transformation.* New York: McGraw Hill-Trade.

Shizhong, Dong, Danian Zhang, and Milton R. Larson. 1990. *Trade and Investment Opportunities in China.* Westport, Conn.: Quorum Books.

Slater, Joanna. 1999. "One-Stop Shop." *Far Eastern Economic Review,* 162 (29):14.

Spulber, Daniel F. 1998. *The Market Makers: How Leading Companies Create and Win Markets.* New York: Business Week Books.

Studwell, Joe. 2003. *The China Dream.* New York: Grove Press.

Walton, Julie. 2002. "PRC Trade Data." *The China Business Review,* 29 (6):46–48.

Zeng, Xianwu. 2002. "Trading Rights after China's WTO Entry." *The China Business Review,* 29 (1):16–20.

PART 2

MANAGING AND MANEUVERING IN THE NEW CHINESE ECONOMY

Chapter 4

FRANCHISING AS AN EXPANSION STRATEGY IN CHINA

Ichiro Enomoto, Zhen Ji, Warit Jintanawan, Yvette Mangalindan, Lee Purcell, and Michael Simonton

On the surface, gaining entry into China's market is an extremely attractive proposition for multinational franchisors, largely because of China's overall market size, its long-term growth potential, and the dramatic rise in disposable income among its rapidly expanding urban population. Indeed, the country's growing affluence and its status as the world's largest consumer market have attracted many established foreign brands to open franchised stores in China. Despite these opportunities, however, multinational franchisors still face significant challenges in establishing a presence in China, whether it is working with China's ambiguous and ever-changing legal environment, selecting a legal structure for franchising, or identifying the most suitable marketing, financing, and logistics strategies.

Franchising involves a business relationship between two parties—franchisor and franchisee—that can be broadly characterized by three fundamental criteria. First, the franchisee is granted the right to use the franchisor's trademark and name. In exchange, the franchisor is entitled to exercise varying levels of control and provide assistance to the franchisee. Lastly, the franchisee must make required payments (both up-front and periodic) to the franchisor in the form of fees and royalties.

In this chapter, we identify the opportunities and analyze the barriers that exist in pursuing a franchising strategy in China. To better understand the issues surrounding the franchising business model and highlight the key decisions new entrants in China must make, we focus on multinational casual-dining franchises, which are enjoying growing acceptance and popularity in the country.

A number of factors have contributed to the market potential of casual-dining franchisors in China. First, China's urban population, which is the target market for casual dining, has expanded at a 5 percent compound annual growth rate over the past five years, a trend that is expected to continue. The per-capita disposable income of this group has accelerated considerably in the past decade, revealing an explosive 41 percent compound annual growth from 1990 to 2000. Smaller household units and hectic lifestyles have also led to an increase in meals eaten outside the home. These factors have contributed to continued brisk growth in the overall dining market as disposable incomes continue to grow.

Furthermore, surveys have shown that Chinese consumers have a strong interest in sampling non-Chinese cuisines. Western fast-food restaurants that meet the demand for convenience and cleanliness—local fast-food restaurants have failed in the domain of hygiene—are likely to boost the popularity of multinational food chains among Chinese consumers. Indeed, for multinational casual-dining enterprises seeking global expansion opportunities, these factors make China all the more attractive. The next step, then, is deciding whether franchising is the best entry strategy.

BENEFITS TO FRANCHISING IN CHINA

With China becoming a highly attractive and lucrative market, the use of franchising to capitalize on this business potential is an attractive solution for many new entrants. We have identified six key attributes and benefits of the franchising model that are relevant in China:

1. A Recent History of Private Restaurant Ownership

The restaurant sector was one of the first domains the government opened to private ownership in the early 1980s, and by 2001, roughly 95 percent of dining establishments were individually owned. Many believe these figures indicate a vast pool of potential entrepreneurs/franchisees with a basic understanding of the economics of owning and operating a restaurant business.

2. A Win-Win Proposition

Franchising in China combines the western know-how of franchisors with the local market expertise of franchisees. By entering into a franchise, Chinese entrepreneurs are able to obtain the necessary training, support, operations manuals, and financing to begin their own business—something they might not be able to accomplish individually. In return, the franchisor benefits from the franchisee's entrepreneurial instincts and experience with local conditions and *guanxi,* or personal relationships.

3. Minimization of Agency Costs

Franchising minimizes agency costs by aligning the economic interests of the owner/franchisee with the interests of the franchisor. China's diversity and sheer size pose significant challenges in directing operations and promotions from a centralized headquarters. Through franchising, operations can be decentralized, allowing for reduced costs and flexibility in responding to the needs of the local market.

4. Rapid Expansion

Compared with a company-owned model, where all expansion is funded by the chain store parent, franchising generally allows for rapid expansion with limited capital investment from the franchisor. In its purest form, franchise expansion is financed predominantly by the private funds of the entrepreneur and its creditors.

This is particularly advantageous in China, where the country's capital markets are less developed than most western markets, making access to capital for foreign investors more restricted.

5. BRAND CONSISTENCY

Because franchisors typically require strict adherence to company operating procedures and policies, questions about brand consistency are virtually eliminated. Franchised products generally possess consistent quality, enabling franchisors to use the same marketing approaches for all of their stores. However, as we see in the next section, the ability to achieve brand consistency across franchises in China can be challenging, especially in the casual-dining market.

6. ALLEVIATION OF LEGAL OVERSIGHT

In some cases, a franchise model can allow the franchisor to sidestep legal restraints typically placed on foreign-owned companies. Since a Chinese national runs the enterprise, the franchisor may avoid certain restrictions—such as the size of potential local joint venture partners, import maximums, and other restrictions defined in the Foreign Investment in Retailing Provisions—although these requirements have been eased with World Trade Organization (WTO) entry.

CHALLENGES TO FRANCHISING IN CHINA

Although the benefits of franchising in China are compelling, there are challenges that potential entrants should consider. The common thread among the obstacles we found is the extensive knowledge gap relative to western economies. Issues such as educating all relevant parties involved in the process and working within an ambiguous legal system can pose severe challenges to entrants who are unprepared. The franchising concept is still in its infancy in China, with the first legal guidelines written in 1997. As such, lawmakers, entrepreneurs, and consumers have just recently been introduced to franchising, and as expected, there is some confusion and contradiction among these participants that has resulted in the following challenges to franchising in China.

Educating Participants

Considerable effort must be exerted by a business entering the market to build primary awareness not only for the company's product line, but for the franchising concept as well. The franchisor must educate government officials, potential franchisees, creditors, and consumers on the basics of franchising, a process that can consume significant energy, time, and funds.

As cited earlier, 95 percent of restaurants in China are individually owned, which represents a high number of potential franchisees. However, the number of owners who actually possess the sophistication and management expertise to deal effectively with the high volumes (of customers, revenues, employees, and documentation) and strict adherence to consistency typically associated with fast-food franchising is significantly smaller. To this end, Noel Kaplan, former senior vice president for the Asia Pacific region of McDonald's, explained a paradox that exists in finding franchisees in China. Basically, the individuals with the capital to become a franchisee often are not willing to put in the exhaustive work necessary to build the business, while the individuals with the work ethic and entrepreneurial spirit often are unable to accumulate the capital necessary to acquire the franchise rights.

The infancy of the franchising concept was apparent when we attended a franchise expo in Shanghai in which over fifty businesses were attempting to recruit franchisees, predominantly in the food service category. Several organizations, for instance, with only one or two company-owned stores (and presumably low brand awareness) were attempting to franchise. One restaurant chain even had a sixteen-year-old girl heading up the negotiations with prospective franchisees. We also discovered that many of the attendees were laid-off workers from state-owned enterprises who were simply seeking employment and who lacked even a basic knowledge of franchising.

AMBIGUOUS LEGAL ENVIRONMENT

The legal framework in China for franchising is, at best, extremely ambiguous, and preparing a franchise agreement requires a thorough understanding of the Chinese legal system with regards to contracts, trademark rights, leases, and debt collection. To help alleviate the process, the Ministry of Internal Trade established the first comprehensive body of law in November 1997 entitled the "Circular of the Ministry of Domestic Trade Concerning the Promulgation of the Measures for the Administration of Franchising Operations." This set of legislation was designed to standardize franchise operations, establish required provisions for franchise agreements, and set the basic rights and duties of both the franchisees and franchisors. However, it was applicable only to domestic transactions between Chinese citizens and not to foreign master franchise agreements. Further, recent restructuring within the central government of China has resulted in the abolishment of the Ministry of Internal Trade, and these guidelines no longer provide legal recourse to those operating under a franchising model. This situation has led to diverse interpretations of the legality of franchising in China.

The president and chief executive officer (CEO) of McDonald's China, Peter Tan, believes that without the ministry overseeing franchising, it is explicitly illegal in China. And, McDonald's will wait for the new guidelines—which are expected to be announced in 2004—to be handed down before franchising McDonald's in China. However, McDonald's is optimistic about the future of franchising in China and is currently investing resources in due diligence and planning in order to be well positioned when the franchising regulations are handed down.

Yet, if franchising, as McDonald's claims, is illegal, why is there a national franchise association, why was the Institute of Franchising in Asia set up at Beijing Normal University in mid-2003, and why would Shanghai sponsor a franchise expo? Other executives we met expressed their belief that franchising is not illegal per se, but that there is just no current law or government support making it explicitly legal. Indeed, such chains as Kentucky Fried Chicken (KFC), Starbucks, and TGI Friday's have interpreted the status of the regulations somewhat more liberally and have continued to operate under the previous guidelines. They are pursuing their franchising strategy with the expectation that future guidelines will allow even more flexibility and opportunity.

INTELLECTUAL PROPERTY

Concerns related to the protection of intellectual property rights in China have been well publicized across all industries, and as much as any other industry, franchisors must be particularly sensitive to intellectual property considerations related to trademarks. Imitators who offer inconsistent quality and service can negatively impact the brand's image, an image that the franchisor has built through extensive promotional activities. In the end, brand awareness and positive consumer association are critical assets of the franchisor, and intellectual property rights infringement can significantly impact the value of those assets.

Starbucks and KFC have expended efforts to discourage trademark infringement within current markets, particularly within the major markets of Shanghai, Beijing, and Chongqing. Starbucks is currently in a copyright row with a Shanghai coffee shop it claims has copied the U.S.-based company's logo and name. Nonetheless, these companies believe the legal infrastructure in China is sufficient for purposes of intellectual property protection and have had positive results in getting imitators to cease and desist. Suggested strategies for deterring unwanted imitators include:

- Constant monitoring of franchisee, distribution, and marketing channels for product infringement.
- Taking legal action against not only the imitators but also the entire support system, including the manufacturer and distribution channel.
- Providing intellectual property training throughout the franchisee's local management and staff.
- Including in the contract a requirement that the franchisee, suppliers, and distributors report the infringing of products or outlets, if discovered.

Protecting intellectual property can be expensive—identifying imitators can consume valuable human and financial resources. For example, Tony Chen, the head of public and legal affairs for Yum (formerly Tricon Global Restaurants, or Tricon)—parent of KFC and Pizza Hut—explained that it was impractical for his firm to investigate and pursue action against imitators in distant markets they have yet to enter, despite their inclusion in future expansion plans. He did recognize that this could negatively impact the acceptance of the KFC brand in those areas if there were brand-deteriorating imitators, but he also felt that they could not commit resources to combating the problem on any larger scale.

At the franchise expo in Shanghai, we witnessed several China-based firms seeking to build a brand modeled after very identifiable western franchises. For example, the fast-food hamburger establishment Merry Holiday uses a red and yellow color scheme and emphasizes the letter "M" in its promotional materials and signage, making it vaguely distinguishable from McDonald's. Additionally, a coffee chain at the expo featured a green color pattern and a store layout almost identical to Starbucks. There are also reportedly two Burger King restaurants operating in China that are not affiliated with Diageo, the corporate parent of Burger King, which has yet to establish a presence in China. The longer these units operate in China, the more challenging it will be for Burger King to claim rights to its trademark, enter China, and eventually establish a consistent brand image.

RETURN ON INVESTMENT CRITERIA

The up-front investment and associated payout period for a franchisor may be significantly longer in China than in other countries. Potential entrants must be patient and understand that the economic reality of establishing a presence in China may deviate significantly from initial expectations. A company that lacks the financial resources and management commitment to endure unforeseen roadblocks and pitfalls may want to consider a more mature market where there is less uncertainty.

McDonald's, for instance, has been in the China market for approximately ten years and has expended significant resources to building its brand in China. Tan explained that the company's return on investment criterion for China is distinctly different from its operations in other countries because of senior management's long-term commitment to the Chinese market. Less well capitalized firms, or ones more focused on short-term profitability and return on investment, are more likely to exit the China market in favor of one with a friendlier environment.

In addition to patience, a large portion of a firm's long-term commitment is its ability to remain flexible and its willingness to reinvest despite major setbacks. Although franchising is a well-established business model, economic and cultural issues unique to China may require a firm to take a step back and rethink its existing strategy when traditional approaches fail. A good example is Tricon's attempt to open the first Pizza Hut in Beijing in 1990. Eager to enter the Chinese franchising market early, Tricon solicited the partnership of a master franchisee that had a successful franchise track record in Thailand. However, having limited experience in China, the franchisee sold his license to a local Chinese government operator. Little priority or care was given to develop the new operation, since the organization was government run. As a result, Pizza Hut experienced severe quality and brand image issues that affected menu selection, image consistency, and dining services. One Pizza Hut even went so far as to create a makeshift karaoke bar as an attachment to the main restaurant. To address this issue, Tricon immediately repurchased all franchising licenses. Instead of withdrawing from the market, it decided to develop Pizza Hut (and KFC) using corporate stores until the franchising market matured.

THE FRANCHISING DECISION: A SUMMARY

There are considerable benefits to pursuing a franchising strategy in China. Franchising offers the opportunity to combine the operating, marketing, and financing business knowledge of the western franchisor with the local market expertise and entrepreneurial spirit of the franchisee. Franchising properly aligns the interests of the parties involved and allows for rapid expansion; it also offers benefits in the areas of marketing and legal oversight.

Despite these benefits, companies have to overcome sizeable barriers to succeed under a franchise strategy—legal ambiguity creates the possibility for unforeseeable hurdles and difficulties; trademark protection can be costly and time consuming; educating the franchisor's entire constituency on the franchising concept can be a huge drain on financial and human resources; and traditional return on investment criteria used to evaluate investment opportunities in other countries may not be applicable in China. Nevertheless, after considering these pros and cons, China may still be a company's best choice for global expansion. Then, the next step will be deciding which type of franchise agreement to enter into.

SELECTING A FRANCHISE STRUCTURE

Determining the appropriate legal structure or franchise agreement ultimately comes down to the issue of control—the franchisor must either retain a suitable level of legal and financial control in the arrangement or have enough confidence and trust in its local partner to allow the franchisee control in carrying out the mission of the company.

There are four main franchise options available (listed in order from the franchisor having most to least control): joint venture, direct franchise, area development, and master franchise. The franchisor can combine elements from two or more of these legal structures to create an agreement that best fits its enterprise. To reach the final decision, the franchisor needs to weigh the benefits and weaknesses of each structure. The dominant trade-off lies between the level of control versus the time and capital commitment. The more control a franchisor exerts in operations and in the growth implementation, the greater the investment will be in both time and capital resources (Figure 4.1).

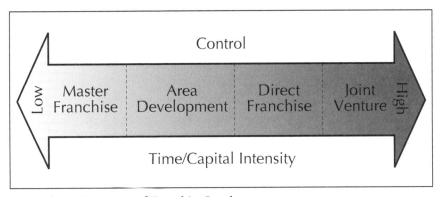

Figure 4.1: Spectrum of Franchise Involvement

JOINT VENTURE

A joint venture is a contractual agreement between two or more parties to undertake a business venture in which profits and losses are shared equally. Although a joint venture is not a type of franchising structure per se, it is an important method of entry and represents the first step toward a franchising model. The franchisor can establish its brand in China and accumulate knowledge about the market while adapting its best practices manual to fit the Chinese market. With this type of arrangement, the franchisor has more control to improve customer experience, operational procedures, and back office functions, thus offering future franchisees a more profitable and consistent brand.

DIRECT (OR UNIT-TO-UNIT) FRANCHISE

In the direct or unit-to-unit franchise, which is the most basic type of franchising structure, the rights to franchise are granted on a store-by-store basis to individual franchisees. Because of the tremendous time investment, the franchisor needs to either excel at identifying, screening, and training potential franchisees or offer a concept that does not require high volume growth. The direct franchise method is best suited for more full-scale dining establishments like Bennigan's or Chili's, which expect to grow at a relatively controlled pace and require fewer units to saturate a market.

AREA DEVELOPMENT FRANCHISE

Under this arrangement, the franchisor grants the rights of franchising for a specific geographic region to a Chinese-based franchisee, but subfranchising (the franchisee offering franchises) is not allowed. Often, the region involves a major market or several medium-sized markets within reasonable proximity of each other. Area development offers less control than a joint venture or a direct franchise arrangement because the franchisee is responsible for such decisions as locations and plans for growth. Because the franchisee bears most of the capital investment and must have its own infrastructure expenses, the franchisee must be well capitalized to meet the franchisor's growth goals. The franchisee takes on the responsibility of monitoring the day-to-day operations of each of its stores while the franchisor follows the traditional western model of building brand awareness and loyalty (while achieving core competencies in purchasing or real estate, for example).

An example of area development can be found with Auntie Anne's mall-based pretzel stores, which used this strategy to expand throughout Asia in the mid-1990s. Currently, KFC is also pursuing an area development strategy in several regions of China. By pursuing such a model, KFC ensures that only the most qualified franchisees are allowed to participate in the program and can maintain tighter control over customer experience and brand perception.

MASTER FRANCHISE

Like the other structures, the master franchise arrangement gives the franchisee the right to open and run units. In addition, the master franchisee has the right to subfranchise to other franchisees and thus assume the role of franchisor. From the franchisor's standpoint, the master franchise arrangement is clearly the least capital- and time-intensive structure, but the trade-off is diminished control. In this regard, it is critical that the master franchisee be an enterprise or partner that the franchisor trusts explicitly. Without a previous working relationship or a high degree of trust, companies are ill-advised to pursue a master franchise structure, particularly early in the entry strategy. An example of a master franchising agreement that has been successful is Hop Hing Fast Food Ltd., which has exclusive franchising agreements with Carl's Jr., Golden Skillet, and Dairy Queen. Its extensive experience with franchising within Asia made it an ideal candidate for the master franchise structure. Given McDonald's long history and level of comfort with the Chinese markets, the master franchise structure would likely suit it as well.

STRUCTURAL VARIATIONS

As previously mentioned, a franchisor has the option of using elements from one or more of these franchising arrangements to develop a structure that suits its particular needs. TGI Friday's, which has established a joint venture in Beijing with its master franchisee, provides the best example of a hybrid arrangement that utilizes several features of franchising structures. The company has established a master franchise structure to allow the flexibility to subfranchise in the future if the opportunity presents itself. Until then, the joint venture intends to place stores in core markets under what looks like a more traditional area development strategy.

KEY OPERATING STRATEGIES FOR SUCCESS

In this section, we discuss some of the key elements to keep in mind when considering a franchising strategy. These include selecting the local partner, choosing an initial market, developing a distribution and supplier network, and settling issues of financing. Each of these is discussed in turn.

SELECTING THE LOCAL PARTNER

One of the most critical elements to an entry strategy in China is selecting a local partner. The right partner can make a significant difference in speeding up entry and expansion time and in minimizing sizeable miscellaneous costs. If anyone understands the importance of finding respectable local partners to help navigate the potential pitfalls of conducting business in China, it is Somkit Tan, president of Superbrand Mall. The Superbrand Mall Corporation, owned by a Thai conglomerate, has invested hundreds of millions of U.S. dollars in the Pudong special economic zone (SEZ) over the past ten years. Tan's advice for multinational firms is that they should approach the People's Republic of China (PRC) with an understanding that "P" represents "patience," "R" stands for "relationships," and "C" stands for "contribution" (see Figure 4.2). Patience means having the willingness to wait significantly longer than initially expected to establish relationships and realize a financial payoff. Relationships relates to the importance of nurturing long-term relationships with business partners and understanding the value Chinese business partners place in knowing and trusting their counterparts. And contribution relates to the

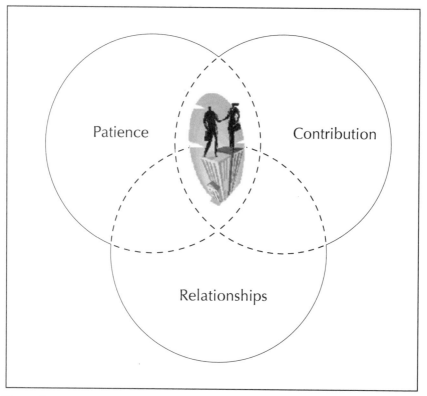

Figure 4.2:   Patience, Relationships, and Contribution (PRC) Diagram

importance that the Chinese government places on contributing time and funds toward the local area. The government views these contributions as signs of serious commitment to long-term business practices.

In addition to understanding your Ps, Rs, and Cs, former McDonald's executive Kaplan advises firms not to assume that a Chinese partner candidate is the most trustworthy and qualified partner just because he speaks fluent English. Although a language barrier can be discouraging, it does not necessarily indicate a lack of skills desired in a local partner. Table 4.1 lists ten favorable characteristics of local partners.

CHOOSING AN INITIAL MARKET

Any multinational casual-dining firm must select a geographic region of China in which to enter. Given the sheer size of China, this decision can seem daunting. The following are some of the choices we came across.

According to Pei Liang, vice secretary general for the China Chain Store Franchising Association, franchisors should start in Beijing to establish critical relationships with national government officials and take advantage of the high tourist volume each year. Tony Chen of KFC, however, supported KFC's strategy of establishing a significant presence in Shanghai because of the area's probusiness atmosphere, the openness of consumers to western products, the high level of tourism, and the market's significant

Table 4.1
Favorable Characteristics of a Local Partner

1.	Trustworthiness
2.	Successful business track record
3.	Local/national government relationships
4.	Strong third-party relationships
5.	Entrepreneurial spirit
6.	Willingness to observe company procedures
7.	Willingness to accept oversight
8.	Access to capital
9.	Management and motivation of local employees
10.	Restaurant experience

long-term growth potential. And while McDonald's has penetrated a number of markets in China under a company-owned strategy, Kaplan expressed his view that new entrants to China may benefit from establishing their presence in Hong Kong and then moving inland toward Shenzhen. He described the probusiness atmosphere and general acceptance of successful Hong Kong firms in the region to support this strategy. In addition, existing management and marketing infrastructure in Hong Kong can be leveraged in nearby markets. Another recommendation is to enter third-tier cities. Although smaller, these markets will also be less competitive, giving the franchisor the ability to achieve profits by capturing a greater portion of a "smaller pie," as well as deter future entrants.

All these recommendations are compelling and the specific circumstances of a given fast-food franchisor will determine the ultimate attractiveness of these possible approaches. Regardless of the market selected, it is crucial that the franchisor recognize that Chinese consumer preferences are as vast as the country's landscape. As a result, management must understand that different markets will likely have different tastes. The product mix and pricing may need to be adapted (within parameters that do not threaten the consistency of the brand) to specific regions in order to optimize the level of acceptance and ultimately the franchisor's profitability. Both McDonald's and KFC have, for instance, adapted their products and their marketing strategies in China to their target segments.

THE DISTRIBUTION AND SUPPLIER NETWORK

In addition to selecting a local partner and choosing an initial market, expansion in China requires the development of a comprehensive, nationwide distribution and supplier network. Currently, domestic distributors and suppliers are ill equipped to handle the level of service demanded by highly competitive firms. Furthermore, outsourcing logistics is a relatively new concept for many manufacturers and retailers in China. However, with China's accession into the WTO, both foreign and domestic firms realize the critical role that logistics and the supply chain play in allowing them to reach market penetration.

Building a Supplier Network
Sourcing inputs that meet the franchisor's standards for quality and consistency without disrupting profitability can pose a significant challenge to potential entrants in China. Three different companies reveal three substantially different strategies for addressing this problem. To ensure consistency with other operations and adherence to its internal standards of quality, TGI Friday's chooses to import roughly 75 percent of its raw (food-related) materials. The advantage of this approach is that TGI Friday's in China is almost identical to stateside operations. The disadvantage is that heavy importing can be expensive and can expose profitability to exchange rate fluctuations.

McDonald's has chosen another route to maintain consistency with its core product. Instead of importing products, McDonald's replicated its supply chain, bringing its key suppliers in other markets, such as potato supplier Simplot, to China. This approach allowed McDonald's to distribute the initial investment burden in China between itself and its suppliers. The risk its suppliers might face from such significant investments was mitigated with long-term supply contracts with McDonald's, a trusted, rapidly growing customer in China. However, this strategy requires significant lead time before suppliers are prepared to meet franchisor demand.

KFC has approached China with yet another strategy for sourcing goods. With its long-established presence in China, KFC has found local suppliers from which to procure its key inputs. Given that chicken is relatively consistent across countries and that it is the primary supply on which KFC relies, the company has benefited from the relative ease and low-cost nature of this strategy.

Infrastructure Constraints
Once supplier issues are resolved, the franchisor must arrange the transport of goods between its supplier network, distribution centers, and end markets. This challenge can be a formidable one, as the logistics market in China is highly fragmented. Recent studies

show that there are over 650,000 wholesale operators servicing just the food, beverage, and tobacco sector alone, most of whom are small-scale operations, with only 10 percent having sales over RMB 10 million (US$1.2 million). China's cold chain infrastructure (the term given to the network of processes and services used to transport and preserve edible products in a temperature-controlled environment) is old, underinvested, and struggling to keep up with the growth in demand. In addition, most investments currently made by multinational firms are for information technology and management development rather than for infrastructure such as roads, trucks, and warehouses. Most retailers either work alone to reach their customers, or they have to rely on numerous local partners or international distribution companies. Although local partners offer the advantage of current relationships and local knowledge, they can often be cumbersome and expensive.

To combat the issue of underdeveloped logistical infrastructure, KFC, which outsources logistics in each of the other ninety-six countries it operates in, invested heavily in its own distribution network, with roughly twenty distribution centers throughout mainland China. Each franchisee is given the choice of using either KFC's distribution network or a third-party distributor for product delivery. Despite the additional fee to use the service, most franchisees opt for KFC to ensure dependable delivery and quality service. Tricon (KFC's parent) is considered to be the only casual-dining organization with such a state-of-the-art system, giving it an enormous competitive advantage over its rivals.

Another option is to build relationships with trusted third-party logistics firms. This option allows casual-dining enterprises to capitalize on a foreign distributor's desire to develop and grow in the Chinese market. Most recently, Wu Mart, a major Beijing retail chain store, and Hutchison Tibbett Britten Logistics (HTB), a British logistics firm, set up a partnership that will give HTB the sole right to provide logistics support to the store's planned expansion into a number of major cities across China. Such a partnership will allow Wu Mart to centralize its supply and delivery system while giving HTB the opportunity to develop its distribution network in China.

FINANCING

Important financing considerations surface throughout different stages of the franchising process, from the time of the market entry decision through executing the expansion plan. The issues center around three primary areas: capital availability for franchisees, lack of equipment leasing options and availability of real estate, and repatriation of capital to the stateside parent.

Access to Capital for Local Partners

Purchasing the franchise rights to a KFC can cost as much as US$1 million. To come up with the capital, entrepreneurs typically have to borrow some of the funds either from family members and friends or through commercial banking channels. In the past, small-business relationships in China were conducted almost exclusively on a cash basis, due to tight credit lending standards and a lack of understanding among the lending community about franchising. But as large chains entered the market, China's credit markets have freed up to some extent. For example, KFC had more than one hundred financially legitimate applicants for a recent franchising opportunity in Shanghai. Chen noted that many banks are now underwriting loans to entrepreneurs based exclusively on the KFC name, without requiring a Tricon guarantee or other type of contingent liability.

Another example of Chinese banks' increasing openness to franchising is the recent arrangement between the Bank of China (BOC) and Kodak, an extensive user of the franchising model in China. Under the arrangement, BOC establishes a comprehensive credit line of US$12 million for Kodak franchisees, thus reducing the up-front capital commitment of a franchisee to roughly US$10,000. Increased access to capital should expand the pool of potential franchisees and allow Kodak (and eventually other franchisors) to identify those franchisees with the strongest work ethic and entrepreneurial spirit instead of the ones with the most funds.

Furthermore, in July 1999, the Shanghai branch of the Industrial and Commercial Bank of China (ICBC) introduced a new mortgage loan program for individuals looking to buy retail space, such as restaurants. This program, which was a first for

China, aimed at encouraging self-employment and reducing unemployment while simultaneously boosting the number of smaller, family- or individually owned establishments. The loans were reserved for relatively large retail spaces, which could be transformed into service-oriented businesses in residential areas, with an average term of five years. These loan programs indicate positive trends in credit availability that should help stimulate local catering initiatives in China.

Additional Costs: Equipment and Real Estate

Often, the franchise fee is only a portion of the up-front costs—under a standard western franchising model, the franchisee also would invest capital in the equipment and in some cases the real estate. According to Kaplan, the equipment leasing market in China is significantly less sophisticated than in the United States, and as such, the franchisor may have to invest in store equipment and lease it to the franchisee, at least until the franchisee can afford to purchase it (after several years of operation). This arrangement could be attractive and offer additional means to generate a return on investment, but it does change the profit dynamics of the franchising business because it requires a higher level of capital commitment from the franchisor.

The availability and financing of real estate can be a major consideration as well, particularly for the pilot and other marquee stores where location is critical. In many cases, real estate is state-owned and can only be leased on a long-term basis (over fifty years). However, under the real estate regulations enacted in 1990, local and foreign investors are allowed to develop, use, and administer real estate.

Other issues related to real estate in China include lease structures that vary significantly from standard U.S. arrangements, the high cost of land relative to its potential for profitability, and the lack of parking in prime locations for foot traffic. However, TGI Friday's overcame this latter hurdle by providing shuttle services to its customers to and from parking garages fifteen minutes away. Additionally, a growing number of shopping centers and malls that are ideal locations for franchised restaurants have been appearing in China. So, while potential entrants should be mindful of these and other capital considerations, franchisors should not view these financing hurdles as prohibitive to a franchising strategy in China.

Repatriation of Profits
In China, restrictions limit the repatriation of profits and capital to the United States or other countries. The State Association of Foreign Exchange (SAFE) in particular requires that foreign companies register a certain percentage of their initial capital investment to ensure that the investment is not overleveraged. There are fairly strict rules that discourage attempts to repatriate the initial investment, making this capital rather illiquid. To avoid this situation, firms should closely evaluate their initial investment or make initial capital contributions in stages to minimize the risk of not being able to pull out overinvested amounts. Although China has been relaxing the restrictions on repatriated profits over the past ten years, SAFE will scrutinize financial information to ensure that repatriated profit has actually been earned and does not represent the initial capital. To alleviate the burden of these restrictions, most franchisors reinvest profits back into China to continue to fund growth.

Also, reinvesting profits provides a natural hedge against currency exchange fluctuations in most cases. The primary exception is in the case of companies that import a significant value of goods. Exchange rate exposure will continue to be a concern for these companies, such as TGI Friday's, which imports over 75 percent of its inputs. In addition, in many cases, the government requires foreign firms to balance foreign exchange to avoid creating a foreign exchange deficit for China. This requirement further emphasizes the benefits of local sourcing.

CONCLUSION

Notwithstanding positive trends in the Chinese market, it is critical that any chain seeking international expansion perform an in-depth evaluation of the opportunities and risks associated with entering

China by way of franchising. The franchisor must find competent and trustworthy local partners, deal with an ambiguous legal system, and control brand consistency. Given the many options for growth, the fast-food enterprise must decide on which geographic markets to enter and which legal structure to use.

Although the challenges may seem daunting, we believe the opportunities and outlook for franchising in China are promising. We hope that the recommendations and insights presented in this chapter will help firms successfully enter China's vast market through this strategy.

BIBLIOGRAPHY

Access Asia Limited. 2001. "Fast Food and Organized Catering in China: A Market Analysis." http://www.accessasia.co.uk/showreport.asp? RptId=56. [Cited October 22, 2001.]

Alon, Ilan. 2001. "Interview: International Franchising in China with Kodak." *Thunderbird International Business Review,* 43 (6):737.

Baldinger, Pamela, and Daniel Reardon. 1992. "Franchises and Fast Food." *China Business Review,* 19 (6):20–21.

Bugg, James. 1994. "China: Franchising's New Frontier." *Franchising World,* 26 (6):8–10.

Burke, Bob, and Carol Wingard. 1997. "The Big Chill." *China Business Review,* 24 (4):12–18.

Carlsson, Carl. 1993. "Franchising Real Estate in the People's Republic of China." *Franchising World,* 25 (5):46.

China Cuisine Association, China General Chamber of Commerce, China National Commercial Information Center. 2002. "Information on the Primary Indexes and Important Commodities Sales of Large Retailers and Catering Industries in China for the Year of 2001." China National Commercial Information Center.

Clifford, Mark. 1998. "Companies: And They're Off." *Far Eastern Economic Review,* 156 (48):76.

Franchise China Conference and Exhibition. 2001. "China's Strong Economy and Growing Consumer Market Set the Stage for Widespread Franchising Growth." http://www.english.franchisechina.com/ HOME.HTM.

Lu, Zhang. 2002. "Kodak Snaps up Franchise Deal with BOC." *China Daily,* January 26.

Pine, Ray, Pingshu Qi, and Hanqin Zhang. 2000. "The Challenges and Opportunities of Franchising in China's Hotel Industry." *International Journal of Contemporary Hospitality Management,* 12:305.

Sheppard, Robert. 1998. "The New Franchising Framework Law and the Future of Franchising in China." http://www.globalsources.com/.

Watson, James L., ed. 1997. *Golden Arches East: McDonald's in East Asia.* Stanford, Calif.: Stanford University Press.

"The WTO and Distribution: The Locals Know." 2001. *China Economic Quarterly,* 5:40.

Chapter 5

OVERCOMING THE LEADERSHIP GAP

Anthony Chen, Alyson Gampel, and
Milan Sevak

A tidal wave of foreign investment, rapidly changing socioeconomic dynamics, and urban migration have radically transformed China's business landscape. Over the past twenty years, China has undergone tremendous change as the government sought to move from an economy that is largely state owned to one that is leaning increasingly toward private enterprise. Domestic firms have grown and prospered with the expansion of export markets. China's accession to the World Trade Organization (WTO) has opened up tremendous opportunities for foreign companies to conduct business with one of the world's largest potential consumer markets. But along with these opportunities come challenges, such as finding and developing leadership talent to navigate China's evolving business environment. Multinational corporations (MNCs) and native Chinese companies alike struggle to develop effective managers that are able to lead in this new economy.

One challenge that companies face is redefining the concept of leadership. Rooted in Confucianism and the Legalist school of thought, the prevailing leadership style in China has been described as paternalistic. Researchers have identified three distinct elements of paternalistic leadership: authoritarianism, benevolence, and moral integrity. Authoritarian leaders (usually male) demand unquestioning obedience from employees and assert their absolute control over subordinates. Benevolent leaders are interested in the well-being of the employee, as well as the employee's family. Moral leaders inspire identification and respect from employees by demonstrating superior personal qualities. In *Management and Organizations in the Chinese Context,* researchers Jing-Lih Farh and Bor-Shiuan Cheng describe the paternalistic leadership style as combining "strong discipline and authority with fatherly benevolence and moral integrity couched in a personalistic atmosphere."

We first examine the historical and cultural context in which the prevailing paternalistic leadership style developed. Next, we analyze this leadership style in light of China's rapidly changing political and economic environment and identify the characteristics needed to manage in this environment. Finally, we provide recommendations to MNCs and domestic companies for developing effective leaders and managers who can successfully navigate China's rapidly evolving business environment.

PATERNALISTIC LEADERSHIP IN CHINA

The paternalistic leadership style is rooted in three thousand years of imperial rule. Under Confucianism (551–479 B.C.), which became the official orthodoxy for China during the Han Dynasty, the family was the basic building block of society, and the father's authority over family members was absolute. Although a similar power structure existed all over the world, in the West, the patriarch's authority was assumed to derive from God. Because the Chinese had no all-powerful god to legitimize patriarchal authority, the father-son relationship as laid out in Confucianism defined patriarchy in China.

The developing Legalist school of thought, conceived more than two thousand years ago, further solidified this relationship. Its "Three Bonds" stated that the emperor was the ruler of the minister, the father was the ruler of the son, and the husband was the ruler of the wife. Thus, as the imperial rulers politicized the Confucian social order by embracing patriarchy, they were also able to solidify their absolute authority through the tenets of the Legalist school. The Chinese have made the family model the prototype for almost all forms of organizations, including business. In fact, researchers have argued that the modern Chinese business structure can be directly linked to the history of patriarchy: The owner or manager plays the father's role, and subordinates or employees play the son.

Although no statistics are available, the majority of overseas Chinese businesses are family affairs. A dominant family member, usually the father, is the head of the business. Other family members occupy key posts, and employees lower down the hierarchy look to the father and other members of the family for leadership. As the private sector in mainland China grows, observers have found that practice repeated there. That is, decision making and power in Chinese firms remain highly concentrated. Consequently, respect for authority and power is a driving force in the workplace.

Like the authoritative model, the benevolent leadership model also finds its basis in the Confucian ideal of mutually harmonious relationships. According to Farh and Cheng, the Three Bonds implies that "the ideal social relations are 'benevolent ruler with loyal minister,' 'kind father with filial son,' 'righteous husband with submissive wife.'" In modern China, benevolent leadership is greatly reinforced by the concept of *bao,* or reciprocity. Favors done for one another are often considered a type of social investment for which future returns are expected. As such, a boss will display benevolent behaviors in an effort to create a sense of indebtedness in his employees. While all cultures have norms of reciprocity, in China the concept of *bao* maintains a higher degree of consciousness in people's minds. *Bao* is also the foundation of *guanxi,* or personal connections, which are prominent in both business and social relations in China. Another implication of mutually harmonious relationships can be seen in the concept of "face." According to Min Chen in *Asian Management Systems,* "face" refers to a combination of dignity, self-respect, and status as perceived by others, implying that responses in public must be carefully monitored so as not to lead to loss of face. Whereas negative reactions, such as anger or threats toward employees, can lead to loss of face, public recognition for exemplary accomplishments at work can lead to increased face. In addition, the workplace traditionally provided for the employees in all aspects, from housing to medical care—the "iron rice bowl" policy, and there is a continuing expectation that the owner or manager will care for the employees.

According to Confucianism, the benevolent leader is also a moral leader. The *Analects* of Confucius stress the importance of cultivating individual virtues, particularly in the realm of governance, and stress that leading the people with virtue and regulating them by the rules of propriety will lead to a sense of shame and righteous behavior. The ideal of moral leadership has held through time and also has been reinforced by the Legalist tradition; imperial leaders supported the Confucian values and demonstrated their superior virtue through mastering the Confucian classics.

CHALLENGES TO PATERNALISTIC LEADERSHIP

Recent developments in China's political and economic climate have put stresses on the old style of Chinese leadership. Strict adherence to the centralized, top-down style of decision making is no longer effective in today's marketplace. With increasing confidence to challenge authority and unprecedented opportunities to influence change, today's generation of business leaders faces a conflict between the demands of the new business and political environment and the historically rooted paternalistic style of leadership.

In China, the value of submission to authority was first significantly challenged in the early 1950s during the agricultural land reforms. The property-holding class was put on trial and had its land taken away. The Cultural Revolution (1966–76) further attacked the foundations of authoritative leadership as young Red Guards assaulted formerly powerful Communist Party members. Even after the Red Guards were exiled and Party members returned to their positions, their level of authority was never the same. Although Party members were able to exert their power by controlling scarce resources, researchers Godwin Chu and Yanan Ju explain in *The Great Wall in Ruins: Communication and Cultural Change in China* that "this submission is no longer willingly expressed, but reluctantly extracted and intensely resented." Survey research confirms that the generation that was most heavily influenced by the Cultural Revolution—the age group that would have been targeted for joining the Red Guard—had significantly lower scores regarding respect for authority. Accordingly, although the basic leadership style has not changed dramatically in the last fifty years, the unquestioning acceptance of this style is decreasing.

A NEW ECONOMIC ENVIRONMENT

Solidified by China's recent entry into the WTO, the current economic reform movement has accelerated the ongoing reevaluation of what makes for effective and acceptable managerial leadership in China. In 1997, the 15th Communist Party Congress called for identifying new ownership structures for state-owned enterprises (SOEs) as a prerequisite for strengthening the economy. Thomas Lee Boam, minister-counselor of commercial affairs at the U.S. embassy in China, noted that SOEs currently employ 70 percent of all workers in China yet produce only 30 percent of all goods and services. In contrast, private firms employ 30 percent of China's workforce but produce 70 percent of all goods and services. Nevertheless, efforts to streamline production in China's SOEs so far have met with resistance because of concerns that massive job cuts may result in social unrest, explained Qiang Lu, the PRC human capital practice leader in the China office of William M. Mercer, an international human resources consulting firm. Such resistance, in addition to the potential for labor unrest, reflects China's deep-rooted reliance on the paternalistic style of leadership. Yet problems with the workplace environment, including health and safety standards, are behind China's approximately 100,000 labor disputes each year.

As multinational firms invest in China, they bring with them an influx of competitive pressure to the country's SOEs. Twenty years after the policy shift, China has mapped out a development plan for about 1,000 of its largest industrial SOEs (out of a total of 118,000) to enable them to compete successfully in this new global market. This development process involves examining current leadership style to determine what will be effective in this new economy. For MNCs, the task is to introduce and incorporate global practices in a nascent market.

THE LEADERSHIP GAP

The move from a planned economy to a market-driven economy calls for entirely new managerial and leadership skills, skills that are currently in short supply. Chinese executives now need to take a more customer-focused approach in their operations. This type of marketing mind-set is completely foreign to the typical Chinese leader, whose primary concerns in a planned economy have been to appease government supervisors, meet production quotas, and ensure employment. Because the government dictated supply and demand, the planned economy business leader in China had absolutely no incentive or need to think about operational efficiency, market segmentation, or workforce development. While a market economy is characterized by a focus on the customer and a need to maximize efficiency, the planned economy lacks these characteristics.

In John Stuttard's *The New Silk Road,* Jack Perkowski, chairman and chief executive officer of ASIMCO Technologies Limited (an independent diversified manufacturer with seventeen joint ventures and two wholly owned companies in China), explained that almost all managers could be described as bureaucratic before 1978. Since then, a new class of very entrepreneurial managers has been created. According to Perkowski, this trend, which began in the southern part of China in Guangdong Province, has now spread to all of China.

While a market economy emphasizes marketing, financial, and operational savvy, the planned economy places more importance on government relationships and *guanxi.* The government-established levels of supply and demand in a planned economy made a strong relationship with relevant government officials essential. By contrast, when the market controls supply and demand, governmental relationships have less bearing on the success or failure of an enterprise. Rather, success in a market economy is driven by the ability of management to understand the market's competitive forces, the diversity of customers' needs, and the importance of innovation and strategic focus. Because the Chinese government seeks to maintain a strong role in the market economy, however, government relationships will continue to be important in business, albeit to a lesser degree than in the past.

Adding to the leadership gap in China is the short supply of talented executives. In a 2002 article in *China International Business* titled "The Head Hunt Is On," Henry Clough reported that the new wave of thirty-something Chinese executives are "among the wealthiest people in China, and the hottest properties in the labor market." Demand for managerial talent from the junior to senior levels has continued to exceed supply and has led to a growth in salaries that matches gross domestic product (GDP) growth. As Clough stated, "Bright young things are finding themselves in positions that their Western contemporaries could not hope to reach."

The dearth of competent executives will likely continue for the next several years as China develops its own cadre of managers. Several universities have started masters in business administration (M.B.A.) courses either independently or in partnership with western universities, but the impact will not be felt for some time. By enrolling in M.B.A. programs, promising Chinese leaders will be better equipped to compete in the new economy. Although an M.B.A. from abroad may be prized, an education from a Chinese university that models those in the West can certainly serve the same purpose. Zhi-xue Zhang, associate professor at the Guanghua School of Management, spent six months at the Kellogg School of Management in the United States and returned with frameworks, strategies, and tactics that faculty could then teach to their Chinese students. The Chinese European International Business School (CEIBS) in Shanghai also focuses on teaching western models to future Chinese leaders. Equipped with the tools gained through an M.B.A., Chinese leaders can succeed in both worlds—local markets and international business.

Although MNCs often supplement local management with western executives, this practice has not been without problems. As Perkowski pointed out, "We find that an expatriate must be quite outstanding . . . with enough experience to overcome the credibility issue." Although expatriates may bring an initial level of marketing insight and knowledge of management practices, consultants lament that foreign talent is often rejected. According to Brian Sun, an executive search consultant for E-sia Consulting in Shanghai, this disdain for foreign leaders is partly due to the high salaries they command but more so to their lack of specific knowledge on Chinese issues like tax regulation and government relationships. Expatriate managers are sometimes appointed with little awareness of China, its cultural differences, and the existing organizational support. This lack of awareness leads to further problems.

Addressing the Leadership Gap

With domestic talent in such short supply and expatriates lacking local knowledge, it is important that China develop new leaders with some of the qualities demanded of "western" business leaders: strategic thinking, sensitivity to external market dynamics, and international experience. The new leaders will also need to integrate China's rich traditions of moral and benevolent leadership that were part of the paternalistic style. All companies doing business in China—both foreign and domestic—will need to learn how to develop local talent according to the demands of the unique Chinese context if they are to generate sustainable profits.

Whereas regular factory laborers and their immediate supervisors tend to be local hires, middle and upper levels of management in MNCs are likely to be foreign. However, the steep average cost of the average expatriate leader (approximately US$250,000 per year) is a strong financial incentive for MNCs to develop and employ local leaders. Accordingly, both MNCs and native Chinese companies are proactively nurturing local managers. For example, with a conscious effort toward developing local talent, 60 percent of Nike's management staff are Chinese nationals, and the company is taking additional measures to increase this number. Trey Hentz, an expatriate manufacturing operations director for the Nike Guangzhou Liaison office, has run Nike's operations in a number of Asian countries, including China, and has trained ten Chinese nationals who will be taking over from expatriates like himself. He has an acute understanding of China's culturally shaped business milieu and recognizes the relevance of *guanxi,* the importance of building friendships to get the job done. Toward this end, Hentz often goes golfing or hiking with his team on the weekends. He believes it is important to invest in training and support when grooming a Chinese national to take over leadership roles. Hentz offers this advice to MNCs wanting to develop local leadership in China:

- Hire for the future, not just for the job that is at hand.
- Set clear expectations covering a span of at least two years.
- Support mistakes that can offer lessons.
- Defend your employees and staff in time of need.
- Direct your trainees to peers for advice; do not do it all yourself.
- Have patience and understand the learning curve.
- Be ready to admit when you have made the wrong choice. Do not continue to pour excessive resources and time into someone who is not making it.

As Hentz sees it, a measure of one's performance as a manager is how well employees do in their new role. Did the company invest the necessary money and effort to set them up for success? If so, Hentz believes this investment will produce capable leaders. Nike serves as a good example of an MNC whose expatriates proactively invest in the development of Chinese nationals. Much like most MNCs' global human resource development strategies, Nike realizes that the most sustainable and cost-effective business model is to aggressively localize the senior management through extensive exposure to good expatriate role models.

Another example of successful leadership development is Legend, China's largest information technology (IT) company. Aside from being known for his strategic thinking and sensitivity to the external market environment, Legend's current chairman, Liu Chuanzhi, is recognized for developing leaders within the ranks of the company. Atypical of most Chinese business leaders, Liu proactively identified two young star employees very early in their careers. As they rose through the ranks, Liu strategically provided them with growth and development opportunities. When the two promising employees reached the uppermost ranks in the company structure, Liu divided the company into two, giving each his own company to run. Wei Guo became the CEO of Digital China and Chin Ran Yang became the CEO of Legend. Liu's focus on developing home-grown managers who are attuned to local conditions was a key step in his goal of further extending Legend's advantage in the computer market and solidifying the company's "legendary" status in China.

Not all companies have the internal resources of these two well-established success stories. Companies looking to develop home-grown leaders can seek the services of the consulting and training firms that have opened offices in China. These firms can help MNCs and SOEs with leadership development, presentation and communication skills, and the determination of which competencies and skills a particular position requires.

CHALLENGES OF LEADERSHIP DEVELOPMENT

Despite a company's best efforts and intentions, there are challenges to overcome with leadership development. First, as in the West, there is competition for talent. As Clough indicated, "The danger for employers who invest heavily in developing their staff into the crème de la crème of the labor market is that those staff members will be singled out by headhunters and bombarded with alternative job offers." Thus, companies will have to work to retain their staff by providing opportunities for advancement, training, and attractive compensation. For instance, Bayer China has focused on trying to build a professional environment and reward progress, not through higher pay, but through greater responsibility. This approach has resulted in very low turnover of personnel because the career structure within the company offers opportunities for advancement. Advancement also ties in with a reward structure that is linked to increased "face" for the employee.

Another challenge that companies have to deal with in China is existing laws governing the mobility of workers. For example, Nike struggles with high turnover at its manufacturing plant, because the workers, mostly eighteen- to twenty-one-year-olds, are allowed to work for the manufacturer for only a few years before they are required by Chinese law to return to their native towns. This law removes both the incentive and the ability to train workers for management positions.

THE NEW CHINESE LEADER

The Chinese market represents one of the most uncertain and complicated markets on the globe. New competitors and government regulations have created rapid changes in market dynamics. The new Chinese leader must be able to navigate these constant pressures and changes while remaining focused on organizational goals. Fundamental changes in leadership style, priorities, and skills are required, and the new leadership style is much more participative than the top-down, black-box decision making of previous times. Figure 5.1 summarizes the shift in thinking that needs to be achieved.

DELEGATION SKILLS

Chinese leaders of the past did not need to be efficient or delegate well—their main priorities were to produce a certain volume and keep people employed. Power was centralized, and one leader made all the decisions, explained Lu of William M. Mercer. This belief system that the leader should make all the decisions created a general unwillingness among subordinates to act independently. Moreover, this power structure can lead to an "escalation of commitment" in which a leader may hesitate to correct a poor decision. In the past, government relationships provided safety nets for leaders, but in a market-driven environment, leaders must accept the consequences of their decisions.

Even if a traditional leader wanted to, he was not equipped to share power effectively, Lu added. However, the willingness and ability to delegate responsibilities is critical to developing successful leaders. Strong leaders will be able to empower and trust subordinates with more and more decision making—not just with tasks.

Figure 5.1: The New Leadership Approach, Priorities, and Skills

The new Chinese leader will need to divest notions of the authoritarian leadership and reframe the moral leadership concept. Leaders who manage during this transition to the market economy will learn to be moral leaders not through public demonstration of virtue but by developing those corporate virtues in their employees.

COMMUNICATION SKILLS

Strong managers must also be able to communicate effectively—not only with employees and customers, but in the case of MNCs, with headquarters in other countries as well. At Nike, for instance, a

Chinese national needs to be able to communicate with colleagues in China *and* those in the home office in the United States in order to be effective, keeping in mind that foreign colleagues may not always be familiar with China's cultural differences. Moreover, given the role of relationships and regulations in China, the manager needs to ensure that expectations are managed and the home office understands the processes involved in local decision making. In many ways, the Chinese national needs to be better at communication than an expatriate. However, the senior managers in the home office must also be aware of cultural differences and adjust their expectations to be supportive of their Chinese employees and counterparts.

SOUND BUSINESS JUDGMENT

In a highly uncertain and rapidly changing environment, Chinese leaders will be required to make more decisions that are critical to the survival of the business. Simply stated, leaders can no longer rely on the government to set organizational objectives. In this environment, successful Chinese leaders will need to understand external market conditions, especially changes in government regulations, and to identify opportunities that the organization can use to its competitive advantage. Additionally, leaders must anticipate and exploit changes in market demand, industry competition, and long-term market trends. Marketing and customer relations become higher priorities, whereas quotas and governmental relations become lower priorities. Another judgment call that Chinese leaders need to be able to make involves product quality. Hentz noted that, especially in China, the pressure to meet delivery needs can compromise product quality. He explained, "The key is to have good enough judgment to know when you can take a risk and compromise, when you cannot compromise, and when you need to ask for a second opinion."

MARKET MENTALITY

To make good judgments, a leader needs to have the right mind-set. As such, successful business leaders must understand the economics and preferences of their customers, who only recently obtained the right to make their own choices. Understanding consumers and their needs, preferences, and values will be crucial to the survival and long-term sustainability of these Chinese organizations. Although this focus on customers seems like second nature to most western businesspeople, it is a new concept for a Chinese leadership that has known only the structure and confines of a planned economy. Indeed, Mercer's Lu notes that often the firm's first step in consulting engagements with native Chinese companies is to educate the client on the new mind-set before it can focus on specific strategies to develop leadership.

THE NEW *GUANXI*

Given the changing relationship between the government and the economy, the new Chinese leader will need to be skilled in effectively negotiating between these two worlds. Over the course of four years, Zhang interviewed hundreds of business leaders and concluded that one of the key indicators of success is knowing how to work within the context of the potentially debilitating governmental structure. On the outside, Chinese leaders will do almost anything to appease government officials, but in the inside, they stubbornly pursue their own agenda. Zhang depicts this concept graphically (see Figure 5.2) with a square representing the leader's pursuit of her or his own agenda and the surrounding circle representing the image she or he presents to the outside world. As can be seen, the exterior stresses the need for harmony in relationships, although the internal agenda may be at odds with business partners or government.

MEETING THE MANAGERIAL CHALLENGE

Identifying and motivating local managers is likely to continue to be a challenge in the near future. Several companies operating in China have addressed this problem in a number of ways. We draw on some of these examples.

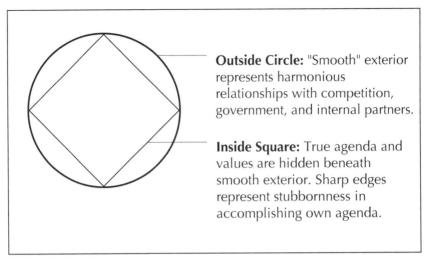

Outside Circle: "Smooth" exterior represents harmonious relationships with competition, government, and internal partners.

Inside Square: True agenda and values are hidden beneath smooth exterior. Sharp edges represent stubbornness in accomplishing own agenda.

Figure 5.2:   Shapes Metaphor of Leadership

HIRING THE BEST

Companies have turned to the best universities and colleges to recruit and train the best talent. They have also turned to the overseas Chinese community to staff their businesses. There they find people with significant experience living and working overseas, who hold M.B.A. degrees, and who have the advantage of being Chinese. Companies like ASIMCO have also tried to identify and hire the best managers from existing SOEs. But hiring is only one aspect of the issue. Companies also have to address the challenges of retaining talented workers through training, rewarding good performance, and motivating managers.

TRAINING PROGRAMS

Companies in China are acutely aware of the importance of training programs to build their human capital and business. Some, such as John Swire and Sons, Lucent, and Johnson and Johnson have put into place programs for their employees that include technical or sales training. The programs may involve several weeks of in-country or overseas training. These programs also provide companies with an opportunity to identify those most inclined to adopt western managerial attitudes and skills. Based on interviews with expatriate managers, researchers Andrew Sargeant and Stephen Frenkel found that more and more companies are going beyond the simple and basic training programs to provide more advanced educational programs.

REWARD SYSTEM

In *The New Silk Road,* Richard Conybeare, director of John Swire and Sons, pointed out that when workers from state-owned factories are hired, they tend to be loyal to the Communist Party or to the state. They have to be convinced to be loyal to the business. According to Conybeare, "This requires a proper payroll and reward system, so that you can identify the people who do a good job and reward them accordingly." With employee attitudes driven by the "iron rice bowl" policy, rewards in the form of benefits and other allowances can be important. As noted earlier, Bayer China, which has a low turnover rate, also rewards progress through greater responsibility. Thus, rewards may take the form of different kinds of incentives. The importance of "face" also suggests that recognition for achievement through career progression can help retention and encourage performance.

DEVELOPING LOCAL TALENT

Although the high cost of expatriates may be an incentive for developing local talent, the real benefit of localization is understanding the local market. For the Chinese employee, localization translates into career progress. For the corporation, localization allows it to compete more effectively. MNCs should continue to delegate, develop, and trust local leadership. One major mistake that MNC expatriates often make is micromanaging local leaders. This communicates an inherent mistrust in their abilities, as Nike's Hentz points out. Rather, trusting and challenging the local management will motivate them to strive for the next level of leadership responsibilities. Companies should provide local talent the opportunity to test their newly acquired business skills in a safe environment. Additionally, MNCs should learn the local business culture by developing native talent and forging relationships with local experts. For example, when bidding for certain projects, many western firms fail to understand the complexities of transactions with government officials and Chinese company management. Developing home-gown talent should make MNCs more attuned to such elements of the local business environment. Without a good understanding of the culture, companies will have little or no chance for success against their local competitors.

THE IMPORTANCE OF *GUANXI*

MNCs need to recognize the importance of friendships and relationships in the Chinese business culture. Zhang noted, "With good relationships, they will do anything for you," even beyond the professional context. However, good relationships do not necessarily mean good business. As Boam indicated, *"Guanxi* makes a good business work; *guanxi* does not salvage a business that never had a prayer." Multinational corporate executives must strive for a proper, balanced understanding of *guanxi*. As Dr. Richard Latham, president of Limited Technologies International—China, explained in *The New Silk Road,* networking and the importance of relationships is a global phenomenon. However, in the Chinese context, he has found that "it is an almost consuming aspect of Chinese life. . . . At every meeting, social or business, the Chinese participants are working on some aspect of the relationship."

CONCLUSION

"Leadership" is a vague term—it can mean different things to different people. A thesaurus connects the term to management, control, direction, and guidance. As these synonyms suggest, putting a clear definition to leadership can be tricky. In this chapter, we have relied on a more general definition: leadership as influence. True leaders are those who can influence positive change in their organization. True leaders influence their surroundings, their subordinates, their managers, their organizations, and ultimately, their country. In this context, China's new leaders will need to use the skills suggested in this chapter to influence how business is conducted in China and capture the growing market's vast potential.

Leadership development cannot take place on its own, however. The importance of *guanxi* and cultural norms for conducting business in China mandates that the identification, training, and development of local business leaders be key aspects of the operating strategy of MNCs and SOEs. Companies that commit resources to develop home-grown talent will ensure that they have a competitive advantage in China's rapidly changing market.

BIBLIOGRAPHY

Ambler, Tim, and Morgen Witzel. 2000. *Doing Business in China.* New York: Routledge.

Bellah, Robert. 1970. "Father and Son in Christianity and Confucianism." In *Beyond Belief: Essays on Religion in a Post-Traditional World.* New York: Harper and Row.

Chen, Min. 1995. *Asian Management Systems.* International Thomson Business Press.

Chu, Godwin, and Yanan Ju. 1993. *The Great Wall in Ruins: Communication and Cultural Change in China.* New York: State University of New York Press.

Clough, Henry. 2002. "The Head Hunt Is On." *China International Business,* 172 (March):49–51.

Farh, Jing-Lih, and Bor-Shiuan Cheng. 2000. "A Cultural Analysis of Paternalistic Leadership in Chinese Organizations." In *Management and Organizations in the Chinese Context.* London: Macmillan Press.

Holt, Wilma F. 1998. "1998 National Distinguished Principals." *Verona American School.* http://www.naesp.org/SpecialProjects/ndpbios15.htm.

Sargeant, Andrew, and Stephen Frenkel. 1998. "Managing People in China: Perceptions of Expatriate Managers." *Journal of World Business,* 33 (1):17–34.

Stuttard, John B. 2000. *The New Silk Road: Secrets of Business Success in China Today.* New York: John Wiley and Sons.

Tsui, Anne, and Jing-Lih Farh. 1997. "Where Guanxi Matters: Relational Demography and Guanxi and Technology." *Work and Occupations,* 24 (1):56–79.

Yang, K. 1993. "Chinese Social Orientation: An Integrative Analysis." In *Psychotherapy for the Chinese.* Hong Kong: The Chinese University of Hong Kong.

Yang, L. 1957. "The Concept of Bao as a Basis for Social Relations in China." In *Chinese Thought and Institutions.* Chicago: University of Chicago Press.

Chapter 6

COMBATING PIRACY
THROUGH *GUANXI*

Daniel Beck, Stephanie Feldman,
Hernan Grimoldi, and
Susanna Ver Eecke

An increasingly sophisticated and low-cost manufacturing base has made China a leading manufacturer and exporter of consumer goods. Yet the country is also regarded largely as the worst perpetrator of intellectual property rights (IPR) violations in the world. Counterfeiting runs rampant in almost every industry, from computer software to personal hygiene products, and is a major cost of doing business in China. Counterfeiting is estimated to be a US$16 billion business in China, with counterfeits constituting 15 percent to 20 percent of all branded goods made in the country. China topped the list of source countries for counterfeit goods and accounted for nearly half the value of goods seized by U.S. customs in 2002, with about US$47 million in infringing goods. Although China's entrance into the World Trade Organization (WTO) has forced the country to focus on improving IPR protection through legal reform, inadequate laws and ineffective enforcement have resulted in little progress. Furthermore, because counterfeiting is such a lucrative business for China, the government has had little incentive to change.

IPR violations exist in many different forms in China—counterfeiting, piracy, duplication, creation of fake and shoddy goods, and trademark infringement. Here, we broadly refer to all IPR violations as counterfeiting, although our focus is primarily on unlawful production of nondurable consumer goods. Counterfeiting these types of goods typically takes two forms: overbuilding, or legitimate factories producing additional product beyond what they are approved to make, and cloning, or reproducing exact replicas of products or packaging, often by reverse engineering.

Over the years, a number of tactics have been used to fight counterfeiting. However, as counterfeiters become more sophisticated, short-term measures, such as product enhancements, packaging changes, and product raids, are becoming increasingly ineffective. Clearly, a longer term strategy that fights counterfeiting at its source is needed—one that influences Chinese legislation, encourages IPR enforcement, and stifles demand. Such a strategy requires companies to have a good understanding of the situation in China, the willingness to work hard to gain trust, as well as the required financial and human resources, which is a massive task for any individual company.

The situation can probably be helped by *guanxi,* the concept of personal connections and their associated obligations that drives business and government affairs in China. Over the past three years, a consortium of multinational corporations has been striving as a group to protect their IPR using various means. Known as the Quality Brands Protection Committee (QBPC), this organization is a consortium of like-minded firms that are all facing a threat to their bottom line from counterfeiting. With the ultimate goal of creating lasting brand protection, they have combined their efforts and *guanxi* to persuade the government to enact stricter anticounterfeiting laws and enforce them. Can the QBPC be a viable long-term strategy for combating counterfeiting in China? We explore the notion of *guanxi,* how it relates to the protection of IPR in China, and whether the QBPC can serve as an effective vehicle for multinational corporations to cultivate *guanxi* and combat piracy in China.

Drivers of Counterfeiting in China

Several cultural, geographic, and economic factors are drivers of widespread counterfeiting in China. From a cultural standpoint, counterfeiting is typically seen as a legitimate way to make a living and not as a cultural taboo. This attitude can be traced back to the Confucian ideal that ideas are not proprietary but rather for the benefit of all. Only in those cases where consumers are harmed do the Chinese demand retribution. Furthermore, the Chinese do not feel it is the central government's responsibility to protect multinational companies from IPR violations. As one former government official told us, multinational companies already enjoy a host of tax benefits and manufacturing cost advantages from the Chinese government. Therefore, it is incumbent on the individual company to protect its own intellectual property.

Geography also plays a role in the prevalence of counterfeiting. The central government faces considerable obstacles in trying to control local administrations across China and enforce IPR. *New York Times* journalist Craig Smith described the situation: "China's central government is more like an emperor trying to control a far-flung network of unruly fiefs than an all-seeing Big Brother whose commands are instantly obeyed." This phenomenon is known in China as local protectionism, which represents an obstacle for anti-counterfeiting efforts. Local officials and law enforcement agencies hoping to maintain order, increase employment, and generate income in their provinces often encourage and, in some cases, even participate in the illegal businesses. Furthermore, local officials, who often have power over the police and judges in their area, occasionally offer protection to counterfeiters in exchange for bribes.

China's efforts to combat unemployment and poverty also act as a stimulus for counterfeiting. The counterfeiting business employs a significant number of people in China and generates much-needed income in the villages where counterfeiting factories are located. Most counterfeiters run small- and middle-size enterprises and are self-employed; closing factories and firing workers will mean cutting off a valuable stream of income and will disrupt the social order the Chinese government desperately tries to maintain.

In fact, a war on counterfeits could lead to rebellion and civil disobedience. In recent years, for instance, there have been cases in which villagers physically defended their workplaces from official raiders. This threat is even more formidable as unemployment in some parts of China begins to rise. As state-owned companies continue to go bankrupt and lower grain prices force farmers to move to the cities, several million people will become unemployed in the coming years. Because there is a growing dependence on small businesses in the private sector to generate income and jobs, government officials are more likely to turn a blind eye to illegal counterfeiting activities. Similarly, judges may rule in favor of a local factory that produces counterfeits if it saves Chinese jobs, and government officials are more likely to implicitly (and in some cases, explicitly) support ambitious "entrepreneurs" who set up counterfeiting operations.

TRADITIONAL ANTICOUNTERFEITING STRATEGIES

In an effort to protect themselves, multinational corporations have adopted a number of strategic anticounterfeiting measures. Some of the most common techniques include differentiating products, differentiating packaging, coopting offenders, educating stakeholders, lobbying for legislation, advertising, and conducting investigation and surveillance. However, most of these measures have been employed in China with only marginal, short-term success.

The corporations whose brands are most at risk from counterfeiting are producers of consumer goods. Their products tend to lack high levels of complexity and are therefore easy to imitate. These companies have strived to differentiate their products from imitations with hard-to-copy packaging. For example, some companies have used bottles embedded with images that appear only when the bottle is refrigerated, while others use holograms and metallic colors on packaging, making it more costly to duplicate. So far, these tactics have had only minimal and short-term success, largely because counterfeiters have become more sophisticated, with better access to raw materials, distribution channels, and manufacturing technology, as well as the ability to develop packaging that is indistinguishable from the originals. In fact, according to Jack Chang, chairman of QBPC, the counterfeit problems remain serious as the illegal operators are becoming more organized and internationalized.

Lost sales, damaged brand equity, and the global proliferation of fake and shoddy goods are major issues that companies face in China. The following three counterfeiting experiences of LEGO, New Balance, and SC Johnson highlight the difficulties in protecting intellectual property in China.

LEGO

In January 2003, plastic toy maker LEGO won a landmark case against a Chinese company that had copied its blocks illegitimately. Initially deemed a huge success, the costs LEGO had to incur in bringing this case to court far outweighed the benefits. The offender was ordered to print an official apology in the *Beijing Daily* newspaper, stop production of the duplicated toys, and turn over the toy molds to be destroyed. LEGO also received a small monetary settlement. However, the amount, RMB 67,000 (approximately US$8,000) most likely fell short of the lost sales and legal expenses incurred by the company.

LEGO's experience is typical of the few counterfeiting cases that do reach the courts each year. For example, in 1998, monetary settlements for counterfeiting infringements represented a mere 7.5 percent of a company's anticounterfeiting expenses. Moreover, the enforcement of the ruling will stop the counterfeiting activities of only one Chinese company. Indeed, lawyers for LEGO, when touring the Hong Kong Toy Fair in March 2003, found outright imitations of their products at several stands, with most of the manufacturers located in China.

NEW BALANCE

Other companies have been even less successful in their legal attempts. At the end of 1999, New Balance discovered that its main Chinese supplier was overrunning its plant to make excess products that it could sell "on the side." Both the disproportionate volumes of materials purchased by the supplier and complaints from

Japanese retailers about merchandise retailed at a third of its recommended retail price led New Balance to cancel its distribution agreement with its Chinese partner. In fear that the overload might leave China for overseas markets, New Balance offered to buy the spare finished goods, but the former Chinese supplier rejected the proposition and started shipping shoes to various countries in Europe. After official raids that seized around 100,000 pairs of athletic shoes, New Balance filed suit against its former partner at the end of 2000. The judge, however, ruled against New Balance, and counterfeit sneakers were sold in Australia, the United States, and several European countries.

SC JOHNSON

A raid on a counterfeit manufacturer of SC Johnson's Red Bird™ shoe polish highlighted the sophistication of counterfeit operations and the challenges of differentiating counterfeits from real products (see Figure 6.1). In 2002, SC Johnson was also surprised to find that counterfeiters had beaten them to market with a new fragrance for Glade air fresheners by three months.

GUANXI AS A BUSINESS STRATEGY

The search for a viable strategy to fight intellectual property rights violations inspired multinational corporations to look to the Chinese culture for solutions, and as a result they came to recognize the importance of cultivating *guanxi* (i.e., relationships) as a business strategy. In western culture, law is used as a framework in dealing with the outside world; legitimate business operations involving international and political relations are governed by a system that determines the accepted outcomes of each type of interaction. The Chinese legal system, in contrast, is plagued by ambiguity and a lack of structure, making legal interpretation a very subjective process. According to researcher Yiming Tang, "Such personal interpretation of law promotes *guanxi*. Thus, *guanxi* is cultivated as a substitute for reliable government and an established rule of law."

Figure 6.1:   SC Johnson Red Bird™ Shoe Polish and Counterfeit Product

Source: Courtesy SC Johnson

Therefore, amidst government efforts to improve the legal and administrative system, many companies still rely on *guanxi* when conducting business.

The uniqueness of *guanxi* is deeply rooted in Confucius's three principles of *li* (structure), *ren* (gentleness and love), and *xiao* (loyalty and obedience). *Li* provides social resources, structure, and status for *guanxi* to take root, while *ren* and *xiao* cultivate people's positive attitude toward each other, which creates an environment for *guanxi* to develop. Also, Confucianism emphasizes the importance of hierarchical order. Tang has argued that when legal frameworks necessary for an open-market economy are still not well defined, Confucian ideals provide the basis of all personal, political, and business relations in China with an emphasis on ethics rather than law and that *guanxi* is the ultimate source of power and authority.

Most people would agree that *guanxi* is an integral part of conducting business in China. Cultivating *guanxi* with the right network of people—in both the private and public sectors—is absolutely crucial to a company's success. *Guanxi* is particularly relevant in today's increasingly global marketplace as multinational companies compete with each other and with local companies to reach over one billion Chinese consumers. Relationships with buyers, suppliers, partners, and government must be carefully crafted; otherwise, companies may find it difficult to conduct their day-to-day operations in China. Despite its clear importance to multinational companies entering the Chinese market, *guanxi* remains a somewhat nebulous concept to the western world. Many multinational companies struggle to understand what *guanxi* is, why it is relevant to them, and most importantly, how they can leverage it in their operation.

Many multinational firms have tried to cultivate *guanxi* in China through a variety of means, including organizing and attending consortiums, building partnerships with established Chinese companies, making donations to local governments, and engaging in constructive collaboration with the central government. In particular, multinational corporations and local companies have spent considerable resources, investing both time and money to form relationships with the leaders of China's powerful government institutions and state-owned enterprises. These investments may range from securing a job for an official's family member to paying a sum of money. They may also involve arranging a sweetheart deal for the Chinese party in exchange for protecting the company from burdensome regulations.

THE QBPC'S STRATEGY AGAINST PIRACY

QBPC, the twenty-first century embodiment of *guanxi,* has established itself as the liaison between branded multinational companies and the central government. Members of QBPC expend tremendous effort to win respect and trust from the Chinese government. As a group, QBPC lobbies the government for better anticounterfeiting measures in China, educates government officials and consumers on the dangers of counterfeiting, and provides a forum for multinational companies to share best practices in their fight against counterfeiting.

The Anti-Counterfeiting Coalition (ACC), the QBPC's predecessor, was started in 1998 by several multinational companies determined to combat the growing problem of counterfeiting in China. With few connections in the government and no perceived legitimacy among enforcement agencies, the organization made little headway toward its goal. According to Patrick Wang, vice chairman of the QBPC, the number of counterfeit goods was proliferating so rapidly that many companies felt frustrated and helpless. Furthermore, the Chinese legal structure was ill-equipped to deal with the issues of counterfeiting—laws were prone to misinterpretation, there was little legal precedence, and in the area of enforcement, local protectionism superceded national law.

In March 2000, the ACC reorganized itself under the China Association of Enterprises with Foreign Investment (CAEFI) as the Quality Brands Protection Committee. Its mission was "to work cooperatively with the Chinese Central and local governments, local industry, and other organizations to make positive contributions to anti-counterfeiting efforts in the People's Republic of China." The QBPC's earliest efforts were focused almost entirely on helping individual companies in their fights against counterfeiters. However, as counterfeit goods proliferated, it became apparent that more comprehensive measures were needed, so the organization began hunting down the counterfeiters and providing support for IPR violation enforcement. The goal was to identify the parties who were participating in and, more importantly, financially supporting the counterfeiting operations. The objective was to target the source of the counterfeiting—the suppliers of machinery, finances, and raw materials—in order to prevent infringement on trademarks before it began. As the QBPC delved deeper into these activities, it found that counterfeiters were not isolated, independent parties but rings of individuals who were highly sophisticated in organized crime.

Over time, QBPC's fight against counterfeiting has evolved into long-term strategies that focus on the central government's policies and infrastructure for IPR protection. In addition to influencing legislation, the efforts of the QBPC in preventing IPR violations have been directed toward educating individuals about the illegality of producing and buying counterfeit goods. The QBPC currently lobbies for more stringent laws that enable companies to seek much greater monetary rewards from perpetrators, which should serve as a financial deterrent. Similarly, by educating local enforcement agencies and urging them to take on more responsibilities to combat counterfeiting, the committee hopes to create a barrier to further violations of IPR.

With eighty-one companies and over US$19 billion invested in China, the QBPC has sufficient clout to capture the attention of the central government. Its members include Johnson and Johnson, Gillette, Procter and Gamble, Reebok, Nike, Microsoft, and Coca-Cola. This impressive roster has lent credibility to the organization, and its collective voice has drawn attention to the counterfeiting problem and attracted the interest of the central government. These companies have also contributed significant human and financial resources toward attaining the QBPC's objectives.

QBPC chairman Jack Chang described the evolution of QBPC's strategy as akin to fighting a forest fire: "Step one is fire fighting; step two is catching arsonists; step three is fire prevention" (Figure 6.2). The three-step process involves working internally to build IPR awareness within the companies; it also involves working externally with the government and the general public to fight counterfeiting at its source. Throughout the QBPC's evolution, one objective has remained salient—to fight counterfeiting by developing a partnership with the government. By establishing *guanxi* with various levels of the central and provincial governments, the QBPC has gained legitimacy and a level of success that no individual company could have achieved on its own.

The QBPC is organized under a steering committee of elected chairs and voting members and sets its agenda in a series of committees organized around such areas as best practices/enforcement, communications, customs, government cooperation, legal, and membership services. The organization is also subdivided into twelve industry working groups ranging from apparel to small appliances, which allows companies within specific industries to

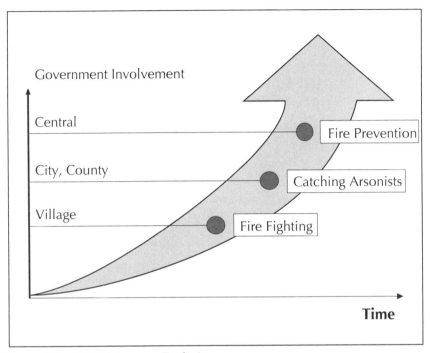

Figure 6.2:   QBPC Strategy Evolution

share best practices and lobby the government as a larger group. Figure 6.3 shows the organizational structure of the QBPC.

THE PROBLEM OF INEFFECTIVE ENFORCEMENT

Under its WTO obligations, China is required to implement effective enforcement procedures for its IPR laws and provide remedies that have a deterrent effect. Although there have been changes in the country's trademark legislation and patent and copyright laws, enforcement—particularly criminal enforcement—is weak and has failed to provide a deterrent effect. The main impediments to effective enforcement are overlapping government agencies and local protectionism. The jurisdictional and functional boundaries of law enforcement agencies in China are often unclear or they overlap, which affects the efficient handling of cases. In particular, this hampers the transfer of cases from the administrative to the criminal enforcement agencies, which in turn undermines prosecution as an

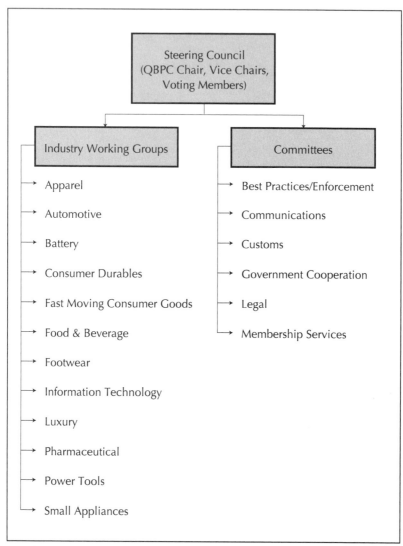

Figure 6.3: QBPC Structure

effective deterrent. Currently, two central government administrative agencies have jurisdiction in this area: the State Administration of Industry and Commerce (SAIC), which is responsible for preventing the counterfeit of registered trademarks, and the State General Administration for Quality Supervision, Inspection and Quarantine (SAQSIQ), which is responsible for preventing the sale of "fake and inferior goods." As seen in Figure 6.4, both these central government administrative agencies have local subagencies, the Administration of Industry and Commerce (AIC) and Technical Supervision Bureau (TSB), respectively, that carry out investigations and raids.

One challenge these agencies face is distinguishing between a trademark infringement and an inferior good, an often murky area. Activity that is classified as criminal under product quality law may be ignored because AIC, the local agency investigating the situation, may not find any trademark infringements. In addition, although each administrative agency has its own enforcement group with the authority to seize infringing products and impose fines, neither agency has the power to make arrests. Moreover, an administrative agency has little incentive to transfer a case for criminal prosecution to the local enforcement agency, the Public Security Bureau (PSB), because the administrative agency must give up its authority and potential income when it makes these transfers. As a result, the administrative agencies routinely apply sanctions instead of criminal punishments. Furthermore, the sanctions are at times overly lenient because transferring such cases to public security authorities is difficult and because the plea for leniency by the offenders themselves is often accepted. Finally,

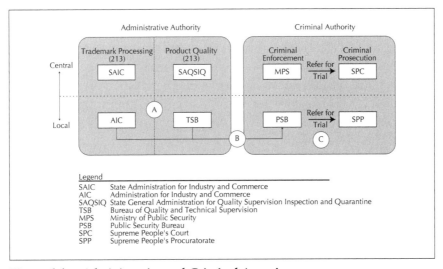

Figure 6.4: Administrative and Criminal Agencies

even when all administrative parties are willing, insufficient funding and out-of-date law enforcement equipment hamper the ability of the agencies handling the cases.

For an IPR violation to result in a criminal prosecution, the case needs to be transferred to a criminal authority (Figure 6.4). It used to be the case that neither the Ministry of Public Security (MPS), the central criminal enforcement agency, nor the local enforcement agency (i.e., the PSB) would consider IPR violations their purview. As a result, convincing the criminal authorities to get involved was a major challenge. However, in December 2002, the Economic Crime Investigation Bureau (ECIB) of the MPS issued an explicit instruction to the provincial ECIBs that IPR crimes should be a top priority. In addition, QBPC members are getting more support from PSB as well as from prosecutors. Once the PSB takes charge and refers the case to the prosecutor's office for approval of the arrest, the likelihood that the case will actually be tried by a Supreme People's Procuratorate (SPP) increases dramatically. In fact, 74 percent of these cases now result in convictions.

Local protectionism presents further obstacles for the central government in enforcing IPR across China. In the face of the opportunities (albeit illegal) provided by counterfeiting, local officials often refuse to cooperate in infringement cases involving local enterprises if the cases are brought to their attention by an outside source. The practice of local protectionism covertly protects the regional manufacturers and sellers of counterfeit goods and continues to pose overwhelming barriers to criminal enforcement.

In light of the enforcement challenges posed by inefficient government agencies and local protectionism, the number of IPR violations that are punished is unsurprisingly low. With a paltry 504 cases (0.2 percent) of all investigated cases transferred to the criminal courts, one can readily see that the threat of criminal prosecution is almost nonexistent (Figure 6.5). Of the IPR violations examined by the central government administrative agencies, only 3 percent or so of the offenders are shut down. Are the administrative agencies simply being too lenient? One can sense the enormity of the challenges caused by the overlapping agencies and local protectionism by comparing the numbers of shutdowns to the numbers of

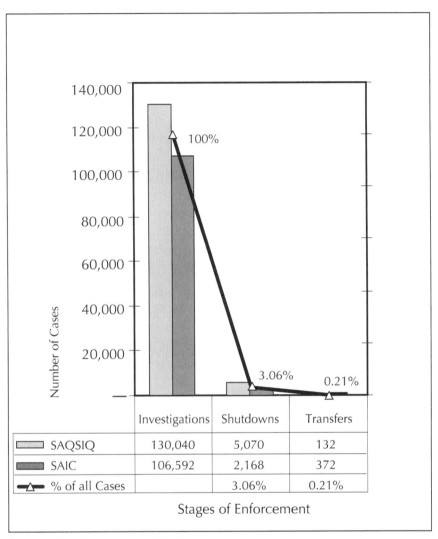

Figure 6.5: Enforcement Challenges

transfers. Logic dictates that if a factory is shut down for trademark infringement or product quality issues, someone (e.g., factory owners) should be taken to court. However, from the numbers, we see that this happens only in a marginal number of cases. In light of these statistics, any raid that results in a successful prosecution is a significant accomplishment.

INFLUENCING LEGISLATION

Current IPR laws are vague and easy to sidestep, and the punishments are not large enough to deter counterfeiting. Consequently, the QBPC considers influencing legislation a long-term effort. The timeline in Figure 6.6 shows the results of the QBPC's efforts to provide input to the central government regarding critical legislative developments. The desired legislative changes are numerous and intricate, and the details are beyond the scope of this chapter; however, the general theme behind all the QBPC's legislative efforts is clarifying criminal liability standards, setting clear criteria for the transfer of cases from administrative authorities to criminal authorities, clarifying the rules of evidence, and increasing the level of damages for those convicted of IPR violations (including fines, prison time, and seizure of equipment used for counterfeiting). The elements above the timeline show specific government actions, and the elements below show QBPC efforts to build *guanxi* with the correct government officials.

According to QBPC chairman Jack Chang, "The best way to build *guanxi* is to prove to be a valued partner. The more we can

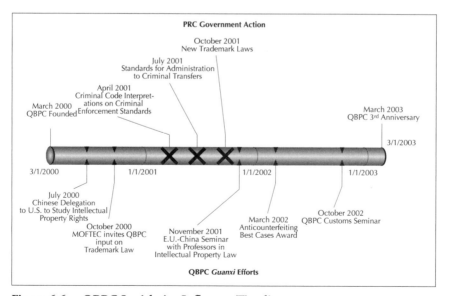

Figure 6.6: QBPC Legislative Influence Timeline

assist the central government in their goal of combating IPR violations, the more valuable we become." The way to ensure that QBPC and its members are viewed as valued partners is "through working sincerely and professionally to win the respect and trust from the Chinese government." The high point of the QBPC's legislative efforts was having almost 100 percent of its trademark law suggestions incorporated into the October 2001 trademark law. Although IPR-related infringements cannot be wiped out overnight, the progress suggests that improvements will slowly occur. A report released by the QBPC in mid-2003 showed that half of the 213 enterprises surveyed thought the counterfeiting problem had improved after the government launched a nationwide campaign in 2001. The report also suggests that counterfeiters lost some market share from 1999 to 2000, although the quantity of fake products did not decline. However, the general perception is that government support is improving—the government intends to issue new criminal liability standards, and the PSB is eager to take on more counterfeiting cases. Furthermore, China recently established its own antipiracy organization, the Anti-Piracy Committee, in late 2002 to coordinate antipiracy efforts initiated by different regions, industries, departments, and individuals.

MAKING PROGRESS ON IPR PROTECTION

Although the central government has been increasingly responsive to calls for reforms in criminal enforcement against counterfeiting, most criminal enforcement actions have yet to yield noticeable results. Observers feel that awareness of IPR issues has been increasing, particularly with China's entry into the WTO, and the coastal regions are most likely to be the first to improve on enforcement. The underdeveloped areas are likely to take a much longer time to come in line with China's IPR commitments. Although influencing legislation has been QBPC's most strategic initiative since its inception in the late 1990s, *guanxi* developed at various government levels by the QBPC has also helped member firms in their pursuit of criminal action, as the following cases indicate.

Gillette

Three years ago, Gillette, Energizer, and five other battery makers conducted several raids on over twenty factories, during which they found and seized almost four million counterfeited batteries. This effort was a success mainly because Gillette, a QBPC member along with Energizer, conducted the raid in partnership with the local administrative AIC officials in Yiwu City, Zhejiang Province. Due to the size of the seizure and its positive relationship with Gillette, the Yiwu AIC transferred the case to the local criminal agency, the PSB, which referred the case to the prosecutor's office for approval of the arrest. After considering more evidence gathered by the PSB, the Yiwu Court tried and convicted two men on the illegal production of fake trademark products and imposed a two-year imprisonment with a fine of RMB 35,000 (approximately US$4,200). The progress made through the *guanxi* developed by the QBPC is evident in this successful outcome.

Nike

In 1999, the General Administration of Customs (GAC) seized thirty shipments of counterfeited Nike goods. Regulations stipulate that in cases where a shipment of suspected fake products is detained, the onus is on the brand owner to post a bond with GAC in the same amount as the value of the shipment. That bond is used as liability insurance by GAC in the event the shipment proves to be legitimate and damages are owed to the parties involved. Thus, while Nike was pleased that the GAC had seized these fake products, the cost of bonds for thirty shipments was extremely high and placed a huge financial burden on its China operations. Thanks to the trust and respect that Nike had developed with the government's International Property Rights Division through the QBPC, however, a mutually satisfactory solution was devised—the director of the division suggested Nike and GAC sign a memorandum of understanding that committed Nike to meeting any financial obligations for liability in the case of an improperly seized shipment without requiring the company to post a bond. Nike was allowed to issue a bank guarantee and waive the bond requirement, freeing millions of dollars in capital that would otherwise have been tied up in bonds.

Other Examples

In addition to Gillette and Nike, there are several other successful examples of how the QBPC's efforts and *guanxi* developed at various government levels helped member firms in their pursuit of IPR protection. For instance, two men convicted of large-scale manufacture of Procter and Gamble products were sentenced to one year in prison and fined in Guanxi province. In Shandong, more than RMB 2 million (US$240,000) worth of equipment was seized at a chemical factory, and the culprit was sentenced to jail and fined. Hewlett-Packard (HP), working in conjunction with the Chinese authorities, seized US$1.2 million in counterfeit computer monitors in 2002 during a raid on an illicit operation in the southern province of Guangdong. A team of HP security personnel, working closely with QBPC, had been investigating the operation for more than two months and was able to gather evidence to trigger a Technical Supervision Bureau raid. In addition, from June 2001 to 2002, Johnson and Johnson established thirty-eight criminal cases against factories counterfeiting its products and against the distributors involved. Over the previous three years, the total criminal cases was two.

THE ROAD AHEAD

Clearly, the QBPC has made significant headway in its efforts to fight counterfeiting; however, there is still a long road ahead. Although legislation reform has yielded significant progress, legal enforcement and the provision of incentives to fight counterfeiting still lag behind. Local officials are expected to generate employment and revenue by any means possible and simultaneously to enforce anticounterfeiting laws. The QBPC can play a role in closing the gap between legislation reform and legal enforcement. One way is for the QBPC to educate local officials on the importance of growth and employment through legitimate businesses. For instance, the Development Research Center of the State Council has detailed losses to Chinese companies in lost sales and damaged brand equity, losses to the government in unpaid taxes, and the damages to the public from counterfeit drugs and shoddy goods.

Because local governments act in their own best interest, even if it means implicitly or explicitly supporting illegal counterfeiting factories, a good understanding between the parties and relationships needs to be cultivated at several levels of government. As noted earlier, companies can individually cultivate *guanxi* at the local level by forging partnerships with the government to support local citizens. As John Yam, external relations director of greater China for Procter and Gamble, noted, "We want the local government to have the same commitment at the local level where the enforcement occurs." Existing local government complacency is most evident in the gap between national counterfeiting investigations and local factory shutdowns. Cultivating relationships at the local level may help crack down on complacency within the local governments.

The QBPC could also focus on attracting local companies to further increase the organization's local recognition and *guanxi*. As local companies slowly embrace the notion of building brands, they in turn will become adversely affected by counterfeiting and will seek to protect their products. Because an indigenous software industry and competitive consumer brands depend on a sound IPR regime, it is likely that homegrown industries with internationally and nationally known brand names will eventually become the loudest voices demanding action by government agencies.

Attention in China is now being focused on effective enforcement, although it is likely that a long struggle remains ahead. The government is trying to silence overseas critics through public demonstrations of success in the fight against copyright breaches. For instance, a record 42 million pirated DVDs and CDs were publicly destroyed across China. On the intellectual property rights front, Chinese courts dealt with and closed 23,636 cases over the period 1998–2002, which was 40 percent more than in the previous five-year period. However, the commitment at the top level to protect intellectual property in China needs to trickle down to provinces, cities, towns, and villages through education, discipline, and training. China's mass media, especially television, and the Internet have opened new channels for public viewing and information—IPR-consciousness is rising in China, and the media coverage of violations and IPR court cases has played an important role. China's compliance is a long-term effort requiring extensive transformation, and the QBPC can help this process through reform and education.

CONCLUSION

The QBPC offers multinational corporations an effective way to work cooperatively with the Chinese government to protect their IPR. By relying on a broad-based strategy of developing *guanxi* at various levels of government through hard work and professionalism, the QBPC has succeeded in influencing the Chinese government where individual firms have failed. Its legitimacy and influence will continue to grow as new players enter the Chinese market. While eighty-one members is an impressive milestone, a comparison between current member companies' collective US$19 billion investment over several years and the US$57 billion foreign direct investment in China in 2002 indicates that a large number of multinational corporations are yet to become members of QBPC.

QBPC can enhance its presence by expanding its membership to include both multinational corporations and local companies, perhaps by leveraging one of its greatest draws, the Industry Working Groups (IWGs). Many industries are currently represented in the twelve existing IWGs. These groups are a major asset for the QBPC because they serve as a forum for companies to share best practices in their China operations. The QBPC can, therefore, offer a comprehensive solution for member companies by combining lobbying with industry-specific tactical suggestions for fighting counterfeiting. As the experience of QBPC shows, foreign companies can successfully fight IPR violations through trade and industry associations, whose involvement is likely to help both enforcement and legislation. Ultimately, the eradication of counterfeiting will benefit both the companies and the local communities, as precious resources that are otherwise spent fighting counterfeiters will be reinvested in manufacturing and in turn help fuel the development of the local economies.

BIBLIOGRAPHY

Ang, Audra. 2003. "Lego Beats Chinese Pirates." *The Associated Press,* January 27.

"The Battle against Chinese Piracy Is Turning to the Courts." 2003. *South China Morning Post.* http://www.apcoworldwide.com/content/pdfs/Chris_Murck_SCMP.pdf. March 1, 2003.

Behar, Richard. 2002. "Beijing's Phony War on Fakes." *Fortune,* October 30.

British Broadcasting Corporation. 2003. "Lego Defeats the Chinese Pirates." *BBC News World Edition,* January 21.

Brown, Owen. 2002. "Piracy Remains Rampant after China Joined WTO." *The Wall Street Journal,* December 11.

"China's Corruption Crackdown." 2003. *FriedlNet,* March 16. http://www.friedlnet.com/news/03031602.htm.

"China Steps up Fight against Counterfeiting." 2003. *CHINAdaily Online,* November 12. http://www1.chinadaily.com.cn/en/doc/2003-11/12/content_280915.htm.

The Economist Intelligence Unit. 2002. "The World in Figures." *The Economist,* December.

———. 2003. "China: A Good Year." *EIU Online,* March. http://db.eiu.com.

Galvin, Adrianne, Trisha Garces, Jason Hecker, and Sarah Levendusky. 2002. "Strategic Options to Combat Piracy." In *Kellogg on Global Issues in Management: Building Competitive Advantage in Global Markets,* edited by Anuradha Dayal-Gulati. Evanston, Ill.: Kellogg School of Management.

Goodman, Peter S. 2002. "China's Killer Headache: Fake Pharmaceuticals." *Washington Post,* August 30.

Green, Stephen. 2002. "Something Old, Something Hu." *The Economist,* December.

Hackley, Carol Ann, and Qingwen Dong. 2001. "American Public Relations Networking Encounters China's Guanxi." *Public Relations Quarterly,* Summer.

"IPR and the WTO: Can the WTO Solve China's IPR Problems?" 2002. *AmCham China Newsletter,* March. http://www.qbpc.org.cn/pressroom/wto-solve-ipr.htm.

Kahn, Gabriel. 2002. "For New Balance, a Surprise: China Partner Became Rival." *The Wall Street Journal,* December 19.

"Lego Wins Copyright Action in Beijing." 2003. *Lehman, Lee and Xu: China Intellectual Property Law Newsletter,* February 4. http://beijing.lehman-law.com/newsletter/ip/archives/20030204.htm.

McGregor, Richard. 2000. "Why China Is a Copybook Case." *Financial Times,* December.

McKinsey, Kitty. 2003. "Watching for Chinese Knock-Offs." *Electronic Business,* January.

Moga, Thomas T., and Jonathan Raiti. 2002. "The TRIPS Agreement and China." *China Business Review,* 29 (6):12–18.

Morrison, Wayne M. 2001. "China's Economic Conditions." CRS Issue Brief for Congress, December 27.

Pearce, John A., II, and Richard B. Robinson, Jr. 2000. "Cultivating *Guanxi* as a Foreign Investor Strategy." *Business Horizons,* 43 (1):31–38.

Quality Brands Protection Committee. 2000. "CAEFI Quality Brands Protection Committee Pamphlet." http://www.qbpc.org.

———. 2000. "Executive Summary." http://www.qbpc.org.

———. 2002. "Update on Counterfeiting in China." September 16. http://www.qbpc.org.

———. 2003. "Criminal Punishment Strengthened in Anti-Counterfeiting Campaign." May 2. http://www.qbpc.org.cn/press-room/27-nov-2000.htm.

———. 2003. "Overseas and Domestic Enterprises Affirm the Market Disorder Rectification Campaign and Call for Increased Criminal Prosecution against Counterfeiting." July 22. http://www.qbpc.org.cn/press-room/2003-07-22-BJ-en.htm.

Rae, Sheila. 2002. "The Ins and Outs of Chinese Government Relations." AMCHAM China Brief, July-August.

Roberts, Dexter, Frederik Balfour, Paul Magnusson, Pete Engardio, and Jennifer Lee. 2000. "China's Pirates." *Business Week International Edition,* June 5.

Seligman, Scott D. 1999. "*Guanxi:* Grease for the Wheels of China." *The China Business Review,* September-October.

Smith, Craig. 2000. "Piracy: A Concern as the China Trade Opens Up." *The New York Times,* October 5.

Sullivan, Laurie. 2002. "HP Cracks down on Counterfeit PC Parts in China." *EBN Online,* June 26. http://www.ebnonline.com/story/OEG20020626S0013.

Tang, Yiming. Forthcoming. "How to Start and Maintain *Guanxi* in the Business Context in China, Hong Kong and Singapore: A Proposed Research Framework." In *International and Cross Cultural Marketing.* Sidney, Australia: Macquarie University Press.

World Trade Organization. 2003. "Frequently Asked Questions about TRIPS in the WTO." December 11. http://www.wto.org/english/tratop_e/trips_e/tripfq_e.htm.

PART 3

UNDERSTANDING MARKETING IN CHINA

Chapter 7

SPORTS MARKETING IN CHINA

*Colby Maher, Brady Countryman, and
Jessica Yang*

Sports marketing broadly refers to the use of sports as a marketing medium to reach a consumer segment, whether in the form of advertising, recognition programs, promotions, television programming, or sponsorship of teams and events. For sportswear companies such as Nike and Li Ning, sports have created the market for their core sportswear products. For other companies, such as soft drink, cigarette, or mobile phone makers, sports are tools used to reach their target audiences. Indeed, sports marketing has become such a seamless component of many multinational corporations' (MNCs) marketing strategies that we can immediately picture their advertisements and their products because of their association with sports. Concurrently, the globalization of media and worldwide broadcasting of sporting events have made what was once a national demand for sports into a mass, worldwide phenomenon. This global appeal is increasingly being employed by MNCs to deploy a consistent marketing strategy in all their markets.

Global sports marketing campaigns, however, still need to be tailored to specific countries, regions, and markets. The vast potential consumer market in China presents certain challenges for companies looking to use sports marketing because sports are not heavily integrated into the Chinese culture. Sports in China have not historically been practiced by the masses, and in recent decades, most sports development has been focused only on athletes who show international champion potential. This fact of Chinese culture necessitates that MNCs using sports to market their products must consider China's cultural and socioeconomic dynamics when developing and implementing a sports marketing strategy.

In this chapter, we examine the sports marketing strategy used by several MNCs operating in China to develop an insight into what constitutes successful sports marketing campaigns in this nascent market. In doing so, we focus on some aspects of sports marketing strategies of U.S.-based MNCs that already have a presence in China. From our research and interviews, we notice four converging cultural and socioeconomic forces that are leading to four emerging trends.

CONVERGING CULTURAL AND SOCIOECONOMIC FORCES

The four converging cultural and socioeconomic forces are: (1) China's importance as a consumer market; (2) the importance of branding in China; (3) the evolution of the Chinese consumer; and (4) the growing interest and participation in sports by the Chinese consumer. These forces form the foundation on which companies can rely when using sports marketing strategies and tactics in the Chinese market. Their convergence can be illustrated as a prism with the four forces entering the prism from different angles and combining to form four trends (Figure 7.1). We discuss each of the four forces in greater detail below.

CHINA AS AN IMPORTANT CONSUMER MARKET

> "MNCs looking to experience growth have to
> go to China."
> —*Peter Tan, president and CEO of*
> *McDonald's, Greater China*

For the past couple of decades, the western business world has viewed China as the next great potential market for significant growth. Many

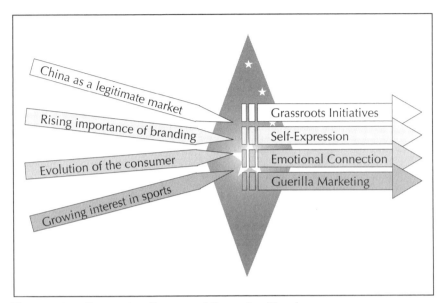

Figure 7.1:   Converging Forces and Emerging Trends

of the MNCs that tried to enter the market have not been successful. For instance, General Electric (GE) has struggled in China over the last two decades. Still, with China's entry into the World Trade Organization (WTO), industries that were previously highly restricted in China (e.g., insurance, banking, and telecommunications) will become open to foreign investment. In addition, with the evolution of contract law, business practices are slowly becoming more aligned with international standards. Companies are recognizing China's movement toward internationally accepted business practices and are investing in China at increasing rates. Net foreign direct investment (FDI) increased by about 25 percent in 2002 and is estimated to be US$48 billion in 2003, about the same level as in 2002, Severe Acute Respiratory Syndrome (SARS) notwithstanding.

In addition to becoming more conducive to foreign investment, China has become an important consumer market. The increase in disposable income among Chinese consumers has turned China into a viable market for MNCs whose products may not have been affordable in the past. For example, eating at McDonald's is considered an affordable restaurant meal for most American consumers, but for most Chinese citizens, a meal at McDonald's is considered an exceptional expenditure. Yet, an increasing percentage of Chinese consumers are able to afford this luxury. The increase in disposable incomes in China (a rise of over 300 percent from 1990 to 1999 alone) is creating a sizable consumer market that is able to afford products provided by MNCs. This market will continue to grow as disposable incomes increase along with gross domestic product (GDP) and as consumer price inflation stays low.

Importance of Branding in China

> "Brands in China are very powerful. You can launch almost any new product with a strong brand."
> —*Kevin Kong, IMG, senior manager*

Throughout most of China's commercial history, branding has not played a significant role in the market. China's early days of industrial development were characterized by state-owned enterprises in which the ability to meet production quotas rather than achieve net profits was considered the key measure of success. When this industrial regulation was lifted, production levels exceeded market needs, and it became apparent that business leaders' management and marketing skills were underdeveloped. The combination of this overcapacity and inexperienced management drove firms to compete through heavy price reductions, and China moved into a phase of hypercompetition. In addition to the debilitating effects of hypercompetition, foreign companies began to enter China and lure Chinese consumers with recognized western brands. Consequently, branding has now become a powerful weapon. Over the long haul, brands are expected to be more important in China than they are internationally.

In some ways, branding in China has become more powerful than in the U.S. market. In the United States, firms carefully evaluate ways in which a brand can be used—when launching new products, firms will use an established brand only when the new product is an obvious extension of the quality or experience implied by the brand. Companies are careful when using brand extensions in the U.S. market because American consumers do not assume that brand excellence in one product category translates to brand excellence in other categories. In China, however, consumers are willing to accept that a strong brand means quality across product categories. This assumption is due in part to historical variability in quality; thus, the reassurance through brand names is important to Chinese consumers. Consequently, brand consciousness is an increasingly significant factor in spending trends—more consumers are making their purchases based on the brand name. A survey by the Central China Television (CCTV)–affiliated Investigation and Consulting Center revealed that 38 percent of Chinese consumers who buy Coca-Cola do so because of its famous brand, while only 19 percent make the purchase based on price.

In China, brands can often be used to sell products that are outside of a brand's traditional product line. The effectiveness of extending brands in innovative ways is demonstrated by the successful clothing lines of Pepsi, a beverage company, and Marlboro, a cigarette manufacturer. Citing Nestlé's launch of a bottled water product, Kevin Kong from IMG noted that a powerful brand allows firms to sell almost anything in China. The Nestlé brand is well known in China, and although most consumers know Nestlé for its chocolate products, the company used the Chinese brand awareness to successfully launch a bottled water product with only a small marketing budget.

EVOLUTION OF THE CHINESE CONSUMER: THE "LITTLE EMPERORS" GROW UP

> "Children are central decision makers who determine
> 65–70 percent of household purchases."
> —*Market Asia Pacific, September*
> *1997*

In effect since 1979, the government's "one child policy" restricts Chinese couples to only one child, with severe financial penalties for having more. Regardless of one's views on this policy, its impact on China's demographics is significant, and its ramification in the marketplace is important. In traditional Chinese culture, children are tended to and doted upon by their grandparents. Thus, when couples are limited to having one child, four grandparents have only a single grandchild upon whom to bestow their attention and affections.

One characteristic of Chinese culture is gift giving in the form of very large sums of money. Grandparents' gifts that were once spread across two or three grandchildren are now lavished on the "onlies." In an article in *Asian Business,* James Irwin described the "onlies" visiting shopping malls, "decked out in fancy designer clothes . . . always under the watchful eye of a doting grandparent." A Market Asia Pacific survey in 1997 found that monetary gifts and the focused attention "Little Emperors" receive has resulted in children being "central decision makers who determine between 60 percent to 70 percent of household purchases." Consequently, this generation influences the spending of a significant proportion of the nation's increasing disposable income.

The Little Emperors, as they grow older, have brought about a shift in the way a generation perceives itself. The Chinese have traditionally identified themselves first as part of the collective and second as individuals. According to Professor Angela Lee at the Kellogg School of Management, Chinese youth, however, are increasingly identifying themselves as individuals first. This shift has had an impact on the type and nature of products Chinese consumers seek—products and brands that are expressions of individualism yet are congruent with their group image. For the Little Emperors, individuality matters, but so does the need to be seen as belonging to a certain group. We discuss this trend and its impact on sports marketing strategies in more detail later in the chapter.

The Little Emperors have both buying power and power in numbers. The company executives we interviewed consistently identified their target consumer as between ten and thirty years old. More than half of China's total current population falls between the ages of five and thirty-five. These demographics and the influence of this key age group have led MNCs to place considerable importance on capturing the Little Emperor consumers and maintaining the relationship as they mature. In the Chinese market, this consumer segment has great potential for MNCs seeking to grow their businesses. The attention these children and young adults have received in their families, their increasing exposure to western thought, and rising household disposable income are creating a sociological shift in Chinese culture. Not only are the Little Emperors large in number, but they influence household purchasing decisions and look to brands to express their individualism.

GROWING INTEREST AND PARTICIPATION IN SPORTS BY THE CHINESE CONSUMER

> "There's nothing like the Western athletic tradition—
> which traces back from the playing fields of Eton to the
> Greco-Roman games—in China's past."
> —*Frank Deford, Sports Illustrated*

China's sports history is filled with traditions in noncompetitive and contemplative sports, such as martial arts and acrobatics, which differ from the tradition of competitive group sports passed down by the Roman and Greek civilizations to the Americas and Europe. According to Frank Deford in *Sports Illustrated,* the Chinese focus on contemplative sports sprang from the Mandarin philosophy in which intellectual pursuits are valued over physical development. Until very recently, because of this philosophy, few Chinese participated in sports activities; instead they viewed their bicycle ride to work as their daily exercise. This perspective changed when Mao visited the West and saw westerners from all walks of life participating in a variety of sports. Mao saw sports as a sign of a developed country and decided that China, too, should enjoy the luxury of sport. "Promote physical culture and sports and build up the people's health," became one of Mao's most frequently quoted slogans. Unfortunately, the resources to bring sports to all Chinese people were limited, so government funding for sports was focused on the athletes who showed the most potential for winning international championships. This focus led to the creation of such schools as the Beijing Sports School, where gifted young athletes are brought to live, study and develop their skills. Achievement on an international level was an important goal for sports then—as it is today. According to a former basketball player in a 2002 *TimeAsia* article, "China views its athletes not as people but as tools that can be used to bring glory and honor to the country."

Despite this focus, the development of sports in China stagnated during the Cultural Revolution (1966–1976). When the Cultural Revolution ended, China emerged as an international leader in technique sports, such as gymnastics and diving, and precision sports, such as table tennis, riflery, and archery. The focus on these sports reflected the underlying belief held by the Chinese that they are genetically disadvantaged. In his article, Deford quotes Susan Bromwell, an anthropologist of Chinese sports, who found in her research that "virtually all Chinese athletes are convinced that they're physically inferior to other races." Because intellectualism is valued over physical development and because of the general Chinese misconception that the Chinese can excel only at technique and precision sports, participation in more internationally popular sports, such as basketball and soccer, has not occurred on a large scale.

The advent of global media is causing a shift in attitudes. Access to media coverage of U.S.-based National Basketball Association (NBA) games and world football (soccer) matches is leading to greater interest and participation in these sports. Now that the NBA roster includes Wang Zhizhi, the first Chinese national to play in that league, more Chinese are watching his team, the Dallas Mavericks. This trend has continued with Yao Ming, the China Basketball Association's (CBA) best player, who now plays for the Houston Rockets. According to a recent article in *Business Week*, the NBA's largest television market outside the United States is now in China. Participation and interest in football are growing as well. With the creation of the professional Chinese Football League (CFL) in 1994, the football industry in China has developed into a multimillion dollar business. In 2002, when China brought the first-ever qualifying Chinese football team to the World Cup, the country was engulfed in football fever. The 2008 Olympic games being awarded to Beijing also brought about a surge in national pride. Recently, Siemens and Adidas-Solomon provided sponsorships for the football league and national teams.

Emerging Sports Marketing Trends in China

How do these trends impact a sports marketing strategy in China? How do increased participation and spectatorship translate into increased consumer spending? How do companies approach their target market? To reach the target consumers, companies need to understand their lifestyle and interests and effectively communicate the image and direction of the company as compatible with this lifestyle. Our research and interviews indicate that four trends have emerged in sports marketing in China:

- Consumer targeting through grassroots initiatives
- Use of trend setting and self-expression as marketing themes
- Establishment of an emotional connection to the consumer
- Use of guerilla marketing tactics

MNCs have created campaigns that target youth through segmentation and grassroots initiatives and try to establish an emotional connection with the consumer. We discuss these trends below.

Consumer Targeting through Grassroots Initiatives

> "Children are not raised playing sports."
> —Yuan Dan, sports management
> director, Beijing Sports School

The lack of youth sports in China has ramifications on many levels. China is beginning to realize that its government-sponsored sports system did not create a pool of talent large enough to sustain professional athletic programs—programs that are necessary to propel the growth of Chinese sports. As Yuan Dan, the sports management director at the Beijing Sports School, explained, only a few Chinese are trained in sports, after being hand-selected during childhood.

This approach limits the overall level of sports participation to only a minute fraction of the population. Because of this practice, premier athletes are not challenged by a large number of qualified athletes and the level of competition suffers. To increase both interest and participation in sports (and thereby increase the pool of competitive athletes), children need access to facilities and opportunities to play organized sports. MNCs have come forward to fill this gap by building more public facilities, sponsoring youth leagues, and creating competitions.

Through these grassroots initiatives, companies are able to reach this target market. The most common support tactic is to sponsor or organize a sporting competition. For instance, Coca-Cola sponsors three-on-three soccer tournaments for secondary school students to capture consumers' tastes and establish their purchasing preferences at a young age. Pepsi is also sponsoring teen soccer, Adidas is funding soccer camps, and Motorola sponsors the College University Basketball Association (CUBA) to build loyalty with the student market segment and learn how to customize products for their tastes and needs.

According to Nike, basketball is more effective than other sports at attracting Nike's target Chinese consumer: the teenage, trend-setting, outgoing male. Nike has built a basketball complex in Shanghai and sponsors its three-on-three basketball tournaments there (Figure 7.2). The walls in the complex have graffiti-like paintings of NBA stars, such as Tim Duncan and Jason Williams, in the style of Asian comic book heroes. The company has also sponsored high school basketball programs in Shanghai. Nike's tight involvement with basketball is rooted in its dominance of the U.S. basketball apparel and footwear market as well as in the licensing contracts it had with the NBA when the league was introduced to China in the early 1990s. Nike's long-term strategy is to weave itself into the fabric of sports in China, according to Terry Rhoads, the former director of sports marketing for Nike-China. To this end, Nike is planning to sponsor a soccer facility in Beijing. Nike has made other investments in sports complexes in the city. Near the intersection of the Second Ring Road and Dongchang'an Jie, one can see basket-

Figure 7.2:   Nike Basketball Complex in Shanghai

Notes: The nameplate of the Nike basketball park says, "Street Dance Storm Basketball Park." The self-expressionism of street punk and hip-hop dance craze parallels similar characteristics of a successful basketball point guard.

Source: Brady Countryman.

ball courts that have Nike's trademark "swoosh" emblazoned on the backboard.

Unlike advertising, sports sponsorships by companies may not directly link to the company's product, yet the benefits in the form of brand recognition and sales can be significant. For instance, under current laws, tobacco companies are prevented from using media exposure to promote their products or brands in China, making it more difficult for a brand of cigarettes to be seen by Chinese consumers. Nevertheless, Mild Seven, a Japanese cigarette company, pushed the boundaries of the tobacco advertising restrictions. With help from Ogilvy and Mather's promotional campaigns department, it devised a marketing strategy using a sports campaign that incorporated the brand's logo and name.

Mild Seven's Chinese name, when translated into English, means "seven stars." Mild Seven capitalized on this meaning and created a sports event called the Outdoor Quest—a competition between top athletes in seven events. The Outdoor Quest is not a standard heptathlon competition. Rather, the events range from biking to kayaking and from cross-country races to off-road inline skating. The settings for the events are picturesque outdoor locations. Ogilvy and Mather's promotional campaign department designed marketing materials used for the Outdoor Quest competition which explicitly advertise the Mild Seven logo with its light blue and yellow color scheme and English brand name. Although these elements are carefully integrated into the design of the marketing materials, the cigarette company does not advertise itself or its product, so the campaign complies with Chinese law. Nevertheless, Mild Seven was able to use the media exposure during the event to promote brand awareness. Mild Seven was a relatively unheard of brand name prior to the Mild Seven Outdoor Quest. The success of this promotional campaign is apparent—Mild Seven has become a leading brand of imported cigarettes in China.

TREND SETTING AND SELF-EXPRESSION AS MARKETING THEMES

"Little Emperors increasingly identify themselves as individuals, rather than part of the collective."
—*Angela Y. Lee, marketing professor,*
Kellogg School of Management

The Chinese consumer is evolving and beginning to see himself or herself as an individual rather than as part of the collective. Experts argue that the Chinese are not *either* individualist *or* collectivist but both at the same time. Indeed, Chinese young adults straddle the traditional values of their parents and the emerging western influences of consumer products and media. They seek out new behavior and attitudes, in some cases against their parents' wishes, and are important trendsetters in certain product segments. Senior executives at advertising firms in China noted that Chinese youth have a strong tendency to do everything in groups and prefer group sporting activities, such as basketball, soccer, and volleyball. Their idea of individualism is congruent with their idea of group behavior.

In the United States, the concept of "cool" often connotes the rebellious youth who somehow stands above the regular crowd rather than blend into it. In China, this type of "cool" has a negative connotation. The Chinese have their own version of "cool": a teen who is always on top of the most up-to-date activities and styles, who blends together the best of the most popular styles. The "cool" Chinese fits the ideal of the group's desired image. This attitude implies that a brand's appeal to the group market should be maximized rather than its appeal to only to a select few. Since an individual's positive reaction can eventually generate group acceptance, owning the "cool" item or engaging in the "cool" activity can be embraced and copied by the target market. For instance, Nike learned that those drawn to the tournaments were its preferred market segment: self-expressive young males who tend to be trendsetters of fashion and attitude. They were the "cool kids" who tended to bring their girlfriends to the tournaments.

Marketers have recognized this cultural shift and promote self-image and self-expression to appeal to this consumer group. For instance, Motorola's 2002 campaign in Asia promotes "Moto," which is self-expression through self-recorded ring tones on a mobile phone. Nike boosted its brand image as the leading sportswear outfitter by promoting basketball and the self-expressive image associated with this sport. In a series of advertisements, Nike featured Chinese basketball players with a prominent player in each advertisement calling attention to his particular talent.

FOCUS ON THE EMOTIONAL CONNECTION TO THE CONSUMER

> "The fond memories of childhood and refreshment that people have when they drink Coke is often more important than a little bit better cola taste. It is this emotional relationship with brands that make them so powerful."
> —BrandSolutions, Inc., 2000

As China's market matures and consumers are faced with increasingly differentiated goods, MNCs are looking to create an emotional relationship with consumers through brand associations. According to independent marketer Joe LePla, "Associations are the mental shortcuts to a company's brand promise . . . influencing in a positive way your customers' senses, minds, and emotions during the buying experience." With brand consciousness increasing, MNCs are using emotion in sports to build relationships with their target consumers. As Nike's founder, chairman, and CEO Phil Knight pointed out in an interview in *Harvard Business Review,* "Emotional ties . . . build long-term relationships with the consumer."

Marketers of low-involvement goods that have a short purchase process, such as soft drinks, do not necessarily focus on trendsetters and image, but on an emotional connection to the consumer. For example, MNCs recently used China's qualification for the 2002 World Cup Finals to build an emotional brand association. Within forty-eight hours of the team's qualification, Coca-Cola released and distributed limited edition World Cup cans in celebration. Coca-Cola used this as an identification approach, whereas Pepsi combined identification and aspirational marketing by appealing to customer emotions. Immediately following China's qualification, Pepsi conducted and distributed emotional interviews with some of the country's most beloved top players. The campaign was called "What Are Your Aspirations?" and included a commercial with Fang Zhiyi, known as the "bad boy" of the team, crying as he expressed his gratitude to the recently deceased founder of the Chinese professional soccer league. Print advertisements capturing the joy when dreams are realized were also used to promote the brand (Figure 7.3). These promotions are an emerging trend in China, as the country is celebrating new national sporting accomplishments and a surge in national pride.

McDonald's also used the emotion of national achievement as a marketing tool following the announcement of Beijing as the host of the 2008 Olympics. McDonald's invited consumers to watch the announcement ceremony in its Beijing restaurants, and when the games were awarded to Beijing, it announced that a free hamburger would be given to every customer in line. Some stores stayed open until 4 A.M. to fulfill this promise. Peter Tan, the CEO of McDonald's China, said this promotion enabled the company to

Figure 7.3: Pepsi Print Advertisement

Notes: This example illustrates emotion being employed at times of national achievement.

Source: Courtesy of Pepsi Corporation. Reprinted with permission.

participate in a community event and national celebration. The combination of national pride, the appeal of sports, and the growing importance of branding is expected to result in about US$1 billion in corporate sponsorships of the Beijing Olympics.

Companies are going beyond national sporting achievements to tap into their customers' emotions, because watching athletes push the limits of performance strikes a chord with viewers. For instance, Pepsi's director of sports marketing, Hanno Leung, produces a weekly soccer show that delves into the personal lives of the company's sponsored athletes. By offering an inside look into these top athletes' lives, Pepsi is able to develop an emotional connection with the consumer—one that it hopes will lead to increased sales of Pepsi's products.

USE OF GUERILLA MARKETING TACTICS

"With regards to guerilla or ambush marketing—the better the marketer you are, the farther you go."
—*Marcus John, IMG Consulting*

Sports marketing and adherence to international standards of business conduct are still in their infancy in China. As a result, guerilla marketing tactics are used to a much greater extent in the Chinese market than in western markets. Guerilla marketing is the use of tactics to imply to consumers that a firm is a sponsor when it truly is not, or is a higher level sponsor than it is for a sporting event (e.g., title versus secondary sponsor). Because enforcement of China's contract laws has been difficult, guerilla marketing has become an acceptable business practice.

According to a senior advertising agency executive in China, "Coca-Cola is most successful when it comes to implementing guerilla marketing." Although Coca-Cola was not a title sponsor of the Chinese national football team, the company used its lower tiered sponsorship in such a way that consumers perceived Coca-Cola to be the title sponsor, unaware that Philips, the actual title sponsor, was associated with the team. As a sponsor, Coca-Cola was licensed to market itself as such, but through heavy promotion of the sponsorship, the company stretched the limits of its license agreement and frequently overshadowed the title sponsor.

Pepsi also employs similar marketing strategies. When China qualified for the World Cup, Pepsi was a sponsor of some of the most recognized athletes on the team but not a sponsor of the Chinese football team. Pepsi used these individual players, plus Pepsi-sponsored leading international football athletes such as David Beckham, the captain of England's Manchester United team, to create a "Pepsi Team." These players appeared wearing Pepsi shirts in ads immediately after China's accomplishment (Figure 7.4). Pepsi also set up promotional booths and events near the World Cup venue and used its athlete sponsorships to attract spectators. Aggressive marketing tactics are also used in other industries. Despite not being an official sponsor of the 2002 World Cup in Japan and Korea, China Unicom set up booths in the vicinity of the venue in order to appear to be affiliated with the event.

CONCLUSION

Although the sports marketing industry is growing in China, sports marketing does not yet have the same impact it does in western societies. For this reason, MNCs find that grassroots initiatives are effective in building sports participation while providing a vehicle to promote products to their target consumer segments. In addition, while targeting youth through grassroots initiatives, MNCs are able to promote self-expression through sports and take advantage of the growing individualism among the younger generations. Targeting this age segment enables MNCs to create an emotional relationship with these consumers at a young age.

With companies exploiting every aspect of their sponsorships, a sponsor may often be overshadowed by competitors' creative and surprising guerilla marketing tactics. However, this challenge is not the only one facing companies that use sports marketing in China. While sponsorships represent a huge step in the free-market direction, government intervention and controls are problematic. Most appointments to Chinese sports governing bodies are political, and

Figure 7.4:   Use of International Soccer Star David Beckham

Notes: As a part of Team Pepsi—David Beckham is featured as a part of Pepsi's International marketing campaign. It can been seen that these two samples of print advertising can be easily customized to the regional markets.

Source: Courtesy of Pepsi Corporation. Reprinted with permission,

appointed officials may not necessarily understand sports management or sports marketing. Furthermore, the absence of good market research data makes the value of a sponsorship difficult to estimate. There are few data on consumer purchasing behavior in China and little local expertise on sports valuation. The value of the property hinges on its ability to offer the sponsor certain assurances of exclusivity and visibility. However, China's shaky contract laws make it difficult to enforce such provisions. The result is that property values are undermined by the risk the sponsors have to take.

Whereas foreign soccer and basketball have become increasingly popular, sponsorship deals for Chinese teams are less popular. Some companies that once sponsored Chinese teams and leagues have withdrawn their support. Television has made sports entertainment big business, and the revenues are a result of cooperation between sports leagues, television broadcasters, and corporate sponsorships in Europe and the United States. Media revenues are the single largest source of income for western sports leagues and teams. In China, however, growing consumer interest in sports does not translate into higher media revenues for sports teams and leagues because of China Television's virtual monopoly over the broadcasting market. Recently Pepsi, Fuji Photo Film, and Virgin Atlantic Airways decided to cancel their sponsorships of certain Chinese teams or allow them to expire. Others have continued to sponsor teams, betting that what has worked with great success in other markets will work in China: sports marketing increases brand exposure. With the Beijing Olympics approaching, along with the increasing Chinese appetite for playing sports, marketers will need to reassess their strategy and capitalize on the opportunities available for raising brand awareness through the medium of sports. So far, sports have never failed to instill great national pride; furthermore, if a team or player endorses a company and its products, so does the fan base. Despite its challenges, the appeal of sports is universal and sports marketing holds considerable promise in China as regulations loosen up, intellectual property enforcement improves, and the market develops. The key to success may be—as Nike's Phil Knight asserted—to "take a chance and learn from it."

BIBLIOGRAPHY

Ambler, Tim, and Morgen Witzel. 2000. *Doing Business in China.* New York: Routledge.

Bennett, Brian. 2002. "Fired up about Football." *Silkroad: The Inflight Magazine of Dragonair,* March.

Cheng, Allen T. 2001. "China Goes for Gold." *Asiaweek.com,* July 13. http://www.asiaweek.com.

"China's Consumer Spending to Rise by 8.7 Percent in 1st Quarter." 2002. *China Intelligence Wire,* April 9.

"China's Economic Structure." 2001. *The Economist,* September 5.

Deford, Frank. 1988. "An Old Dragon Limbers Up." *Sports Illustrated,* August 15.

Edelstein, Jordan, Zack Eleveld, John Peters, and Chris Stengrim. 1998. "Little Emperors . . . Big Business." Final paper for China I, Kellogg Graduate School of Management, Northwestern University.

Hong, Sun, and Peggy Leung. 2001. "Cashing in on Olympic Flame." *AsiaWeek.com,* July 13. http://www.asiaweek.com.

Irwin, James. 2000. "One for All and All for One." *Asian Business,* March 22.

LePla, Joe. 2000. "Success by Association." http://www.workz.com/cgi-bin/ gt/tpl_page.html,template=1&content=1449&nav1=1&. October 9, 2000.

Madden, Normandy. 2001. "Brands Chase Gold in China's 2008 Olympics." *Ad Age Global,* 1 (12):4.

Mejia, Pedro, Amit Nag, and Vicki Nataka. 2002. "The Commercialization of China's Sports System: New Business Models." In *Kellogg on Global Issues in Management—Anthology 2002,* edited by Anuradha Dayal-Gulati. Evanston, Ill.: Kellogg School of Management.

Mo, Crystyl. 2002. "Brick City." *TimeAsia,* 159(7).

Parrott, Stuart. 2002. "The Golden Game." *Asia, Inc.,* March 20.

Schlevogt, Kai-Alexander. 2000. "The Branding Revolution in China." *The China Business Review,* 27 (3):52–57.

United Nations Conference on Trade and Development. 2003. *World Investment Report.* New York: United Nations.

"Where China's 'Little Emperors' Get Their Product Information." 1997. *Market Asia Pacific,* September.

Willigan, Geraldine E. 1992. "High Performance Marketing: An Interview with Nike's Phil Knight." *Harvard Business Review,* July-August.

Chapter 8

Taking Global Brands to Local Success: Marketing Western Snack Foods in China

Tracy Eckert, Juanita Haron, Elizabeth Heintzelman, George Lane, and Jennifer McKnight

The Chinese marketplace continues to experience tremendous change as the country transitions from a closed, state-controlled communist system to a burgeoning market economy that offers a vast array of global products to the country's 1.2 billion consumers. Although this new marketplace has attracted countless multinational companies, these firms soon learn that local success requires a different set of marketing strategies. In other words, simply being western isn't enough. In China today, competitive pressures are strong, with several firms manufacturing similar products and local firms becoming stronger players. Consequently, before a multinational firm can introduce a new product to China, it must first evaluate every aspect of its homegrown marketing strategy to see where adaptations may be necessary—to succeed in the local environment, appropriate adaptation is key. As Bruno Lemagne, president of the Unilever China Group, has stated in *The New Silk Road*, "Adapt better to the local environment, and you will win."

Cultural norms significantly contribute to consumer behavior and consumption patterns, and successful marketers address cultural differences in consumer behavior and consumption patterns by localizing marketing strategies and adapting products to satisfy local values and preferences. Firms that sell culturally neutral products such as aluminum—commodities that serve a universal need and thus are unaffected by culture—could enter China without adapting their products to local expectations. However, firms entering China with culturally specific products, such as automobiles, foods and beverages, and clothing, may need to modify both products and positioning to be successful.

Product adaptation is the way in which the product is modified to conform to local tastes, and product positioning is defined as the attitude or point of view the marketer attempts to convey to the consumer regarding the product and brand. Building on a recent marketing framework developed by Philip Kotler, professor of marketing at the Kellogg School of Management, and Gary Armstrong, professor of marketing at the University of North Carolina Business School, we explore the alternative options available to firms going overseas (Figure 8.1). We use this framework to analyze the snack food industry in China to understand how western firms modify their products and positioning for the Chinese market. Our meetings with executives of U.S. snack food companies and advertising executives and with experts on China

		Product	
		No Change	Adapt
Positioning / Promotion	No Change	Straight Extension	Product Adaptation
	Adapt	Communication Adaptation	Dual Adaptation
	Product Invention - Develop New		

Figure 8.1:   Product and Positioning Strategies

Source: Adapted from Kotler and Armstrong 2000.

and marketing provided valuable insight into how foreign firms can tailor their products and positioning strategies to succeed in China.

THE SNACK FOOD MARKET

Few categories are as sensitive to local culture as snack foods. Since China has one of the oldest and richest food cultures in the world, entrenched habits and refined tastes that have developed over thousands of years present a formidable challenge to western companies and their processed and packaged snack foods. After all, western snack foods were originally created as a response to western markets, where people often eschew freshness in favor of convenience. Needless to say, the habits of Chinese consumers are not the same.

Known as *xiao chi* or "little eats," snacks foods in China are divided into two categories: eastern-style and western-style snacks. On the one hand, eastern-style snacks (e.g., dried and preserved seeds, nuts, beans, meats, shrimp, etc.) are perceived as healthy options and are popular among older segments of the population. These snacks are typically eaten at social occasions during teatime and family gatherings. Western-style snacks (e.g., potato chips, sweets, cookies, popcorn, etc.), on the other hand, are generally purchased and eaten on impulse and are more popular with younger population segments that value taste above nutrition.

Although introducing western snack foods to Chinese consumers is a challenge, the snack foods category in China is a rapidly growing market with immense potential. Valued at just under US$1 billion, the Chinese snack food industry grew over 50 percent from 1995 to 2000. Industry growth was spurred by increased consumer spending, which grew by 41 percent from 1994 to RMB 5.8 trillion (approximately US$701 billion) in 2000. On average, food products and services accounted for 44 percent of consumer expenditures, with snack foods representing a large portion of this spending.

Despite the market's success, distribution constraints are currently impeding the growth of most snack food companies. In contrast to more developed markets, China lacks dominant firms with well-honed and widespread distribution networks. In many cases, distribution consists of individuals carrying products on their bicycles for delivery to mom-and-pop stores for sale to local residents. In the long run, hypermarkets, such as Carrefour and other large chain stores currently spreading through China's larger cities, will likely become a dominant retail channel, which will eventually allow mass-market leaders to emerge. Given the increasing popularity of western-style snack foods, the market potential, and fragmentation, a western snack food company must immediately establish a presence among Chinese consumers to become a dominant player in China. This immediacy is particularly important for capturing the market of the younger generation, whose tastes are evolving rapidly and have not yet formed brand loyalty.

PRODUCT ADAPTATIONS

Understanding Chinese consumers and tailoring products to satisfy their tastes are paramount for successful introduction of a new product in China. With western snack foods in particular, the most effective method for entering the Chinese market is to modify the product to conform to local tastes (Figure 8.1). To be successful in China, where product offerings are often more varied than in the West, product adaptation involves more than just changing a product's flavor—successful western snack food offerings have been modified for the Chinese market in flavor, name, packaging, and shape.

PRODUCT FLAVOR

Snack food companies cater to Chinese consumer interests when developing product flavors, especially when targeting children. For instance, when compiling a list of potential flavors, Frito-Lay researched current snack food flavors in China, evaluated flavors in the company's product portfolio, and generated additional concoctions with the assistance of flavor houses like International Flavors and Fragrances Inc. (IFF) and McCormick and Company. Before settling on American Creamy and Japanese Steak as the first two Cheetos flavors in China, the company tested over six hundred different flavors, from the U.S. cheese flavor to roasted cuttlefish, a dried-squid snack popular in China. Unlike in the United States, where Frito-Lay sells just two flavors of Cheetos, in China, Cheetos come in four different flavors—Japanese steak, American creamy, tomato ketchup, and milk and eggs.

General Mills also relied on flavor houses for assistance in developing flavors for Chinese consumers. Although the company researches snack food flavors already on the market prior to launching new products or flavors, the firm avoids "me too" strategies, preferring instead to lead the snack food market in developing innovative flavors. For example, General Mills was the first firm to offer the American tomato ketchup flavor, which other snack food makers quickly followed by introducing similar "me too" ketchup flavors in their snack food product lines. General Mills now offers Bugles in five different flavors in China—American tomato ketchup, magical char-grilled BBQ, spicy fried chicken, purely delicious original, and enhanced original—and markets four different Kix flavors—Japanese BBQ, Korean BBQ, seafood, and sweet corn.

PRODUCT NAME

In addition to flavors, product name is another important component of product modification. China's 1996 Labeling Law, which stipulates all food packages must include Chinese character labels, provides an opportunity for western firms to brand products with conceptual images and key benefits. Product names often communicate images and attributes that stand out. For instance, the translation of Cheetos' Chinese characters "qi duo" is "many surprises." In China, Cheetos bags are full of "many surprises," namely new product shapes, flavors, and often toys and collectible items. Similarly, Coca-Cola's Chinese characters translate as "delicious happiness," Bugles' as "cute, crispy horn," and Kix's as "network crispy." In all cases, the brand name conveys the product's desired attributes.

PRODUCT PACKAGING

Because it carries the brand name and symbol, packaging is an integral component of product modification in China. The use of colors on packaging is especially important because of the strong significance of colors in Chinese culture. Both General Mills and Frito-Lay, for instance, adopted bright, flashy packaging for their snack foods in China that attracts attention on the shelf, especially from children. But more than drawing attention, colors convey meanings in China. For instance, yellow is a powerful color for packaging, as yellow used to be a color reserved for the Emperor—he alone wore yellow clothing and would grant special permission as an honor to a select few to wear the color. Red is another popular color for snack food packaging; it symbolizes happiness and good luck. Red is often associated with festivities and is used in spring festival decorations and gift-wrapping on special occasions for close friends.

Generally, food package sizes in China are small, and single portion packages of snack foods are the most prevalent in the market. Houses and apartments in China are smaller than the average American home. They typically have less storage space and are equipped with smaller refrigerators. Thus, Chinese consumers are unlikely to "stock up" on food or purchase jumbo-sized packages. Furthermore, small packages lend themselves well to impulse consumption. Food packages also tend to be much stronger in China than in the West, because Chinese consumers believe strength equals quality. In other words, the sturdier the package, the better the product is perceived to be. In light of this belief, General Mills designs packages strong enough to bear the weight of an adult male.

PRODUCT SHAPE

Perhaps because they are used to a variety of snack foods, Chinese consumers often seek snack foods with unique shapes. General Mills again is head of the class by being innovative and responsive. To accommodate the preferences of Chinese snackers, Cheetos flavors come in different shapes—milk and eggs Cheetos are offered in a flat disc shape, tomato ketchup Cheetos are in the shape of round balls, and other Cheetos flavors are offered in the standard Cheetos corn shape like the one used in its U.S. product.

MARKETING STRATEGY: SEGMENTING, TARGETING, AND POSITIONING

A product that adapts to the preferences of the Chinese consumer is only part of the equation. The success of western snack foods also relies on strategic positioning in the Chinese market. The global appeal of explicitly American brands (e.g., Levi's, Marlboro, and Coca-Cola) suggests that while Chinese consumers may reject the unfamiliar flavors of western snack foods, they are likely to respond favorably to a product that appeals to their aspirational desires. Although an all-American appeal may have easily opened doors a decade ago when western products were new and readily accepted, today's Chinese market is more competitive, consisting of several major players with more discerning consumers. According to a 2001 *Access Asia* market report, "Basically, foreign goods can no longer rely on exoticism in order to attract sales, but now have to compete with domestic products on key elements of quality, packaging, price, renown and service." When simply being western is no longer a compelling proposition, marketers must develop insights based on marketing research to create new strategies. To fully understand how snack foods companies should position their products in China, we need to gain a better understanding of the immediate customer.

Like any market, the Chinese snack food market can be segmented on many factors, including demographics (age and family size), geography (region of the country), psychographics (lifestyle), and behavior characteristics (occasions of use). The two most relevant segmentation factors for the Chinese snack food market are demographics and behavior characteristics.

DEMOGRAPHICS

Bernd Schmitt, a China marketing expert at Columbia University and the China-Europe International Business School, has stated that until recently, "understanding of the Chinese consumer market has been severely limited due to the lack of reliable data regarding consumer perceptions and consumption patterns. As a result, little is known about Chinese consumer behavior and how to segment the market." Because of the lack of knowledge about consumers, demographic segmentation is currently used by a vast majority of consumer good marketers, including those marketing western snack foods.

In many markets, companies segment the market by age to reach people who have common needs that are driven by their stage of life. In China, historical factors unique to the country offer even more compelling reasons to segment the market based on age. People across different age groups do not differ just in terms of their life stage but also in terms of their political beliefs and experiences. The rapid rate of change for China's political and social influences has a profound effect on consumers segmented based on age and other demographics. According to Wen-Wen Paquette Wang, marketing director for General Mills, the trends and events that define a generation, such as political movements, product introductions, and technological advances, change so rapidly in China that it only takes a few years for generations to be formed. The result is that people separated in age by only a few years may identify with a completely different generation. Wang said that although General Mills targets mostly younger buyers, it has found major differences in buying habits even within a narrow age range in the young consumers segment.

While adults over sixty have been affected by the Cultural Revolution and have lived a majority of their lives under Communist rule, people under twenty have grown up in a more open China, and in many places, especially the urban areas, they are accustomed to using western products. Baiping Shen, director of strategic planning, PRC, for Leo Burnett in Shanghai, indicated that western snack food companies often target age groups based on the product attributes considered important to each group. Whereas adults are focused on taste quality, younger people are interested in novelty characteristics like coloring and flavor. Table 8.1 indicates the relative importance of various product attributes to these segments.

Table 8.1
Importance of Product Attributes to Adults and Children

Product Attribute	Importance to Adults	Importance to Children
Taste quality	****	**
Flavors	**	****
Texture/crisp	***	*
Shape	*	***
Coloring	—	****

Source: Leo Burnett, Shanghai, 2003. Reprinted with permission.

MARKETING TO LITTLE EMPERORS

Often called "little emperors" because of the extravagant amount of attention and resources devoted to them by their parents and grandparents, Chinese children are targeted by many western companies for two reasons. First, because the children have been exposed to western products and ideas their entire lives, they are much more likely than adults to try new western products. Second, the one-child policy, coupled with the rise in China's income level, means that many of these "onlies" have a large amount of disposable income to spend on consumer goods. For instance, when entering China, Kentucky Fried Chicken targeted this group because it knew that the "little emperors" would be indulged, even though the product was not of conventional Chinese tastes and might not appeal to the parents or grandparents.

OCCASIONS OF USE

Although demographic variables such as age may serve as good proxies for different needs, recent research, such as that conducted by Bernd Schmitt and Guido DeBoeck, is shedding light on meaningful differences between groups of Chinese consumers based on psychographics and behavior characteristics. One behavior characteristic that is particularly relevant to the snack food market is occasions of use. Partly because western snack foods have been only recently introduced into the Chinese market and partly because they are simply western, their occasions of use are very different both from those of traditional Chinese snack foods and from how western cultures consume western snack foods. Typically, they are not consumed with a meal or as a meal replacement, as they may be in the West, but are instead usually eaten on a whim to satisfy an impulse. According to an industry source, targeting on usage occasions is critical because it allows companies to create the same consumption platform across different markets. When targeting specific usage occasions, companies can position their brands to appeal to the entire family and be considered everyday products.

IMPLICATIONS FOR PRODUCT POSITIONING—EXCITING AND NEW

By segmenting the market based on demographics and occasions of use, western marketers have created desire for their snack food products by positioning them as an exciting experience while simultaneously emphasizing novelty through new flavors, packaging, promotions, or tie-ins. General Mills, for instance, positions Bugles as fantasy for the teen market and often includes mermaids and video game features in its commercials. This degree of innovation parallels the pace of change in China's very dynamic society. The "little emperors" segment is particularly receptive to this "exciting and new" message because of the social popularity of consuming trendy foods. In Jun Jing's study of China's "little emperors," a young Chinese boy noted, "Whenever there is a new product that I have not tried before, I buy it immediately. I have to try new things. Otherwise, when classmates are chatting, if everyone has tried something and you have not tried it, then you have nothing to say." In the current Chinese marketplace, creating an aura of excitement and newness around one's snack food product is the key to gaining entry into the snack food category. By adopting this strategy, western firms are able to motivate young Chinese consumers to experiment with new snack food products.

In addition to creating excitement about their products, western firms must connect their product to local cultural habits to gain the acceptance of Chinese consumers. For instance, people in China have historically consumed sugar-water purchased from street vendors. When Coca-Cola first launched its signature product in

China, Chinese people were able to make the product personally relevant by comparing it to this familiar sugar-water—they could imagine themselves using the product, which provided a category point of reference.

In contrast to Coca-Cola, a global cereal manufacturer failed to make this cultural connection in developing its positioning strategy. This manufacturer entered the Chinese market with its standard cold cereal product and positioned it as a healthy breakfast alternative. The product was short-lived because the company overlooked two breakfast attributes that are important to Chinese consumers. First, taste, not health, is the most important attribute for breakfast food in China; and second, Chinese prefer warm breakfast foods such as congee (rice porridge) and dim sum to cold cereal. Shen believes that the launch would have been successful if the company had positioned its cold cereal as a quick lunch or after-school snack instead of a breakfast food.

CONCLUSION

The successful western snack foods company is the one that enters the Chinese market with a dual adaptation strategy that modifies the product to conform to local tastes and then positions it strategically to young consumers. To enter China's snack food market today, a product must be exciting and new, which is why so many multinational companies are performing significant amounts of marketing research to develop innovative flavors, shapes, names, and packaging. However, even novelty in product adaptation needs to be accompanied by a positioning strategy that connects with local habits and tastes to succeed in that market.

Some of the key recommendations that follow from our study are:

- *Creating Brand Loyalty:* Being fun and new may be the price of entry into the snack food market today, but innovation is not a long-term point of differentiation, as new products can and are easily copied by competitors.

Consumers are increasingly assimilating western habits but have not yet developed loyalty for particular western brands. The extent of counterfeiting in China indicates that the importance of branding is likely to increase owing to the reassurance that brand names are a signal of quality. With a growing middle class, brand loyalty is also likely to increase as consumers use branded goods to convey status and achievement. Western firms must build brand loyalty now to ensure market share in the future.

- *Connecting with the Chinese Consumer:* Chinese consumers are becoming increasingly sophisticated and will no longer accept a product simply because it is western. There is an opportunity for western firms to develop more sophisticated marketing campaigns to appeal to these more sophisticated consumers. Such campaigns should leverage the product's appeal to young consumers and focus on specific usage occasions. Additionally, they should try to segment based on attitudes and aspirations. The company that connects with consumers on these higher-order characteristics will create deeper, more meaningful relationships between the consumer and the brand.

- *Growing Importance of Regions to Category Expansion:* As the current big-city markets gradually become saturated, western firms hoping to reach more of China's 1.2 billion people will need to start thinking about the subtle cultural differences between the regions of China and the corresponding changes in product and positioning that these differences imply. As they expand, western firms will also need to consider the distribution constraints involved in trying to reach all the provinces in China. Targeting underserved areas where there is little competition may enable western firms to establish market dominance.

BIBLIOGRAPHY

Access Asia Limited. 2001. "Savoury Snacks in China: A Market Analysis."
    5 October. http://www.accessasia.co.uk/showreport.asp?RptId=180.

Ambler, Tim, and Morgen Witzel. 2000. *Doing Business in China.* London:
    Routledge.

Collins, Glen. 1994. "Chinese to Get a Taste of Cheeseless Cheetos," *New
    York Times,* September 2.

DeBoeck, Guido, and Bernd Schmitt. 1998. "Consumer Segmentation in
    China: Identifying Differential Patterns in Consumption Preferences
    Using Self-Organizing Maps." In *Visual Explorations in Finance,* edit-
    ed by Guido DeBoeck and Teavo Kohonen. London: Springer.

Jing, Jun. 2000. *Feeding China's Little Emperors: Food, Children, and Social
    Change.* Stanford, Calif.: Stanford University Press.

Karat, Clare-Marie, and John Karat. 1996. "World-wide CHI: Perspectives
    on Design and Internationalization." *SIGCHI Bulletin* 28 (1). www.
    acm.org/sigchi/bulletin/1996.1/international.html.

Kotler, Philip, and Gary Armstrong. 2000. *Principles of Marketing.* 9th ed.
    New York: Prentice Hall.

Schmitt, Bernd. 1998. "Consumer Segmentation in China." *Marketing Issues
    in Transitional Economies.* www.globalbrands.org/resources/online/aca-
    demic.htm.

Stuttard, John B. 2000. "Clever and Sensible Adaptation Is Key." *The New
    Silk Road: Secrets of Business Success in China Today.* New York: John
    Wiley and Sons.

Chapter 9

THE CHALLENGE OF WINNING LOCAL CLIENTS FOR MULTINATIONAL ADVERTISING AGENCIES

Kristen Mitchell, Scott Rupp, and
James Steckart

As domestic consumer demand grows rapidly, China has become an important market for multinational media companies. Media conglomerates and investors alike are attracted by China's huge potential advertising business as Chinese consumers' spending power increases. Yet media platforms in China—television, radio, newspapers, and the like—remain tightly regulated. Deregulation remains unlikely in the near term, even in the wake of China's accession to the World Trade Organization (WTO). There are frustratingly few ways for foreigners to ride the gathering wave in Chinese media. The ad agency business is the key exception. Multinational advertising agencies (MNAAs) have been allowed to operate as minority joint venture partners since 1986, when Dentsu Young and Rubicam became the first MNAA joint venture operating in China. Since then, the Chinese advertising industry has experienced tremendous growth.

Advertising spending grew at a compound annual rate of 22 percent to US$8.3 billion from 1990 to 2000 (see Table 9.1). Although annual growth rates have slowed since 1997, the rate of

Table 9.1

Advertising Expenditures in China, 1990–2000 (in US$ millions)

Year	Newspapers	Magazines	TV	Radio	Cinema	Outdoor	Internet	Total	Growth
1990	$330	$127	$491	$49	$11	$102	$—	$1,110	—
1991	$392	$136	$608	$62	$11	$106	$—	$1,316	18.5%
1992	$569	$162	$807	$93	$10	$143	$—	$1,784	35.6%
1993	$988	$182	$997	$131	$9	$236	$—	$2,542	42.5%
1994	$1,253	$260	$1,346	$165	$8	$362	$—	$3,394	33.5%
1995	$1,345	$278	$1,743	$215	$6	$368	$—	$3,955	16.5%
1996	$1,589	$328	$2,184	$224	$6	$393	$—	$4,724	19.4%
1997	$2,036	$376	$2,615	$268	$11	$560	$—	$5,865	24.1%
1998	$2,139	$365	$2,994	$293	$10	$637	$—	$6,438	9.8%
1999	$2,466	$463	$3,317	$269	$3	$741	$—	$7,260	12.8%
2000	$3,081	$611	$3,537	$320	$2	$765	$14	$8,330	14.7%

1990–2000 CAGR: 22.3%

Source: Data courtesy of Zenith Optimedia Group.

Note: Statistics include mainland China and Hong Kong. Assumes exchange rate of RMB 8.28 and HK$ 7.76.

CAGR = Compound annual growth rate

growth is still 10 percent or more. Annual growth in 2001 was above 10 percent as well and brought an estimated US$10 billion to the industry despite one of the worst worldwide advertising slumps in many years. With these dramatic growth rates, China has emerged as the second-largest advertising market in Asia behind Japan (see Table 9.2), and it is the world's fifth-largest advertising market. Industry associations and analysts predict that China will be among the top three advertising markets in the world by 2015, if it is not the largest.

China's entry into the WTO is expected to lead to further growth of the advertising industry. As China lowers trade barriers, advertising spending by new entrants in the country's market is expected to increase. Branding is likely to become an increasingly important differentiator, and local firms are likely to respond to greater competition between consumer products by increasing their advertising expenditures. In addition, all restrictions on foreign ownership of advertising agencies will be eliminated in 2004, allowing MNAAs to operate wholly owned subsidiaries in China.

Table 9.2
Asian Advertising Spending (in US$ millions)

Country	2000 Ad Spending
Japan	$42,003
China (including Hong Kong)	8,330
South Korea	6,575
Australia	4,509
Taiwan	1,887
India	1,587
Thailand	1,473
Indonesia	938
Singapore	872
Malaysia	818
New Zealand	679
Philippines	486
Pakistan	132
Vietnam	131
Cambodia	41
Laos	5
Asia Pacific total	$70,464

Source: Data courtesy of Zenith Optimedia Group.

Table 9.3
Chinese Versus U.S. Ad Spending (in US$ millions)

	United States	China
2000 ad spending (US$ million)	$250,000	$8,330
Population (millions)	270	1,300
Ad spending per capita	$925.93	$6.41
Ad spending as percent of GDP*	2.5%	0.45%

Source: Data courtesy of Zenith Optimedia Group and Deutsche Banc Alex. Brown.

* GDP percent for China based on mainland China as spending and GDP.

Even without the competitive pressures from foreign entrants driving increased advertising spending, demographics alone suggest dramatic future growth. Advertising spending in the United States for the year 2000 was US$250 billion on a population base of 270 million people, or roughly US$926 per capita per year (Table 9.3). China's advertising industry spent US$8.3 billion for the year 2000 on a population base of 1.3 billion, or only US$6.41 per capita. If per capita ad spending in China reaches only 21 percent of the current U.S. level (roughly US$194 per capita), its advertising industry would match that of the United States. Furthermore, U.S. ad spending as a percentage of gross domestic product (GDP) is 2.5 percent, compared to only 0.45 percent in China. If ad spending in China increases to a comparable percentage of today's GDP, the industry will triple current levels. Ad agencies, which typically earn percentage commissions on advertising expenditures by clients, are poised to capture this dramatic growth.

THE REVENUE MIX OF MNAAS

The dramatic growth in ad spending is reflected in an equally dramatic increase in the number of advertising firms registered in mainland China. Between 1990 and 2001, the number of advertising agencies increased sevenfold, to 78,300. Since the early 1990s, MNAAs have dominated the top ten agencies in China. In 1995, the top ten ad agencies were all international. Current information for total billings by these agencies in China is not available, but an estimate based on minimum market share figures

Table 9.4
Market Share of Top Agencies (in US$1,000)

Top Ten Agencies (1995)	1995 Billings
1. Saatchi and Saatchi Advertising, Beijing/Guanzhou	$12,464
2. JWT Thompson China, Beijing	$8,544
3. Ogilvy and Mather, Beijing	$7,877
4. Leo Burnett Co., Guanzhou	$7,702
5. McCann-Erickson Guangming, Beijing	$7,598
6. DMB and B, Guanzhou	$6,346
7. Grey China, Beijing	$4,833
8. Bates China, Beijing	$3,953
9. Beijing Dentsu Advertising, Beijing	$3,355
10. Euro RSCG Ball Partnership, Beijing	$3,206
Total billings of top ten agencies	$65,878
1995 advertising expenditure—mainland China only	$2,007,006
Commission revenue potential*	$200,701
Implied market share of top ten agencies†	33%

Source: Data from International Advertising Resource Center.

* Assumed 10 percent commission rate.

† Actual commission paid most likely lower, implying even higher market share for the top ten agencies.

from 1995 suggests that power lies in the hands of a few multinational agencies (Table 9.4).

Clearly, the MNAAs dominate the ad agency business in China, with smaller players competing in a fragmented market with many subspecialties (e.g., public relations, below-the-line services, regional focuses, interactive agencies). The majority of clients and billings of MNAAs come from international brands. One agency reported that billings from international clients accounted for 70 percent of total revenue.

Yet ad spending in China is dominated by local brands. In fact, as Table 9.5 shows, the top ten advertisers in mainland China in 2000 accounted for 15 percent of total ad spending and with all local brands. (However, in 2002, *Ad Age* reported that Procter and Gamble had cracked the top ten with its Safeguard and Crest brands.)

It is interesting to note that local brands dominate ad spending but not the revenue mix of the dominant agencies. We believe that three factors are at play:

Table 9.5
Top Advertisers and Categories (in US$1,000)

Top 10 Brands		Top 10 Product Categories	
Brand	2000 Ad Spending	Category	2000 Ad Spending
Naobaijin Health Products	$124,793	Tonic and vitamins	$1,288,220
Gai Zhong Gai (Ca)	114,576	OTC Chinese medicine	528,274
Puxue Oral Solution	78,300	Residential property	377,391
Yandi Medicine	75,164	Professional services	272,992
Beyoung Gusui Strong Powder	61,842	Communications	251,994
Dongfeng Yanfan X.F.M.L. Cr	52,889	Cough cold preparations	250,579
Huiren Shenbao	49,943	Shampoo and conditioners	230,373
Palm Handwriting	48,193	Wines and spirits	229,959
Huiren Wuji Baifeng Pill	47,592	Skincare	220,323
Palm Handwriting Lianbiwan	45,821	Mobile phones and accessories	180,051
Total	$699,113	Total	$3,831,157
Percent of mainland China ad spending	15%	Percent of mainland China ad spending	80%

Source: Data courtesy of Nielsen Media Research 2003.

1. Local brands spread their agency business across several non-dominant Chinese agencies on a regional basis. This practice has prevented any single Chinese advertising firm from cracking the top ten agencies at the national level.
2. Local companies pay reduced commissions to Chinese agencies, far below "standard" commissions charged by MNAAs, resulting in lower billing and market share figures.
3. Some local companies may handle advertising in-house and not use agencies at all.

Clearly, revenue would increase dramatically if MNAAs could win the business of local brands that dominate advertising spending in China, while still charging their standard billing rates.

MNAAs in China have been quite successful in capturing the domestic business of preexisting multinational clients that have entered China. MNAAs have also successfully won "China-only" business from multinational advertisers with whom they did not have a prior relationship in other national markets. As Geoffrey Fowler of the *Wall Street Journal* notes, international ad agencies have transformed Chinese advertising from drab, propaganda-like messages into a modern, lively medium. China's entries for the advertising industry's Clio Awards have multiplied tenfold since 1999 and Chinese ads won their first Clios in 2002. Most recently, a team from Leo Burnett China came up with several winning ideas for a new global ad campaign for McDonald's.

These successes suggest that MNAAs have a reasonably secure position with their existing worldwide and other non-Chinese clients. Furthermore, given their track records of execution in China and the potentially higher comfort level that non-Chinese advertisers have when working with more familiar multinational agencies, MNAAs are likely to continue to capture business from new entrants into China with whom they have relationships in other territories. In sum, the agencies can expect revenue to grow in a fashion that corresponds with ad spending of multinational advertisers in China. That growth rate should be quite robust given the

Chinese economy's expansion and the increasing spending power of its consumers.

Benefiting from this "rising tide" alone, however, is not a sustainable strategy of competitive advantage. Winning large, local clients is the key to growth and should be the long-term strategic focus for MNAAs in China. According to Robert Swartz, managing director of Ogilvy and Mather in Beijing, "China will support huge domestic brands." A senior executive at one of the top agencies indicated a goal of achieving a fifty-fifty split between international and local clients.

Winning large accounts from local advertisers is a strategic priority for MNAAs for several reasons. Winning large local clients will drive growth for the MNAAs and will lead to greater scale. Scale matters in the advertising business, because it creates leverage with media outlets and clients. Scale also creates the ability to offer a range of strategic marketing services, as well as a larger revenue base from which the agency can fund investments in market research and regional offices. Moreover, working with local brand advertisers will give MNAAs a deeper understanding of Chinese business practices, Chinese consumers, and the competitive landscape for specific product categories. This knowledge will make MNAAs a more valuable strategic partner to both Chinese and multinational clients. Finally, as competitive pressures require greater advertising by all players in China, local companies may increasingly value the strategic benefits that advertising agencies can deliver. Local brands are currently the biggest advertisers in China, and local agencies, despite their smaller size today, may well pose a significant competitive threat to MNAAs, particularly on a regional basis.

THE MYTHS AND REALITIES OF OPERATING MNAAS IN CHINA

What are the barriers to winning local clients? Do MNAAs operate in a level playing field when trying to win local clients? The press, trade, and academic literature seem to hold several misconceptions about the Chinese advertising industry. Together, they suggest potentially significant impediments to MNAAs in China. These commonly held myths include competitive disadvantages related to government regulation, price discrimination by media outlets, lack of reliable market data, and cumbersome ownership structures required by Chinese law. However, we believe these impediments are not major issues. In fact, competition among local and international agencies is quite fierce and efficient. We discuss some of these perceptions below.

Myth 1: MNAAs Face Unequal Access to Media Time and Face Price Discrimination by Media Outlets

There have been allegations that state ownership and tight control of Chinese media have posed a challenge to MNAAs by limiting their access to advertising space and time. In the mid-1990s, research suggested that advertising agencies could not freely choose media outlets and that preferential treatment was given to Chinese clients purchasing media time directly. However, the situation appears to have changed significantly since this research was conducted.

In our meetings with both MNAAs and local Chinese agencies, these problems no longer seemed to be an issue. MNAAs did not report any price discrimination in media buying or disadvantaged access to time slots or media platforms. In fact, Chinese agencies indicated that they outsourced media buying for their clients because they lacked the size and scale to independently purchase media on favorable terms. The local agencies reported that the larger MNAAs were big buyers of airtime and were able to secure better terms for media buys than Chinese agencies.

Myth 2: MNAAs Face Confusing, Subjective Local Regulation of Advertising Content That Often Does Not Apply to Local Advertisers

Advertising content is indeed subject to regulation in China. Images of police, sexuality, Mao Zedong, protests, as well as challenges to authority and claims of being "the best" are not permitted. The regulations are difficult to interpret, and there are indications they were enforced on an unpredictable, local, case-by-case basis, leading to confusion and frustration among agencies. Current sources suggest these problems may continue today. According to a 2002 report by the American Chamber of Commerce, "Inconsistent implementation of these regulations at the local level has resulted in significant loss and confusion for multinationals and is tantamount to protectionism, as local firms are exempt from such restrictions." The Chamber of Commerce also reported that current legislation limits pretax advertising expenditures to 8 percent of sales, which might impede entry by firms accustomed to spending much more in a new market.

Meetings with agency executives, however, indicate that regulation of advertising content is in fact not quite as fickle and cumbersome as it is perceived to be. Although restrictions on creative expression (in terms of state censorship) have not disappeared, ad agencies have become more adept at dealing with them. Hiring experienced and dedicated staff to interface with regulatory bodies addresses the operational challenge of complying with the law and prevents delays that might otherwise occur in receiving approval for the advertising. The MNAAs with whom we met did not indicate that regulation was a significant problem, nor did they feel that they were treated differently than local agencies. More specifically, they did not believe local agencies enjoyed an advantage with regulators on behalf of their clients. Finally, as a senior executive at an ad agency noted, the 8 percent of sales ad-spending cap was either abolished or no longer enforced.

MYTH 3: LACK OF RELIABLE AUDIENCE AND DEMOGRAPHIC DATA POSE A SIGNIFICANT CHALLENGE

As Ogilvy and Mather's Swartz stated, "China has 5,000 years of history and one year of statistics." Indeed, statistics in China are in short supply, and those that do exist are not always reliable. Chinese agencies we met with suggested that the lack of data, combined with their greater knowledge of the local consumers and market, gave them an advantage over MNAAs in planning and executing effective local campaigns.

The lack of data is certainly a problem, but it does not impede the MNAAs' ability to differentiate themselves from local agencies. Several studies note that the Chinese are tired of advertisements presented in "ordinary or boring ways" dominated by slogans, a legacy of the Cultural Revolution. An earlier study in the mid-1990s indicated that half of the most impressive television commercials were from foreign agencies. In addition, MNAAs have years of experience conducting market studies, focus groups, and consumer research in geographies all over the world. As we discuss later in this chapter, all of the major MNAAs have developed their proprietary research methods, which is a major value-added service that MNAAs can offer to their clients. Furthermore, all of the MNAAs that we met with employ the vast majority of their staff (over 80 percent) locally. The advertising industry pays considerably more than other fields in China, and the market for creative talent has increased substantially during the last five to six years. These local staffers, combined with sophisticated proprietary research, have helped MNAAs gain insights into the mind of the Chinese consumer.

Myth 4: Regulations Governing the Structuring of Joint Ventures Could Become an Operational Nightmare for MNAAs

Chinese law restricts MNAAs to minority ownership positions in joint venture agencies, and these partnership structures could be operationally cumbersome for MNAAs. Indeed, all of the MNAAs we met with except one were minority or fifty-fifty partners in joint ventures with Chinese companies (the exception had a majority position). However, the repeal of these restrictions in 2004 as part of China's accession to the WTO may lead to significant changes in the ownership structure of joint ventures operated under MNAA brands.

Our meetings with MNAAs indicated, however, that their Chinese joint venture partners for the most part were silent partners without any operational role. Maintaining healthy joint venture partner relationships did not seem to be impeding operations. None of the MNAAs with whom we met reported an interest in changing the ownership structure of their joint ventures for operational reasons.[1]

The operating reality of MNAAs is quite different from the myths about the industry, which demonstrates how rapidly the Chinese advertising industry is evolving. The discrepancy is also reflective of the limited information available on the Chinese advertising industry. What then are the biggest challenges facing MNAAs today?

MNAA: SUPPLIER OR STRATEGIC PARTNER?

One of the biggest challenges for MNAAs is overcoming the local client's view of the advertising agency as a mere supplier rather than as a strategic partner. In the eyes of Chinese firms, advertising agencies supply their creative skills, graphic design ability, or production expertise to the client's ideas and strategic branding plans. The advertising agency essentially has a limited role: taking the client's message and creatively packaging and distributing it to the public. In contrast, the western view of the role of the ad agency is as collaborator and strategic marketing partner. The view of the advertising agency merely as a supplier limits all areas of the agency-client relationship in China, including pricing, length of projects and partnerships, degree of cooperation from client top management, and agency-client commitment. To succeed in China, MNAAs need to alter the supplier mind-set and redefine the agency role more in line with that in most parts of the world. However, this task is easier said than done. Meanwhile, the role of the advertising agency as supplier has given rise to several related challenges, most notably price competition and short-term projects.

One of the most challenging aspects of entering the Chinese market for the MNAA is that in China, unlike in more developed markets, price is one of the principal criteria by which agencies are evaluated. Because local clients view advertising as a commodity, they are focused on the price tag of the pitch, rather than the quality or strategic value of the product. Although Chinese companies invite many agencies to pitch for a new advertising campaign, they often end up choosing the firm that offers the lowest price—usually the local advertising agency. In some cases, the low-cost firm executes "borrowed" ideas from unsuccessful MNAA pitches. This price competition is indicative of the low value that Chinese companies place on agencies' creative capital and strategic insights.

To get its foot in the door with local clients, at least one MNAA indicated it has begun to compete on price. Other MNAAs, pointing to their own policies of not lowering their standard pricing parameters, mentioned that they sometimes would hear about MNAA competitors bidding at 20 percent of their standard price. This short-term strategy lowers the perceived value of their services just when the MNAAs should be justifying and emphasizing the strategic value of their expertise. Conversely, one may argue that in an environment where private firms may be price sensitive, competing on price may allow MNAAs to get some exposure and develop relationships with clients. In keeping with this supplier mindset, local firms often contract with advertising firms on a job-by-job basis. As one ad executive told us, "The ad industry is so young—firms want to date, not marry." Although MNAAs have been able to establish long-term relationships with foreign advertisers in China, local clients are not used to contracting advertising firms on a long-term basis. However, for the MNAAs, successful partnerships on a project-by-project basis can build trust and eventually lead to a long-term strategic partnership. Saatchi and Saatchi recently developed a long-term partnership with a Chinese state-owned enterprise (SOE) after being assigned a series of challenging short-term projects. By collaborating with the client on several small projects, Saatchi and Saatchi was able to convince the client of the agency's strategic value in China's competitive cell phone market. Over time, the SOE's management learned the value of working with an MNAA in a competitive market.

MNAAs' COMPETITIVE ADVANTAGE AS A STRATEGIC PARTNER

In their quest to become a strategic partner for local clients rather than an advertising services supplier, MNAAs have a major competitive advantage with their institutional know-how and time-tested strategic branding approaches. The largest western agencies all have rich company histories: Ogilvy and Mather was founded in 1948, Grey Advertising in 1917, and J. Walter Thompson in 1864. These histories shape their culture and, more importantly, their advertising and branding approach. In comparison, communist rule effectively blocked all mass advertising in China until the market-oriented reforms in the late 1970s, giving local firms at most twenty years or so of institutional history. In fact, Chinese citizens over forty years old came of age in a world free of mass advertising. Even though employees of local agencies have been able to study, work with, and learn from the MNAAs in the last twenty years, the Chinese advertising agencies are still relatively young and inexperienced. Their relative position on the learning curve contrasts and highlights the institutional advantages of the MNAAs. As Baiping Shen, director of strategic planning, PRC, for Leo Burnett, said, "Local firms have very good single ideas or campaign executions, but they don't understand the long-term strategy. They lack a systematic approach to [building] brand equity."

Discussions with leading MNAAs regarding their own perceived core competencies and, more importantly, their plans for new business expansion indicate that the most pronounced competitive advantage for MNAAs rests in three specific client strategy areas: (1) market data collection and knowledge management, (2) strategic market segmentation, and (3) new product introduction and branding. Besides possessing a strategic competitive advantage in client services, MNAAs have advantages over local advertising agencies in two key operating areas: (4) capital resources for regional office development and national coverage, and (5) an established, methodical approach to managing their own company brands.

As we discuss in the following sections, MNAAs can showcase these competitive advantages to local clients and demonstrate how these areas are critical to achieving advertising success and increasing sales.

Market Data Collection and Knowledge Management
Demographic statistics and growth figures are notoriously unreliable in China. Hence, data are more often used to illustrate or suggest trends than to give precise information. Although data are

much more accessible now than before, their unreliability implies that the data need to be independently verified and interpreted. All of the major MNAAs have developed their own tracking surveys and primary research methods. For instance, one advertising executive mentioned that his firm recently revamped its primary qualitative research methods in China. Instead of using focus groups, it now relied on one-on-one interviews at home because of the Chinese consumers' discomfort with expressing their opinion about product brands in front of others. MNAAs often conduct their own market research, using proprietary data collection methods and analytical models to gain a better understanding of the marketplace. In particular, they rely on well-proven qualitative research methods to shed light on consumers' perceptions and attitudes toward key product traits, which in turn helps gauge market success. In comparison, Chinese market research tends to be based on feedback from salesmen, test introductions, and personal field experience.

Given their global structure, MNAAs generally have much larger market research and consumer insights departments than local agencies. These resources have allowed them to develop proprietary research models that deconstruct the emotional relationships that people have with brands and benchmark these brands against their competition. Many have models that can reliably and quantitatively predict in-market performance and even tell their clients which advertisement elicited the emotions that will most affect future purchasing behavior. These models are often used to forecast the right mix of channels and media spending. Ogilvy calls it "360 Degree Brand Management," Grey calls it "Synchronized Marketing," and all major MNAAs have their own proven quantitative models that give direction on strategically coordinated messages across consumer touch-points. A good understanding of psychographic research in crafting marketing campaigns is crucial and can itself be marketed as a competitive advantage. MNAAs are careful, however, in interpreting the results of the quantitative research because they are still learning about the psychology of the Chinese consumer. Often, the responses offer only a fuzzy segmentation scheme, and furthermore, there are significant regional differences. Indeed, advertising in China can get complicated for the MNAAs because of cultural differences and potential problems with translation, especially given the subtleties of the Chinese script and spoken language. Therefore, foreign expertise and knowledge need to be coupled with local staff and insights.

Strategic Market Segmentation

The ability of MNAAs to leverage their consumer insight will only increase as the growing demand economy splinters what has been until recently a homogeneous consumer market. In particular, two important demographic trends—the growth of a middle class with purchasing power, and the increasingly western attitudes of the younger Chinese consumer—orchestrate the shift from broadly targeted "everyman" brands to the more narrowly targeted niche products. Conventional wisdom heard time and time again in China is that the younger generation, coming of age in predominantly single-child homes, with ready access to media and advertising, is a fundamentally more jaded, knowledgeable consumer with very different attitudes and responsiveness to advertising. These macrodemographic trends make targeted marketing potentially more profitable. As the Chinese consumer becomes more heterogeneous in tastes and perceptions, companies will need better information for strategic segmentation. This change presents an opportunity for MNAAs, because they should be able to attract local clients by showcasing their modeling and segmentation expertise.

New Product Introduction and Branding

The challenge that MNAAs face lies in their ability to demonstrate the value of strategic segmentation. Niche and new product introduction is one area where this segmentation expertise is crucial. More than one agency mentioned that new product introduction is an area where local firms are more willing to pay for the expertise of MNAAs; as such, new product launch campaigns are opportunities for MNAAs to get their foot in the door. In addition to new product introduction, branding work, such as product rebranding and corporate brand hierarchy development, is another area where local clients are typically more willing to pay a premium for the expertise of MNAAs. MNAAs are valued for this work because companies such as Ogilvy and Mather and Leo Burnett have widely disseminated branding frameworks and are generally recognized as branding experts. Equally important, local clients that are highly focused on corporate branding efforts are on average more aware of the financial value of a well-thought-out branding strategy and are thus more likely to pay for it. As a result, competencies in new product development and branding should figure prominently in the strategies of MNAAs to new local clients.

Capital Resources for Regional Office Development
There are no truly "national" campaigns in China because consumer tastes and perceptions are very localized. Consumer attitudes, perceptions, and per-capita incomes vary widely between coastal and inland markets and urban and rural areas and are severe enough to necessitate region-specific campaigns and sometimes even region-specific product attributes. This variation means that national brands, such as Legend Computers and Tsingtao beer, have to bear the additional costs of dealing with multiple local agencies in different regions. An MNAA would have the capacity to handle the coordination of multiple regions and could, if necessary, open a satellite office in key client cities. When China is ready to support national megabrands, the deep pockets of the MNAA global parents will be a key competitive advantage. Until such time, the sheer size of the Chinese market presents a major obstacle for both MNAAs and local agencies. There are numerous major metropolitan areas, and each region is a self-contained market. A local agency may be able to focus on a particular region and dominate it. As regional commerce barriers begin to erode, MNAAs will have to closely monitor the expansion strategies of their largest local competitors and prioritize regional targets throughout China.

Stewards of Their Own Brands in China
Finally, MNAAs are able to focus their advertising expertise inward and leverage the power of their strong brand names within the advertising industry. Successful firms have a concrete strategy for building their own brands within China and promoting their own expertise. Ogilvy and Mather, for instance, were quick to publish

David Ogilvy's classic books on advertising in Chinese in the early 1980s and continue to hold seminars and provide marketing education materials to enhance their "premium" agency status.

From Supplier to Strategic Partner

Although MNAAs have several competitive advantages, leveraging them into strategic relationships with local clients requires focusing on client education, developing collaborative relationships, choosing clients wisely, securing access to senior managers, and investing in staff training and development. We discuss each of these in the following sections.

Collaborative Client Education

Chinese clients are not fully aware of the benefits of working with an MNAA. Thus, client education will continue to be critical to winning clients and, ultimately, shifting the mind-set of Chinese firms away from viewing advertising firms merely as suppliers. To market a new product, a firm uses informational advertising that communicates the benefit of the product. Along the same lines, selling the value of MNAA services and shifting the mind-set of the Chinese firms require the distribution of information about the benefits of hiring an MNAA. Forums, seminars, and conferences are tools for advertising agencies to teach basic marketing strategy and demonstrate the value of their services. Foreign advertising agencies seeking a piece of the pie are well advised to formalize the education effort, perhaps by publishing monthly case studies and circulating them to past clients and/or chief executive officers (CEOs) of potential clients. In addition, agencies may wish to borrow a local strategy and develop relationships with advertising and marketing departments at Chinese universities. By educating advertising students and becoming thought leaders on Chinese marketing and advertising, MNAAs can build their brand name with future managers and tap talented students to join their firms.

Although we have emphasized the importance of the MNAA as educator, the MNAA also needs to listen and learn from the client. Collaboration between the MNAA and the local client is critical. Leo Burnett's Shen notes that one key to his firm's success is the understanding that local companies do not want to be told what they do not know. These clients want to work collaboratively with an ad agency and be treated with respect. When presented with an unfamiliar subject, some executives may instinctively say no to new ideas. MNAAs should be sensitive to this issue during initial projects as they bring the client up to speed on the language of branding and marketing.

Choosing Clients Wisely and Securing Access to Senior Management

Some clients prefer collaboration, whereas other clients are not used to working in a collaborative relationship. Executives from leading agencies in China, such as Leo Burnett and Saatchi and Saatchi, reported that they choose their local clients carefully and take on clients that will be receptive to a collaborative relationship. Access to senior management of a potential client is an indicator of the degree of collaboration. When access to senior management is limited, MNAAs have less opportunity to educate decision makers on marketing strategy and branding decisions. Senior management of local firms may not appreciate the strategic value of sales and marketing at first, and gaining access to them is critical for changing the MNAA-as-supplier mind-set. To develop a successful collaborative relationship, it is important that the MNAA have a good understanding of the needs of the local client and have access to top management.

Keeping Local Employees Satisfied

Another "mission-critical" priority for any MNAA whose objective is to build a large local client base is staff development and training. Developing and retaining local employees should be an ongoing cost of conducting business for any firm committed to winning in the Chinese market. Although the majority of the staff at MNAAs is local, the sentiment within the industry is that employee turnover rates are higher within MNAAs and that this affects the quality of the work.

MNAAs need to increase employee loyalty within the company. MNAAs do need to have a high percentage of nationals in the office; however, they can take some very clear steps to increase a local employee's sense of ownership and job satisfaction, for example, incentive pay and bonuses, explicit criteria for promotion, and rotational training programs for promising managers (see chapter 4 for a discussion of some of these strategies). Local employees must know that the agency is a meritocracy, with good performance leading to increased responsibility.

Furthermore, maintaining high employee retention rates is essential in attracting new clients. A renewed emphasis on continuity of personnel is a signal of agency commitment to the clients; it also ensures the continuity of product management teams. To accomplish this continuity, MNAAs need to take a two-pronged approach: (1) focus on Chinese local employee satisfaction; and (2) fundamentally rethink the current system of expatriate employee placement. Globally, the advertising industry has traditionally experienced a higher employee turnover rate than other industries. Anecdotal evidence from China suggests that employee turnover in both the MNAAs and local agencies is extremely high. The reasons for the lack of employee loyalty are varied. First, expatriate workers who are paid based on the home office pay scale make substantially more money than local employees. Second, according to Barry Colman of Grey Relationship Marketing in Shanghai, there is a perception that the top jobs, such as managing director and creative director, will always go to expatriate employees brought in from the home office. Thus, many nationals often spend a few years learning the business and then leave to start their own agency.

To address these issues, MNAAs ought to focus on employee development. The benefits of doing so are many: A more engaged local employee base with an ownership mentality effectively reduces vulnerability to poaching, combats local agency competitive advantage, and offers better services to the local clients. Finally, nurturing local Chinese employees may help foster increased cooperation with joint venture partners and increased transfer of knowledge from local agency partners. As Shen said, the local agency campaigns are "more intrinsically Chinese . . . somehow closer to market." It is hubris indeed to assume there is no value to be had from the local agency partners and employees. Besides providing insights into subtle cultural nuances, these relationships with local employees and partners can also help navigate government relations.

Expatriate Employee Placement

Most expatriate employee positions tend to be short-term. According to Shen, "The Japanese companies send in expats for ten years plus. They really get to know the market and they're able to make long-term strategic decisions. It still seems that the Western agencies see a China posting simply as a necessary stop for up-and-coming managers. . . . They seem to see China not as an important market in its own right, but simply as a branch of Hong Kong." The view that the China offices were often revolving doors for senior managers on the executive fast-track was echoed consistently.

A high turnover of senior management leads to a continuous and costly climb on the learning curve that affects the performance of the local office executive team. Although shorter time commitments are likely to be more appealing to the expatriate staff, there is a powerful benefit in having longer-term employees. Some MNAAs, such as Leo Burnett, have simply phased out expatriates and filled top positions with Chinese executives. Although the salary cost savings are high, this practice requires more effort to imbue the local corporate culture with the MNAA's global culture, approach, and quality standards. Agencies have attempted to achieve this goal in different ways. Tom Doctoroff, chief executive of Greater China J. Walter Thompson, challenges his staff to beat him in table tennis, which they play in the office conference room. According to Doctoroff, this encourages creativity, independence of thought, and a freedom to challenge the hierarchical structure that is commonplace in most Chinese companies. Other policies are also in place to ensure that MNAAs offer the same benefits of continuity and long-term strategy, which includes encouraging expatriate staff to come for substantial periods of time, such as five years or more, and to actively mentor and train local staff.

CONCLUSION

Many Chinese companies, facing fierce competition from international rivals post-WTO entry, need to develop strong branding strategies as part of their overall competitive positioning. Yet they have little experience or knowledge about how to do so. Some may not even realize that they need to do so. This situation presents a tremendous opportunity for MNAAs. The value that they can bring to bear for local brands is considerable. Over the long-term, China could potentially become the biggest advertising economy in the world. So far, MNAAs have made good progress securing an initial position in the market. However, China is more than just one of many markets where MNAAs should establish a presence to serve existing global clients. It is a massive market in its own right, with indigenous brands that will continue to have a significant (if not dominant) presence in the Chinese economy. Local Chinese brands may well become global brands in the future, and MNAAs could help them expand beyond their domestic borders. Thus, MNAAs should strategically position themselves to serve these local brands and take advantage of the growing opportunity for their strategic services. We summarize the strategies presented in this chapter for winning local clients in Table 9.6.

To win local clients, MNAAs must ensure that their China operations are much more than satellite offices. By focusing on their core product and service strengths, taking a long-term approach to

Table 9.6
Key Operating Strategies for MNAAs to Gain Local Clients

1.	Focus on a long-term relationship: build trust project by project
2.	Educate clients on benefit of product (case studies, conferences, university events)
3.	Choose local clients carefully and set expectations up front
4.	Secure access to senior managers
5.	Leverage the unique competitive advantage of the MNAA • Market data collection and knowledge management • Strategic market segmentation • New product introduction and branding focus • Capital resources for rapid regional office development
6.	Act as brand stewards and carefully manage MNAA brand
7.	Continued focus on local staff development

client relationship building, acknowledging the threat local agencies could pose, and making investments in people and offices in China's regional centers, MNAAs can position themselves to serve leading local brands and become dominant players in one of the most promising media markets in the world. With the growth potential of advertising in China, winning local clients is crucial not just for the long-term success of the local offices of multinational agencies but to the overall growth and strategic positioning of the MNAAs themselves.

NOTES

1. We were unable to assess, however, whether parent companies of the MNAAs might want to consolidate ownership of these joint ventures for nonoperational reasons once full ownership is permitted in 2004.

BIBLIOGRAPHY

Ambler, Tim, and Morgan Witzel. 2000. *Doing Business in China.* New York: Routledge.

American Chamber of Commerce. 2003. "People's Republic of China." http://www.amcham-china.org.cn/publications/white/2002/en-27.htm.

Chung, Olivia. 2002. "Sales Rocket to 80B Yuan." *The Standard,* November 7.

Everett, Andre, and Yim-Yu Wong. 1999. "Capitalist Promotion Meets Communist Regulation: Advertising Agencies and the Media in China." Presented at Business Forum: Los Angeles.

Fowler, Goeffrey. 2003. "China's Edgy Advertising." *Wall Street Journal,* October 27.

Ha, Louisa. 1996. "Concerns over Advertising Practices in a Developing Country: An Examination of China's New Advertising Regulations." *International Journal of Advertising,* 15 (2):91–102.

International Advertising Resource Center. 2003. http://www.bgsu.edu/departments/tcom/faculty/ha/intlad1.html.

Lague, David. 2001. "Advertising's New Mecca." *Far Eastern Economic Review,* 164 (16):62–63.

Lin, Carolyn. 2001. "Cultural Values Reflected in Chinese and American Television Advertising." *Journal of Advertising*, 30 (4):83–94.

Madden, Normandy. 2002. "Shanghai Rises as Asia's Newest Marketing Capital." *Advertising Age*, October 14.

Marcus, D., J. Dix, W. Hammond, and D. Mitchelson. 2003. "Broadcasting Signals." *DB Alex. Brown Equity Research*, April 22.

MediaChina Net! 2003. http://english.mediachina.net/index.jsp.

Nielsen Media Research. 2003. "Asia Pacific AdEx." Nielsen Media Research.

———. 2003. "China AdEx." Nielsen Media Research.

Prendergast, Gerard, and Yi-Zheng Shi. 2001. "Client Perceptions of Advertising and Advertising Agencies: A China Study." *Journal of Marketing Communications*, 7 (2):47–63.

Sin, L. Y. M., S. Ho, and S. L. M. So. 2000. "Research on Advertising in Mainland China: A Review and Assessment." *Asia Pacific Journal of Marketing and Logistics*, 12 (1):37–65.

Tharpe, Marye. 2003. "Advertising Agencies in China." http://www. ou.edu/class/jmc3333/chinaag.htm.

Tompkins, Richard. 2002. "WPP Buys into Chinese Agency." *The Financial Times*, November 5.

Wang, Jian. 2000. *Foreign Advertising in China: Becoming Global, Becoming Local*. Ames: Iowa State University Press.

ZenithOptimedia Group. 2003. *Market and MediaFact Pocket Book: Asia Pacific*. http://www.zenithoptimedia.com/pubsmain.htm.

Zhou, D., Z. Weijiong, and V. Ilan. 2002. "Advertising Trends in Urban China." *Journal of Advertising Research*, 42 (3):73–81.

PART 4

LOOKING TO THE FUTURE

Chapter 10

DELIVERING ON THE DREAM: 2008 OLYMPICS IN BEIJING

Christopher Butler, Patrick Eggen,
Brian Ericson, and Jason Greenwald

On July 28, 2001, the International Olympic Committee (IOC) named Beijing as the host city for the 2008 Olympic Summer Games. In addition to affirming China's status as a world power, this distinction has fueled an urban development project of grandiose scale. The prestige associated with the games has provided the government an extraordinary opportunity to compress twenty-plus years of public work initiatives into a seven-year period. Indeed, there have been several recent success stories of the Olympics serving as an accelerator of urban development for the host city. Prior to hosting the Olympic Games, both Seoul in 1988 and Barcelona in 1992 underwent extensive modernization projects and emerged as truly "global" cities. Beijing intends to raise the stakes even further. Immediately after winning the bid, the Beijing Organizing Committee for the Games of the Twenty-ninth Olympiad (BOCOG) released a strategic plan that outlined an ambitious seven-year, US$34 billion development project featuring new highways, new railways, urban regeneration, and environmental initiatives. Professor John MacAloon, one of the world's most renowned Olympic anthropologists, has declared that the Beijing Olympic preparation plan could be "the world's largest single urban development project since the building of the Pyramids."

It is crucial to differentiate between the ephemeral impact of a seventeen-day "mega-event" and the more profound long-term macroeconomic impact and intangible legacy of the Olympics. Many host cities have mistakenly viewed the Olympic Games as a short-term economic boon, and most economists deride the idea of hosting the Olympics as irresponsible fiscal behavior. Professor Victor Matheson, a leading sports economist, cites the inordinate amount of capital devoted to specialized sports facilities—projects that have limited post–Olympic Games utility for the general public and serve as a long-term burden to taxpayers. Most analysts also maintain that host cities tend to overestimate the positive short-term economic impact of the Olympics and fail to account for displacement and substitution factors that offset incoming revenue. For example, visitors often spend money at sporting events instead of other local activities, resulting in a simple reallocation of revenues rather than a true net increase in local economic activity.

Although these criticisms have some merit, we focus here on the potential long-term impact of Beijing 2008. The fundamental challenge for Beijing is to minimize the construction of Olympic-specific investments that will have only short-term benefits and instead allocate capital to general infrastructure and other projects that will generate long-term value to the economy and citizens of Beijing.

THE LEGACY OF THE OLYMPICS

There are several different ways to fund the Olympics (Figure 10.1). The games of Munich (1972), Montreal (1976), and Moscow (1980) were financed almost exclusively with government subsidies and generated massive deficits because organizers devoted an extraordinary portion of overall investment to specialized facilities and lacked any sustainable plan for these facilities post-Games. To avoid this scenario, Los Angeles (1984) leveraged existing infrastructure and financed the event through private funds. The Los Angeles Olympics were wildly successful and even recorded a healthy US$250 million profit. The Seoul (1988), Barcelona

(1992), and Sydney (2000) Olympics relied on both public and private funding. Although the Beijing Olympic Games are financed through massive government subsidies, organizers have paid close attention to the lessons of past public-funded games and have devised infrastructure plans that serve a broader range of needs for the economic, social, and cultural life of Beijing.

China intends to use the Olympic Games to focus on the urban development of Beijing, hoping that the massive improvements to infrastructure, combined with the enhanced image of the city, will lead to an enduring economic lift. Melinda McKay and Craig Plumb of Jones Lang LaSalle (JLL), a global real estate management company, noted that "the key to success of hosting the Olympics is largely dependent upon the ability of the city to leverage off the images and perceptions created during the event itself, and to continue delivering on the dream long after the circus has left town." Beijing's massive US$34 billion infrastructure project can be grouped into five "legacy categories":

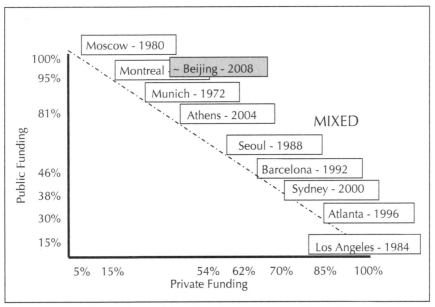

Figure 10.1:   Comparison of Funding Sources across Olympics

Source: Preuss 2000. Reprinted with permission of Professor Holger Preuss.

1. Specialized sports facilities
2. General infrastructure
3. Environmental initiatives
4. Urban regeneration and cultural heritage
5. Tourism promotion and hotel development

In each category, we look at the specific infrastructure projects that Beijing is undertaking and their potential impact on the city.

SPECIALIZED SPORTS FACILITIES

The Olympics obviously require substantial investment in specialized sports facilities. Since the early 1970s, these facility expenditure requirements have increased as the number of new Olympic events has proliferated and many events have shifted from outdoor to indoor locations. A review of past Olympic experiences reveals an evolving strategy of managing the onerous task of constructing an abundance of world-class sporting facilities while maintaining a level of fiscal sanity. Munich (1972) and Montreal (1976) relied almost entirely on government subsidies to finance the construction of a majority of their sports facilities. To further compound problems, the Montreal organizers lacked firm, sustainable plans for utilizing these facilities post-Olympics. The associated expenses ushered the city into a post-Olympics economic hangover. As a result, when the IOC was seeking a host for the 1984 games, there were no initial takers.

The organizers of the 1984 Los Angeles games clearly learned from the lessons of Montreal and relied almost exclusively on existing facilities and private funding. More recently Seoul (1988), Barcelona (1992), and Sydney (2000) have adopted a hybrid strategy: constructing new, specialized facilities where necessary but using existing facilities wherever possible. As McKay and Plumb have noted, there is a movement toward more conservative budgeting by host cities: "Most recent host cities have learnt from the costly mistakes of earlier hosts and have sought to minimize investment in temporary facilities for the Games themselves while maximizing investment in long-term projects." We believe one of the fundamental challenges facing Beijing is leveraging existing facilities as much as possible and minimizing the construction of new specialized sports facilities. This strategy will enable the government to redeploy capital to the construction of general infrastructure, which will generate more long-term value for the overall Beijing economy.

In its action plan, the Beijing Olympic committee initially proposed thirty-seven facility sites for the 2008 games, which included ten existing facilities requiring no additional work, five existing facilities requiring refurbishment, and twenty-two entirely new facilities. The construction and refurbishment of these sports facilities is projected to cost US$1.65 billion, financed mainly with government subsidies. The Beijing budget for sports facilities is only 5 percent of the overall infrastructure budget—a small proportion when compared to other host cities. The Chinese government has invited foreign and domestic firms to bid and present plans for the construction of the new facilities, which include the 80,000-seat National Stadium and the Olympic Village. Although it is unclear whether a foreign firm will ultimately be chosen for these projects, the decision of the Beijing Olympic Committee to open the bidding to international firms is a departure from traditional host city policy (dependence on internal firms) and in keeping with its "opening up the economy" policy.

The stadium investment-related boom will result in many new temporary jobs, most of which are likely to go to unskilled laborers, typically from outside the Beijing region. Moreover, the investment in sports facilities often serves to boost the local economy with temporary jobs for related infrastructure that will be underutilized in the future. Although this short-term employment is certainly beneficial, it is important to view such job creation in the proper context.

Specialized facilities are rarely reused and are expensive to maintain or even tear down. For the 1998 Winter Olympics in Nagano, Japan spent US$19 billion indiscriminately and ultimately steered the city into a post-Olympics economic slump. Similarly, the 2002 World Cup host countries, Korea and Japan, spent US$3 billion constructing twenty new soccer stadiums that, in many cases, were located in cities with no professional franchise and thus no sustainable long-term use. "More attention needs to be paid as to whether there can be some ongoing return and community benefit from Olympic precincts and venues. If such facilities do not have significant post-Game use they can become 'white elephants' and be a long-term burden to taxpayers," warned Olympic scholar Richard Cashman.

The BOCOG recognizes this concern and notes that "full consideration has been given to the post-Olympic use of the sites in the process of determining their location, in their design and in their construction so that they will become an Olympic legacy which Beijing residents can utilize." A majority of the facilities will be concentrated within four areas of Beijing: Olympic Green, Western Community Area, North Scenic Area, and University Area. Although it is encouraging that a majority of these facilities will be fully integrated into the Beijing metropolitan area, it is more critical that Beijing organizers have a long-term "pay-back" plan for the facilities after the Olympic torch has been extinguished. These sports facilities have the potential to provide the citizens of Beijing with recreational venues for decades to come; however, building them is certainly not the most efficient use of public funds given the numerous other challenges the city faces. Zhou Wangcheng, the division chief of the Finance Department at the BOCOG, stated that plans to sell selected athletic venues to private investors before and after the Olympic Games are being considered. However, as yet, no potential buyer market had been targeted. Specialized sports facilities generate ongoing income only if they attract subsequent sporting events. It is critical that these sports facilities generate recurring income through either Chinese professional sport franchises or public recreational use. Alternatively, the BOCOG should develop a realistic "exit" strategy to offset the massive initial investment. Without a concrete post-Olympics plan for these facilities, the legacy of these stadiums will be that of white elephant projects rather than ones that truly contribute to the urban fabric of Beijing.

INFRASTRUCTURE DEVELOPMENT

The Olympics is arguably the premier sporting event in existence today, and the expectations for the host city of the Olympiad are high. When the world turns its attention to Beijing in 2008, it will expect to find not only first-rate sporting facilities but also a world-class city, complete with a fully functioning modern infrastructure that includes efficient transportation, modern utilities, and city-wide telecommunications services.

There has been a trend in recent Olympics to make significant investments in infrastructure projects of developing urban areas. To prepare for the 1992 Olympics, Barcelona invested US$8 billion in roads and transportation, housing, offices, commercial venues, telecommunications, hotels, sports facilities, and environmental infrastructure. Similarly, the planned investment for the 2004 Olympics in Athens is an impressive US$23.8 billion, including investments in road systems, rail transportation, and telecommunications.

Beijing is a developing urban area of one thousand square kilometers with a population of over twelve million. To ease pressure on transportation to central areas and the Olympic Green, city officials are intent on developing a fast, efficient, urban transit system. This system will be based upon new urban "fast roads" and arteries. The three-dimensional transportation system will include multilevel roadways with metro lines, flyovers, and pedestrian crossings that pass under or over the roads.

The current state of Beijing's transportation system, however, is a far cry from this vision. Traffic in the city is continually snarled, a problem compounded by a shortage of north-south roads and expressways, with only 216 kilometers of roads servicing the entire area. The bus system is extremely crowded and moves slowly due to the traffic congestion. Additionally, the fare structure for the bus system is very complex and lacks consistency throughout the city. The only potential escape from the traffic is the rail system, but it is currently very outdated and severely underdeveloped. The two rail lines—the Loop and the Metro—are over thirty years old and serve only 1.2 million passengers per day.

Beijing plans to spend US$11 billion on transportation lead-
ing up to the Olympic Games. The plan is impressively comprehensive, addressing road systems, bus systems, urban rail, and the
airport in significant detail. More importantly, the plan is highly
integrative, providing many transfer points between the different
modes of transportation. For instance, multimodal terminals will be
constructed to transfer between the bus lines and the Metro. We
highlight some of the planned developments in the following sections.

ROAD SYSTEM

The planned transportation infrastructure enhancements include
inner-city expressways, outlying expressways, the ring road system,
urban street networks, and the Intelligent Transportation System
(ITS). Possibly the greatest synergistic component of the transportation architecture is the ambitious plan to install the ITS. The
system will include passenger and incident monitoring for buses
and a tracking system backed by GPS (global positioning system)
for all buses and taxis that will provide real-time traffic management
and video communication. A dedicated geostationary minisatellite
will be linked to a transportation coordination center, where it will
be used for monitoring with the capability of transforming pictures
into virtual reality images. A successful integration of ITS into
Beijing's transportation network will mean improved response times
for emergency personnel and more efficient flow of traffic.

URBAN RAIL SYSTEM

The urban rail system will probably undergo the greatest expansion
of any of the city's transportation systems. The capacity of the rail
system is expected to jump from 1.2 to 5.6 million passengers per
day, a 460 percent increase, and the existing urban rail network will
be tripled. Two key components of the expansion are the
Dongzhimen line, which will connect downtown Beijing directly to
the Beijing Capital International Airport (BCIA), providing easy
access for business travelers and citizens alike, and the Olympic sub-

way. The Olympic subway will be 28 km long with twenty-four stations and will also be closely integrated with other transportation systems. Additionally, the Olympic subway will link ten busy sections of the city and have the capacity to bring 40,000 to 60,000 passengers per hour to the Olympic Green.

In the same spirit of efficiency as the ITS for the road system, five million smart cards will be issued over the next two to three years. Aided by an infrastructure of 100,000 validating, reloading, and issuing machines, smart cards will provide a large-scale, automatic fare collection system. By 2007, banking and other services will be combined with the cards to provide even more convenience.

AIR TRAVEL

The final element to Beijing's transportation plan is expanding capacity for air travel. Beijing Capital International Airport, one of three airports serving the city, is already the largest airport in China, serving thirty-five million passengers per year. For the Olympics, a third runway will be added along with an additional terminal and fifty-five standard gates. As a result, the airport's capacity will increase by 37 percent to forty-eight million passengers per year.

UTILITIES AND TELECOM

Along with an efficient transportation system, Beijing is also working toward an improved infrastructure for utilities and telecommunications. Nearly US$1.8 billion will be invested in modern utilities, primarily focused on increasing the supply of cleaner natural gas, a key element of Beijing's environmental clean-up plans. A second Shanxi-Beijing gas pipeline will be built to increase the supply of natural gas to Beijing by 200 to 300 percent. To facilitate consumption, numerous intracity pipelines and storage facilities will be built, at an estimated cost of US$800 million, in hopes of increasing natural gas usage by 400 to 500 percent by 2008.

On the communication front, the city's basic information technology and telecom infrastructures will be upgraded at a cost of

US$3.6 billion. These investments should provide a platform for widespread Internet use throughout the city.

LEGACY OF INFRASTRUCTURE DEVELOPMENT

Nearly all of Beijing's urban infrastructure projects are investments in durable assets that will last for years, if not decades, to come. A fast, urban public transportation system will facilitate the movement of people and goods in the local area. Additionally, all the transportation options will be designed as one integrated system that simplifies transfer between modes of travel. Finally, the system of expressways connecting all towns with populations of 50,000 or more to Beijing will expand domestic growth by encouraging the movement of goods and people in the entire region. However, any major city improvement must take into account the flexibility of long-term forecasts and the pace of technology development. These factors, coupled with the scale of the project, can greatly affect its success. The accelerated pace of work due to the coming Olympics makes it vital that the planned development is in keeping with Beijing's long-term needs.

ENVIRONMENTAL INITIATIVES

Early in the bidding process for the 2008 Olympics, Beijing's massive environmental problems attracted great criticism. Indeed, on many pollution-plagued days in Beijing, just walking around can be uncomfortable, let alone competing in an Olympic decathlon. Beijing wisely viewed this glaring weakness as an opportunity for improvement and committed to a radical environmental turnaround project, boldly promising the city would have cleaner air than Paris (a competing bid city) by 2008. The International Olympic Committee—which added "environment" to "sport" and "culture" as the third principle of the Olympic movement in 1994—was clearly impressed and gave Beijing its blessing to become the second "Green Games," following the success of Sydney in 2000.

THE FIRST GREEN GAMES IN SYDNEY

Much like Beijing, Sydney made environmental protection one of the cornerstones of its Olympic bid, and its promises in this area were far more ambitious than in any previous Olympic Games. The Sydney Olympic Committee worked closely with Greenpeace and other organizations to incorporate environmental protection into all stages of the planning and development of its Olympic site. Their goal was not only to minimize the impact of the games themselves, but more importantly, to establish a precedent for future development.

Although Sydney proved unable to deliver on all of its promises, it did achieve a number of significant environmental successes:

- An Olympic Village that has since been transformed into the world's largest solar-powered settlement, with 665 homes now owned by the public
- A main Olympic stadium and several other major venues that are also solar powered (and provide excess energy to the rest of the city)
- A car-free environment for the seventeen days of Olympics, with virtually all spectators using public transportation to attend events, dramatically influencing transportation and development patterns post-Olympics in Sydney

THE CHALLENGE AT HAND: ENVIRONMENTAL PROBLEMS AND ECONOMIC COSTS

A visit to Beijing makes it quite apparent that the city has a long way to go in combating its air pollution problems. Recent measurements peg total suspended particles (TSPs), the primary culprit responsible for the thick smog that frequently blankets the city, at two to five times World Health Organization (WHO) standards. Likewise, sulfur dioxide levels exceed China's national standards by 100 percent; nitrogen oxide levels are well over 200 percent of the limit. Astoundingly, these measures actually represent a significant improvement relative to the worst conditions experienced in 1998. Thanks to aggressive environmental efforts in recent years (Beijing's environmental expenditure in 1999 was 4.5 times the national average), sulfur dioxide levels have dropped by 47 percent.

The true measure and extent of these problems, however, is not to be found in these percentages but in their effect on people and the economy. On the economic side, a World Bank study of China estimated that pollution-related illness resulted in a remarkable *4.5 million person-years* of lost labor productivity in 1995 alone. Even more troubling, chronic obstructive pulmonary disease (highly correlated with air particulate levels) is the leading cause of death in China, with a rate of death twice the average for other developing countries and more than five times greater than most developed countries. The American Chemical Society estimated that more than one million deaths a year (one-eighth of total deaths) were attributable to air pollution between 1990 and 1995.

Although quantifying these impacts on health and human life is a challenging and controversial enterprise, several studies estimate the total financial costs of pollution alone at between 2.1 percent to 4.5 percent of China's gross domestic product (GDP). Factor in the estimated financial costs resulting from overall damage to the ecology and the total impact rises from 7.5 percent to 18 percent of China's GDP. Thus, although China is enjoying remarkable economic growth, these numbers suggest that the country is paying a high price for its success.

GREENING BEIJING: WHAT IS BEING DONE

The results of these studies have not been lost on the Chinese government, and numerous efforts have been undertaken to improve environmental conditions in Beijing and China at large even before the Olympic bid was secured. However, most agree that winning the Olympic Games has prompted Beijing to redouble its efforts. According to Robert Walker, managing director for Jones Lang LaSalle in Beijing, "The Olympic Games have been an important stimulus to Beijing's measures to improve the environment in the city."

In terms of financial commitment, the government spent just over US$500 million a year on environmental measures from 1996 to 1998. During the preparation period leading up to the games (2001–2007), the city has budgeted over US$1.2 billion a year for environmental initiatives, an increase of 130 percent. This massive investment (US$8.6 billion in total) nearly matches the enormous budget allocated for transportation infrastructure (US$10.8 billion) and is over six times the size of the budget for developing sports-related venues (US$1.4 billion).

Clearly, one of Beijing's top priorities will continue to be bringing "blue skies" back to the city. To achieve the highly ambitious goal of reaching WHO guidelines for air quality during the Olympic period, Beijing officials realize they must do something to counteract the dramatic increase in private-vehicular transport. As a result of higher household incomes and falling tariffs on foreign autos, the number of vehicles in Beijing increased fourfold between 1986 and 1996, from a mere 260,000 to 1.1 million. The city is hoping the substantial expansion and improvement of the public transportation system will reverse, or at the very least slow, this trend. The city will also enact increasingly strong emissions standards and transform 6,000 public buses and 13,400 taxis to run on cleaner natural gas. The government is also adopting administrative measures to encourage the use of the dominant form of private transport, the ubiquitous bicycle.

Although these measures are expected to significantly lower nitrogen oxide levels, the sulfur dioxide problem will be addressed by taking on heavy industry and power generation, which are responsible for 72 percent of these emissions. Currently, there are 110 heavily polluting factories that ring the inner city. To minimize the negative effects of these factories, they will be moved to new locations outside the fourth ring road, effectively cutting the amount of "inner-city" land devoted to industry in half. Although these relocations will clearly improve conditions in downtown Beijing, it is not clear whether they are a viable long-term solution or a short-term workaround that simply hides the problem.

Unfortunately, smog is not Beijing's only problem—the city is also plagued by water issues, domestic and industrial waste problems, dust storms, and an overall highly fragile ecosystem. Major invest-ments are anticipated to radically expand and modernize Beijing's environmental infrastructure. Numerous water and sewage treat-ment plants will be built with the goal of treating 90 percent of all sewage in modern facilities, up from 42 percent in 2003. New waste treatment systems will enable 80 percent of all industrial solid waste to be reused or recycled and 100 percent of hazardous waste to be treated and safely disposed.

To combat the severe dust storms that blanket the city in 25,700 tons of choking dust every spring, the government will increase the forested area surrounding the central city by 50 percent with a 125-kilometer "tree belt." This city wall is just one compo-nent of the much larger "Green Great Wall" that is being initiated to forestall desertification throughout China. This proposed 2,800-mile network of forest belts is believed to be the largest ecological project in history, with a total cost of US$8 billion over nine years. Although Chinese officials claim this project will halt desertification in its tracks by 2010, many western scientists doubt this can be achieved.

Beijing is also committed to increasing urban green coverage up to 45 percent. A large part of that green development will come within the Olympic Park itself—40 to 50 percent of this newly developed area will be transformed into forested land. Robert Walker of JLL maintains that these new green spaces will "be a last-ing benefit to all residents" and will likely have a significant influ-ence on property values in adjacent areas.

THE LEGACY OF ENVIRONMENTAL ACTIONS

Although it remains to be seen whether Beijing can truly achieve each of these ambitious and far-reaching goals in such a limited time frame, most observers are convinced of Beijing's commitment and believe that the short-term improvements in air and water qual-ity and other measures will be substantial. Environmental improve-ments, including air quality, should lead to a reduction in health-associated costs and increases in overall productivity. Furthermore, some analysts maintain that improvements in the quality of life will encourage more companies to locate in Beijing. Andrew Ness contends in *The China Business Review* that if the changes make Beijing "a far more pleasant place to live and work," then domestic and overseas companies will "create strong and stable demand in the city's office sector."

One domestic sector that clearly will benefit tremendously from these projects and policies is the environmental protection industry, which many experts believe will become one of the major growth sectors in the coming years. As of 2000, more than ten thousand enterprises in China engaged in environmental protection, employing 1.8 million workers and generating an output value of US$13 billion. While this already represents dramatic growth—a six-fold increase in workers and a twenty-five-fold increase in output compared with 1990—experts believe that industry growth will be further accelerated by Beijing's Olympic-related initiatives. According to Xie Xuren, vice minister in charge of the State Economic and Trade Commission (SETC), the industry "will face unprecedented development opportunities and become a new growth point" of China's national economy. However, while some aspects of the sector are already at world-standard levels, most domestic firms lag significantly behind international standards in environmental technology. To maximize the long-term domestic growth benefits, experts concur that China must increase competitiveness in the environmental industry through research and development and capital investment.

In general, the environmental plan outlined seems to be focused on big-ticket, high-tech environmental projects as solutions to the problems rather than fostering long-term changes in attitudes and behavior. Although the current plan will likely generate visible and tangible successes, a long-term solution will necessitate contributions and commitment not only from the government, but from businesses and the public as well. As Xie Zhenhau, director of the State Environmental Protection Administration (SEPA) stated, "All society should be made aware that . . . environmental conservation will be a long and complicated task in China" and that US$8.6 billion and seven years of dedicated efforts will be only a first step in the right direction.

URBAN REGENERATION AND CULTURAL HERITAGE

Olympic host cities have used the games as a catalyst to revitalize run-down and neglected areas and make positive improvements in their real estate market through their location of Olympic parks. As Olympic scholar Holger Preuss observes, this pattern is not surprising given that these former industrial areas are frequently the only affordable land available in the vicinity of the city center. Sydney, for example, built its park in a once-neglected area in the middle-ring riverside wasteland. Prior to the Olympics, this area was home to brickworks and munitions dumps and included largely unusable swamp areas; as a result of the Olympic Games, the area was reborn. It is now one of the most accessible areas in Sydney and has become a thriving residential community. Similarly, Barcelona transformed its waterfront from a run-down area of industrial warehouses and a poorly maintained seaport into a prosperous trading port and a popular commercial district. Based on these and other successes, Preuss has asserted that "it is clear that the Olympics are used to solve urban problems" and that this represents an "essential portion" of the overall macroeconomic benefit of hosting the games.

Yet not all cities experience an immediate payoff from these efforts. Atlanta built Centennial Park in a classic inner-city environment with the hopes of sparking investment from businesses and boosting residential interest. Nearly seven years later, they are just starting to see interest in residential loft apartments in the area, and certain businesses are beginning to see the benefits of being located around the park. "If this trend can be leveraged, the full benefit of the Games may be realized more than five years after the flame was extinguished in Atlanta," stated McKay.

All three of these host cities attempted to improve communities and build new districts out of dire urban areas. While the location of Beijing's Olympic park does not follow that exact prescription, it is in an area Beijing is trying to transform into a new residential and business district. The current plan is to open up the northern part of the city and create a north-south axis to complement the east-west axis that currently exists. This 12-square-kilometer park is expected to be not only a tremendous centerpiece for the Olympic Games and for visitors from around the world but also the foundation stone for a new business and residential district for Beijing. Its development will be dependent on many infrastructure initiatives, such as subway accessibility and the construction of the fifth and sixth ring roads.

POTENTIAL CHANGES IN THE REAL ESTATE MARKET

The improvements in infrastructure and the urban regeneration the host city makes in preparation for the Olympic Games have the potential to significantly alter the real estate market. For instance, Barcelona saw a huge effect on residential markets, with values increasing between nearly 300 percent over the time period 1986–1993. Beijing expects a similar impact on its real estate markets. Current predictions are for another six to seven years of double-digit GDP growth directly related to Olympic urban investment. The real estate markets in the northern district of Beijing, the Chaoyang district, are already starting to experience the effect of the games. Real estate investors are making decisions based on the opening up of the northern portion of Beijing, and many developers have begun to focus on attracting high-end investors, trying to capitalize on the anticipated prestige of the location.

Although the Olympic-related impact for the residential real estate market is typically limited to the medium- to high-quality housing built for the athletes, Beijing predicts that between 10 and 12 million square meters per year of housing completions will occur between 2002 and 2008, the equivalent of 670,000 units. Whether this predicted expansion coincides with the city's plans to remove slum and substandard housing is unclear. Beijing demolished approximately 5 million square meters of substandard housing between 1990 and 2000. The government wants to demolish an additional 9.34 million square meters of older, inner-city housing out of a total of 28 million square meters. This plan has two potential pitfalls. First, it may displace many people unless a clear relocation plan is in place. Second, it runs the danger of inadvertently destroying much of the history, culture, and charm of old Beijing.

Given that Beijing will be developing a new area of the city and expanding the infrastructure to adequately service this area, it seems likely this new business district will experience substantial growth in the office real estate market. Past trends suggest that the Olympic Games have the greatest impact on cities that have relatively small and less mature office real estate markets, such as Barcelona. For cities like Atlanta and Sydney that are already well established, the effects have proven to be "relatively modest." According to Walker, the real estate markets in Beijing "probably stand to benefit more than any other host city in the last twenty years."

CULTURAL HERITAGE

One of the main concerns with awarding Beijing the 2008 games was the human rights issues China has faced in the past. The Olympics will provide a world stage for China to show the strides it has made and will be an ideal opportunity for China to place its culture and heritage on display for the world. Although there has been much fanfare about the 2008 Olympics being the "Green Games" or the "High-Tech Games," the primary focus will be what the BOCOG is calling the People's Olympics, highlighting the history and culture of China. According to the BOCOG, there will be more local residents involved in planning, creating, and implementing these games than in any previous Olympics. As part of the process, the government has set up programs at a local university to educate citizens about the Olympics. The games are being viewed as an opportunity to promote the traditional Chinese culture, to create an awareness of the country's history and the development of Beijing, and to showcase the friendliness and hospitality of its citizens.

The primary Olympic scholar in Beijing, Professor Hai Ren, has stated that the people of Beijing are "very positive" about the games and enthusiastic about the opportunity for the nation to "show itself to the world." Ren also views the Olympics as a golden opportunity for "ordinary people—athletes, coaches, and tourists—to experience and understand China" and argues that getting ordinary citizens involved and providing opportunities for them to interact with visitors are critical to the success of the "People's Olympics" effort.

Preserving and displaying the history of China is also a priority for the BOCOG. Back in the 1950s, the government decided it would be too costly and unmanageable to maintain Beijing's historic center, so that much of the area is becoming neglected and dilapidated. But as the city continues to expand and modernize, city leaders have recognized that these older Beijing neighborhoods bring to life a very important element of the history and culture that is not captured by the city's more famous ancient monuments. With this in mind, the Beijing Municipal Construction Commission issued two regulations in 1999 identifying areas of historic preservation. These areas consisted of approximately 5.6 square kilometers of ancient streets, courtyards, cultural centers, and more. The plan intended to restore these sites gradually back to their original conditions and potentially convert the most attractive ones into public museums. This plan was implemented shortly after the Olympic bid was won, when it was given an accelerated timeline and a substantial restoration budget of US$208 million. Once again, the Olympic Games provided the necessary impetus for an initiative that might have taken much longer to implement, or perhaps not have been implemented at all.

In addition to the plan just described, the government has already spent almost US$40 million during 2000–2003 for the protection and renovation of over one hundred historical and cultural sites. The Forbidden City is also due to receive a face-lift at a cost of almost US$85 million, marking the greatest investment in this cultural landmark since 1911. Finally, plans are in place to expand such city treasures as the National Library, the Gallery of Fine Arts, and the Capital Museum. Beijing is apparently doing everything in its power to display its history and culture while also modernizing and building the infrastructure necessary to host the Olympic Games.

The Legacy of Urban Regeneration and Cultural Heritage

Beijing faces real opportunities for urban regeneration and the preservation and promotion of its cultural heritage. The Olympic park will be a part of the creation of a new business center for Beijing. This initiative, in conjunction with its effects on the residential and office real estate markets, could potentially have a significant impact on the domestic growth of Beijing. It will primarily help move some people out of the crowded city into the suburbs, but it will also attract new businesses and expansion from local companies. Real estate alone, if it follows a similar absorption rate to the other ring roads, will create an abundance of new opportunities. The present absorption rates for apartments are 95 percent within the third ring road, 80 percent between the third and fourth ring roads, and 60 percent along the satellite areas around Beijing's urban fringe. Absorption rates for the north and northwest of the city, where the majority of the Olympic construction is occurring, are expected to rise even higher as the city completes transportation accessibility to this area. The upside is tremendous with the new ring roads and absorption rates predicted to be close to capacity. The potential downside is a flood of new construction that fails to attract investors and eventually turns into a neglected region of the city. Another concern is the fate of the lower-income residents who risk being displaced by the urban revitalization and the demolition of many of the inner-city areas. This important issue needs to be addressed.

The initiatives currently in place for preserving and promoting the city's cultural heritage could lead to gains in tourism and greater national pride in the city. Modernization is a key aspect of a host city for the Olympic Games, but for a city like Beijing, the preservation of the past and the emphasis on culture will play a large role in the legacy effects the city sees after the games are gone.

Hotels and Tourism

Historically, the hotel industry has been one of the first sectors in a developing host country to benefit from the Olympics. Jones Lang

LaSalle examined hotel expansion in the last four Olympic host cities and identified a two-fold increase of hotel room supply in Barcelona and an average boost of 35 percent in the other three cities. All four host cities recorded a sharp uptick in the average daily occupancy rate during the entire Olympic year, averaging 22.6 percent. The BOCOG estimates that the current supply of 85,000 hotel rooms in Beijing will balloon to 130,000 by 2008, resulting in a compound annual growth rate of 6.3 percent. The committee also predicts that Beijing's current selection of top-tier hotels will increase from two hundred to three hundred hotels.

Despite these bullish growth projections, some industry insiders caution against irrational hotel development in response to Olympic fever. Richard Hartman, managing director for Six Continents Hotels, the largest international hotel chain in China, contends that Beijing already has sufficient hotel capacity to handle the 2008 Olympic crush. He warns, "Olympic cities have a track record of having to cope with massive oversupply after the event. We could go back even further to see the almost irrational frenzy to add inventory which takes years to recover." Raffles International's chairman and chief executive officer Richard Helfer echoed Hartman's concerns: "China grew about 7 percent last year, and the Olympics are going to give it that extra impetus. In Beijing, that typically means overbuilding, with a bit of a trough after the event—as shown in many previous Olympics."

Others claim that this growth is warranted but do not believe it is directly a product of the pending Olympics. Instead, they attribute the hotel market expansion to China's recent entry into the WTO, its economic growth in the face of global financial woes, and the appeal of its huge potential market. They argue that each of these factors establish the Chinese hotel market as one of the most attractive regions in the world for developers. "For a city's tourism and convention industries, the long-term payback of the Olympics is potentially profound," noted McKay.

For instance, the Sydney 2000 Olympics has been recognized as the most effective marketing campaign in Australian history, with an estimated US$2 billion of global publicity generated for Sydney and Australia over the last four years. The number of out-of-city visitors to Sydney set an Olympic host city record, and international visits actually increased in the seven months following the Olympic Games, defying previous trends. Barcelona demonstrated a similar ability to leverage its international visibility with foreign tourists. As a result of the urban transformation and publicity from the Olympics, it was catapulted from being the sixteenth-most-popular destination in Europe pre-Olympics to the third by 1999. In the long term, the benefits reaped by these cities' tourist sectors may be one of the Olympics' most important legacies.

The Olympics will serve as a strong impetus for Beijing's burgeoning convention market. Following Sydney's Olympic bid victory announcement, Sydney's convention market increased 34 percent. Sydney, Atlanta, and Barcelona also recorded a significant boost in convention delegates in the year after the Olympics. In fact, Barcelona achieved a 21 percent compound annual growth rate in international convention delegates between 1992 and 1997.

The 2008 Olympics will provide a boost to the local Beijing economy through additional tourism, including ticket and souvenir sales. Although the Beijing games will attract throngs of tourists, the true impact of these tourists must be accurately assessed, taking into account displacement and substitution effects. For instance, Klaus Heinemann argues that many potential tourists will choose not to visit a host city during the Olympic Games to avoid crowds, noise, and increased security risks. Additionally, local citizens often leave the city to escape these inconveniences associated with the games. Finally, an analysis of the net expenditures of Olympic tourists typically reinforces the notion that visitors spend money at sporting events at the expense of other local activities, resulting simply in a redistribution of revenues rather than a true net increase in local economic activity. Thus, the net increase in foreign tourists is of paramount importance to the economic impact.

Another concern is that increased construction by hotel developers will skew short-term hotel room inventory. A more robust strategy for the industry is to focus on long-term, continuous growth. Otherwise, new hotel construction will come to a screeching halt after the Olympics until demand eventually catches up with supply.

Many opportunities exist for foreign firms to participate in advising, investing, or playing some other role in the approximately four hundred new hotel properties. "According to some analysts, it's the biggest potential hotel gold mine in world history," said Lo Young, regional director of marketing in north Asia for Six Continents. Despite this strong investor interest, however, few transactions have occurred, due to a lack of market transparency, strict tenure laws, and concern regarding the ability to repatriate earnings out of China. Foreign investors are also wary of the potential room oversupply dilemma and the impact this supply glut would have on capital values in the medium term.

CONCLUSION

China's vision of the twenty-ninth Olympiad as having an important impact on the city as well as on the country is clearly reflected in the magnitude of its investments. Urban infrastructure, urban regeneration, and the environment have been given the lion's share of the US$34 billion Olympic budget, and of the five legacy categories, these have the highest impact. In comparison, the impact of sports-related facilities and hotels and tourism on the Beijing economy is likely to be limited, as Montreal and other host cities have had the misfortune to learn.

China went to great lengths to secure the bid for the 2008 Olympics, and from all accounts, the country is putting forth extraordinary effort to deliver on the promises made to the IOC and the world. Clearly, the research and planning put into the various aspects of creating an Olympic legacy have been extremely thorough. Because so few projects of this scale are ever pursued, it is nearly impossible to accurately estimate the eventual total cost. However, China must keep tight control of budgets so that future generations are not burdened with any unnecessary debt. A related area of concern is corruption. With a project this size, millions of dollars could easily slip through the cracks unless strict anticorruption measures are in place.

Many experts have questioned whether the initiatives Beijing has proposed for environmental cleanup are financially viable, long-term solutions. A few projects, such as the relocation of factories to areas further from central Beijing, seem particularly short-sighted. In light of Beijing's rapid expansion, this solution will presumably only delay the problem by a few years until these new locations are also densely populated. Many western scientists see this short-sightedness as a disturbing trend in many of China's recent environmental efforts, including the massive Great Green Wall. Dee Williams, from the U.S. Department of Interior, has argued that the country must move beyond micro-level tech fixes and embrace political solutions. Indeed, the Beijing government should look at longer-term measures like updating environmental regulations, changing business practices, and educating the public.

By educating and involving the public and engaging and working with the business community to determine innovative and cost-effective approaches, equitable and sustainable solutions can be achieved. An emphasis should be placed on using clean and renewable energy and recycling waste. Obviously, these approaches will take time to develop, and possibly none of them may truly be "accomplished" before the Olympics, hence resulting in no visible "victories" for the Beijing government. However, with all of the current enthusiasm and emphasis on improving the city, this is the ideal time to seize the momentum and start engaging the public and business communities in the "long and complicated" task of environmental conservation, a legacy that will benefit Beijing for years to come.

The BOCOG has placed significant emphasis on the People's Olympics, with the many benefits shared by all citizens; however, the social costs of preparations in many previous host cities have fallen disproportionately on lower income groups. With the current initiatives, there does not appear to be a definitive plan in place to deal with those displaced by scheduled inner-city demolition. Moreover, the modernization of the city and the growth in the real estate market will likely result in a significant increase in housing costs, making it even more difficult for these citizens to find suitable and affordable housing. The rights and interests of certain social groups should not be sacrificed under the banner of progress, and an action plan should be in place that will take care of the people being displaced.

The eyes of the world will fix on Beijing for eighteen days in July 2008. This is the opportunity for China to present Beijing as a "living postcard," to impress on the world the massive modernization the city has undertaken and the efficient orchestration of the BOCOG to coordinate a seamless execution of the games. For eighteen days in 2008, the whole world will be watching as China delivers on the dream.

BIBLIOGRAPHY

Asian Development Bank. 2000. "Urban Air Quality Management and Practice in Asian Cities." http://www.adb.org/Vehicle-Emissions/ASIA/docs/APMA/beijing.pdf.

Associated Press. 2001. Newswire. September 19.

Baade, Robert, and Victor Matheson. 2000. "Bidding for the Olympics: Fool's Gold?" In *Transatlantic Sport,* edited by Carlos Barros, Murad Ibrahim, and Stefan Szymanski. Cheltenham, U.K.: Edward Elgar Publishing.

The Beijing Organizing Committee for the Games of the XXIX Olympiad. 2001. "Beijing Olympic Action Plan." http://www.beijing-2008.0rg/new_olympic/eolympic/plan.htm.

Brunet, Ferran. 1995. "An Economic Analysis of the Barcelona '92 Olympic Games: Resources, Financing, and Impact." *The Keys of Success: The Social, Sporting, Economic, and Communications Impact of Barcelona '92,* edited by Miguel De Moragas Spa and Miguel Botella. Bellatera, Italy: Universitat Autonoma de Barcelona.

Cashman, Richard. 2003. "Impact of the Games on Olympic Host Cities." Centre d'Estudis Olimpics (Autonomous University of Barcelona).

Finer, Jonathan. 2002. "The Grand Illusion: 2002 World Cup." *Far East Eastern Economic Review,* 165 (9):32–36.

Green Games Watch. 2000. Website. http://www.nccnsw.org.au/member/ggw/.

Greenpeace Australia. 2003. Website. http://www.greenpeace.org.au.

Heinemann, Klaus. 2002. "The Olympic Games: Short-Term Economic Impacts or Long-Term Legacy." Paper Presented at the Symposium on the Legacy of the Olympic Games, Lausanne.

Hellenic Innovation Relay Centre. 2000. "Athens Olympics 2004: World Class Opportunities Worthy of the Great Event." http://www. hirc.gr/events/infra/Org_New percent20Infra percent20Brochure.pdf.

Jones Lang LaSalle. 2001. "Olympics Leave Lasting Legacies on Host Cities." July. http://www.joneslanglasalle.com.hk/Press/2001/070401.htm. Jones Lang LaSalle.

————. 2002. "Jones Lang LaSalle Hotels Turns the Spotlight on China." October. http:// www.joneslanglasallehotels.com/JLLH/JLH.nsf.

Lee, Soonhwan. 2001. "A Review of Economic Impact Studies on Sports Events." *The Sport Journal,* 4 (2).

McKay, Melinda, and Craig Plumb. 2001. *Reaching Beyond the Gold: The Impact of the Olympic Games on Real Estate Markets.* Chicago: Jones Lang LaSalle IP.

Ness, Andrew. 2002. "Blue Skies for the Beijing Olympics." *China Business Review,* 29 (2):48–54.

New South Wales Treasury. 1997. "The Economic Impact of the Sydney Olympic Games." http://www.treasury.nsw.gov.au/pubs/trp97_10/.

O'Grady, Mark. "China's Olympian Transportation Revolution." FTA International Mass Transportation Program. http://www.sites.usatrade. gov/imtp/2008%2001ympics1.doc.

Preuss, Holger. 2000. *Economies of the Olympic Games: Hosting the Games: 1972–2000.* Sydney, Australia: Walla Walla Press.

————. 2002. "Rarely Considered Economic Legacies of the Olympic Games." Paper presented at the Symposium on the Legacy of the Olympic Games.

Price Waterhouse Coopers. 2001. "Business and Economic Impacts of the 2000 Sydney Olympics." Department of State and Regional Development, Australia.

Ratliff, Evan. 2003. "The Green Wall of China." *Wired,* April. http:// www.wired.com/wired/archive/11.04/greenwall.html.

Shellum, Steve. 2002. "A Race of Olympic Proportions Is on as China's Hotel Industry Gets on the Fast Track." *Hotel Online,* April. http:// www.hotel-online.com/News/PR2002_2nd/Apr02_BeijingGold.html.

Stadia Arena InfraSport. "The Opportunity: Transport Infrastructure." Website. http://www.saibeijing.com/transport.html.

U.S. Embassy Beijing. 2000. "The Cost of Environmental Degradation in China." http://www.usembassy-china.org.cn/sandt/CostofPollution-web.html.

World Resources Institute. 1999. "China's Health and Environment: Air Pollution and Health Effects." http://www.wri.org/wr-98-99/prc2air. htm.

Chapter 11

CHINA COPING WITH SARS

Angela Y. Lee

The year 2003 will largely be remembered by the sudden emergence of Severe Acute Respiratory Syndrome (SARS), a potentially fatal viral respiratory disease characterized by pneumonia, high fever, headaches, body aches, diarrhea, or a dry cough. By the end of the summer, nearly 8,100 people throughout the world had fallen sick with the disease, including 774 who died. Although many countries experienced significant SARS outbreaks, China was the country most significantly affected by the disease. The first case of SARS was reported in China's Guangdong Province in February 2003 and quickly spread to Beijing, Guangdong, Hebei, Hong Kong, Inner Mongolia, Jilin, Jiangsu, Shanxi, Shaanxi, Taiwan, and Tianjin. SARS was responsible for 349 deaths on China's mainland and sickened more than 5,000. In Hong Kong alone, over 1,400 people were infected and 298 people died.

To combat the spread of the disease worldwide, the World Health Organization (WHO) issued its first travel advisory against nonessential travels to areas affected by SARS on April 2, 2003. Predictably, the areas first listed on the travel advisory were in China, including the Hong Kong Special Administrative Region of China and the Guangdong Province, followed shortly thereafter by Beijing and Shanxi Province, then Inner Mongolia, Taipei, and Tianjin. Not until June 24 was the travel advisory against Beijing—the last Chinese area that remained on the list—removed.

SARS dealt a heavy blow to China's service sector, especially to tourism and travel-related industries. Many companies suffered huge losses and some were forced out of business because of SARS. However, China's economy as a whole seemed to have weathered the crisis quite well. In fact, the country may even have emerged from the crisis strengthened by the lessons learned.

THE IMPACT OF SARS ON THE CHINESE ECONOMY

The negative effect of SARS was most severe in the airline industry. According to the International Air Transport Association (IATA), out of the US$6.5 billion lost in the global airline industry, US$4 billion of the losses could be directly attributable to SARS, with about half of those losses borne by airlines based in the Asian-Pacific region. Two major Asian airlines, Singapore Airlines and Cathay Pacific Airways, each reported losses well over US$150 million. Extensive losses were due not only to travelers who canceled their travel plans to affected areas, but also to those who avoided travel altogether for fear of catching the virus from fellow travelers who might have come from affected areas.

Once Beijing was taken off the travel advisory list in June, airplane seats began slowly to fill once more. In October, both Singapore Airlines and Cathay Pacific Airways reported that they were back to pre-SARS levels. Based on the airlines' month-to-month improvements, IATA predicted that things would return to normal by the end of 2003, if there were no further outbreaks of SARS.

Despite the fairly quick rebound of the airline industry, SARS dealt a more serious, lingering blow to China's overall service sector, particularly the tourism industry. For instance, holiday celebrations in China typically bring in nearly US$4 billion from tourism. However, the May celebrations were significantly toned down by the Chinese government, who reduced the week-long holiday by two working days to discourage people from traveling and potentially spreading the deadly virus to nonaffected areas. Many tourist attractions and related businesses, such as shops, restaurants, and parks, were closed for a prolonged period.

Predictably, the cancelled public events and overall lack of travel significantly affected hotels in the country. Beijing's five-star hotels reported occupancy rates as low as 1.6 percent during the month of May, when occupancy rates typically range from 70 to 80 percent. In fact, many hotels in Shanghai and Beijing decided to suspend business altogether. China's largest hotel management company, Jin Jiang International Management Corporation, for instance, started to "renovate facilities" in fourteen of its seventeen hotels in Shanghai, including the Peace Hotel. The situation for the smaller hotels was even worse.

Retail sales also dropped dramatically during the second quarter in affected areas, particularly in Hong Kong. Many consumer products companies, including McDonald's, Eastman Kodak, Estée Lauder, Tsingtao beer, Carlsberg, and Canon, reported lower sales as consumer confidence fell. Consumers cut back on spending even as businesses cut prices in the hope of attracting buyers.

Although SARS significantly damaged tourism-related industries, the overall Chinese economy remained strong despite the outbreak, with some sectors even showing healthy growth trends. Compared to the previous year, gross domestic product (GDP) went up 9.9 percent in the first quarter of 2003, although growth slowed down in the second quarter because of SARS, resulting in an 8.2 percent increase for the first half of the year. Manufacturing output grew by 16.2 percent in the first half of 2003, while industrial output experienced a 4.5 percent increase, making it the fastest growth period since 1994.

The computer and technology sectors were relatively unaffected by the outbreak of SARS; computer production rose by 46.6 percent during the first half of 2003 compared to the same period in 2002. Other sectors within the technology industry, such as electronics and information technology, also experienced a 27 percent growth. China's booming hardware sector, which makes up about 20 percent of the world's supply of technology hardware, also seems to have triggered an increase in demand for China's software. Investor confidence remained strong as SARS seemed to have little impact on overall foreign direct investment (FDI). Although FDI did fall by 8.8 percent in June and 37 percent in July relative to the same periods in 2002 because of foreign investors' reluctance to visit China, FDI inflow began to rise again when no new SARS cases were reported. By November 2003, actual utilization of FDI reached nearly US$48 billion—about the same level as 2002.

HOW BUSINESSES RESPONDED TO SARS

China's economy remained strong despite the SARS outbreak largely because most companies employed strategies to effectively deal with the crisis. According to a survey conducted by Mercer Human Resource Consulting of over 260 companies operating in areas affected by SARS, only 4 percent of businesses in Hong Kong, Singapore, and China did not take action to combat SARS. Over half of the companies provided their employees with masks, and 42 percent encouraged their employees to work at home. Travel was restricted by 79 percent of the companies, and 43 percent of them made quarantine compulsory for those staff at risk for SARS.

The Mercer report identified four stages of response to SARS. Sixty-nine percent of companies surveyed in China and 84 percent of companies in Hong Kong reportedly took first-stage actions, which aimed at reducing the exposure of staff to infection by providing comprehensive information on SARS through briefings and bulletin postings. These companies also restricted travel, cancelled meetings, distributed face masks, and increased the frequency of cleaning of office premises. Companies in the second stage of emergency response initiated actions to limit interaction between staff through voluntary or compulsory quarantine or working at home. Employees were encouraged to work flexible hours, and social events were reduced or cancelled. These actions were adopted by 26 percent of companies in China and 53 percent of companies in Hong Kong. The third stage of response, taken by 28 percent of the companies in China, included the provision of special or enforced leave for those at risk. Motorola, for instance, temporarily closed its headquarters in Beijing, asking one thousand employees to work from home after one employee was diagnosed with the disease. Finally, a handful of companies took large-scale action to minimize exposure by freezing recruitment, reducing work hours, and redesigning work flows and practices to adjust to the new situation. Of the companies surveyed, only 5 percent of the companies in Hong Kong and 1 percent of those in China found it necessary to resort to these measures.

As the SARS crisis subsided, companies quickly resumed their pre-SARS level of activities but with a heightened level of awareness and a new set of standard procedures. In the event of another possible attack of SARS, companies are seeking consultations with crisis management professionals, practicing evacuations, and preparing health kits. Motorola, for instance, now provides traveling businessmen with SARS kits completely equipped with masks and thermometers. Cathay Pacific Airways, one of the airlines most affected by SARS, now tracks and disseminates health reports on SARS to all employees. Many companies also have complete contingency plans in place. By anticipating which production line to cut and where to find alternative sources of production, companies are much better prepared to act if a supplier were quarantined due to SARS.

THE GOVERNMENT'S RESPONSE TO SARS

Whether the Chinese government underestimated the unknown coronavirus's lethal potency or it was following its typically conservative policy about sharing information, no information about the presence of SARS in China was announced until April, when the disease had already spread to many parts of the world. Even though the outbreak was devastating Hong Kong's economy, the Chinese government continued to downplay the severity of the threat and stated that SARS was limited to a few cases on the mainland and was under control. Amidst mounting concerns and criticisms at home and abroad, officials in Beijing finally admitted in mid-April that the outbreak was much more severe than they had previously claimed and was still not under control. China's health minister and the mayor of Beijing were removed from key Communist Party posts for the way they mishandled the situation, and the national government acknowledged the need to cooperate with the WHO to track and report the spread of the deadly virus. Meanwhile, SARS continued to spread, with the worse cases reported in Hong Kong, Taiwan, Singapore, and Toronto, Canada. A summary of SARS cases can be seen in Table 11.1.

After the initial missteps, the government announced tough measures to combat the disease: Schools in Beijing were closed, uni-

Table 11.1
Summary of Probable SARS Cases between November 1, 2002, and July 31, 2003

Areas	Female	Male	Total	Median Age (Range)	Number of Deaths	Fatality Ratio (percent)
Australia	4	2	6	15 (1–45)	0	0%
Canada	151	100	251	49 (1–98)	43	17%
China	2674	2607	5327	Pending	349	7%
China, Hong Kong SAR	977	778	1755	40 (0–100)	299	17%
China, Macao SAR	0	1	1	28	0	0%
China, Taiwan	218	128	346	42 (0–93)	37	11%
France	1	6	7	49 (26–56)	1	14%
Germany	4	5	9	44 (4–73)	0	0%
India	0	3	3	25 (25–30)	0	0%
Indonesia	0	2	2	56 (47–65)	0	0%
Italy	1	3	4	30.5 (25–54)	0	0%
Kuwait	1	0	1	50	0	0%
Malaysia	1	4	5	30 (26–84)	2	40%
Mongolia	8	1	9	32 (17–63)	0	0%
New Zealand	1	0	1	67	0	0%
Philippines	8	6	14	41 (29–73)	2	14%
Republic of Ireland	0	1	1	56	0	0%
Republic of Korea	0	3	3	40 (20–80)	0	0%
Romania	0	1	1	52	0	0%
Russian Federation	0	1	1	25	0	0%
Singapore	161	77	238	35 (1–90)	33	14%
South Africa	0	1	1	62	1	100%
Spain	0	1	1	33	0	0%
Sweden	3	2	5	43 (33–55)	0	0%
Switzerland	0	1	1	35	0	0%
Thailand	5	4	9	42 (2–79)	2	22%
United Kingdom	2	2	4	59 (28–74)	0	0%
United States	14	15	29	33 (0–83)	0	0%
Vietnam	39	24	63	43 (20–76)	5	8%
Total			8098		774	9.6%

Source: Data from World Health Organization. (http://www.who.int/csr/sars/country/table2003_09_23/en/).

versity classes were suspended, hospitals were quarantined, and people suspected to be at risk were isolated. All shows, exhibitions, and entertainment activities in public places in areas seriously hit by the SARS epidemic were cancelled. The week-long Labor Day holiday was called off to discourage mass travel. Procedures for the prevention and control of SARS were established and implemented on planes, trains, buses, and ships, and roadblocks were put on city limits to prevent the spread of SARS to other parts of the country.

The government also took steps to improve patient care. In highly affected areas, the number of hospitals accepting SARS patients was increased, treatment areas were expanded, and national twenty-four-hour hotlines were established so people could call for updated information on SARS. Additionally, a national task force, the SARS Control and Prevention Headquarters of the State Council, with a budget of RMB 2 billion (US$243 million) was created to combat SARS. About RMB 20 million would be spent on funding scientific research, but the bulk of the money would go toward treatment of farmers and poor urban residents infected with SARS, toward upgrading county-level hospitals, and toward purchasing SARS-related medical facilities in central and western China. Another RMB 3.5 billion (US$421.7 million) was set aside to establish a nationwide public health network for public health emergencies. Special SARS supervision teams that included medical experts were dispatched to affected areas to monitor and help local governments and hospitals in the tracking and treating of SARS patients. These measures helped the Chinese government regain the confidence of its citizens and the global community.

To alleviate economic damage, a tax relief rescue package was announced by the Ministry of Finance to abolish or reduce many taxes and fees for hotels, airlines, travel agencies, and several other hard-hit members of the service sector. Although the relief might be too late for companies that were already out of business or on the verge of failing, the program was welcomed by many businesses. For airlines, the tax break meant savings of about 3 percent of revenue, and a waiver of the civil aviation construction fees as part of the package translated to further savings of 5 percent of the airlines' domestic revenue and 2 percent of international revenue. The government also worked with airlines and hotels to introduce discounts and vacation packages to attract visitors. All these efforts proved effective. By late September, for instance, most five-star hotels in Hong Kong, such as the Ritz-Carlton and the Island Shangri-La, were reporting an occupancy rate of 80 percent or more.

CONCLUSION

By the time the travel advisory against Beijing was removed on June 24, 2003, more than 8,000 people had been infected with the SARS virus, over 700 people had died, thousands of businesses had closed, and countless jobs had been lost. Still, despite these consequences, the outbreak had a silver lining. To many observers, SARS helped bring countries together—it was through the cooperative efforts of many nations that the outbreak was brought under control.

SARS also hastened reforms in China by inducing the government to a degree of openness toward both its own people and the global community. Before SARS, there was a strong disparity between China's impressive economic development and the openness of the government. The initial mishandling of the SARS situation by government officials was indicative of this lack of transparency. Within the year, however, secrecy in policy was reduced, cooperation with world organizations was enhanced, and progressive reforms in the public health sector were implemented.

Some are skeptical about the change, arguing that the primary motivation was not social reform but economics. Others criticized the policy shift, arguing that the stability of the government rather than the safety and welfare of the people drove the reforms. These criticisms notwithstanding, SARS highlighted the significance and urgency of China's health system reform and brought about much-needed changes in the public health system, especially in the rural areas. With a system in place to combat SARS and additional funding allocated to support and improve the system, the Chinese people can look forward to better health care across the country.

Businesses in China will also benefit from the openness of the government under the new leadership. Although China's service sector was hurt badly, its financial and industrial sectors continue to thrive, and businesses in all sectors can anticipate a political climate and a government bureaucracy that endorse a higher degree of transparency. Although some of these changes may have been the result of China's gradual adoption of a market economy or of its WTO accession, SARS no doubt played an important role as a catalyst.

BIBLIOGRAPHY

"Business China." 2003. *Economist Intelligence Unit,* 29 (21).

"Business: New Routes to the Beach; Travel and Tourism." 2003. *The Economist,* 358 (8335):64.

"Business: Spreading Their Wings; Chinese Firms Abroad." 2003. *The Economist,* 368 (8340):71.

"Cathay to Restore All Flights Halted by SARS Outbreak." 2003. *The Wall Street Journal,* August 28.

"China, US Butt Heads over Taiwan at WHO." 2003. *Asia Times,* May 21.

Connolly, James. 2003. "SARS: A Wake-up Call for Business?" *Financial Executive,* 18 (7):18.

Cosgrove, Julia. 2003. "Asia's Great Bargains." *Business Week,* September 22.

Dean, Jason. 2002. "Taiwan Plays Down Leader's Rhetoric on China—Business Fears Chen Speech Will Raise Political Tension with the Mainland Regime." *The Wall Street Journal,* August 6.

DeLisle, Jacques. 2003. "SARS, Greater China, and the Pathologies of Globalization and Transition." *Science Direct-Orbis,* August 27.

Dolven, Ben. 2003. "China: Bouncing Back from the Brink." *Far Eastern Economic Review,* 166 (34):48.

Estulin, Chaim. 2003. "Alive and Kicking." *Time,* 162 (12):A25.

Garrett, Laurie. 2003. "SARS Forces Change in China: Illness Could Hasten Reforms." *Newsday,* May 18.

"Hong Kong Economy: On the Rebound." 2003. *Economist Intelligence Unit: Business Asia,* September 8.

Hunter, David. 2003. "China: Plenty of Change." *Chemical Week,* 165 (30):5.

Hutzler, Charles. 2003. "Hu Wrestles with Political-Economic Mismatch: China's Transformation of Markets and Society Feeds Democratic Desires." *The Wall Street Journal,* October 20.

McKay, Betsy. 2003. "Leading the News: U.S. Weighs Quarantines for SARS: If Deadly Illness Returns, CDC Wants Tough Steps; Legal Barriers May Arise." *The Wall Street Journal,* October 20.

Neuman, Scott. 2003. "Asian Airlines Rebound from SARS." *The Wall Street Journal,* October 10.

————. 2003. "The Economy: Passenger Traffic on Global Airlines Improved in June." *The Wall Street Journal,* August 5.

"The Political Scene: China Will Not Let Taiwan into the WHO." 2003. *Economist Intelligence Unit Country Report: China,* June 1.

"A Positive SARS Side-Effect." 2003. *Asia Times,* May 27.

Ramstad, Evan. 2003. "Computex, after Postponement Due to SARS, Is Set to Open Today." *Wall Street Journal,* September 22.

Robertson, Jack. 2003. "SARS Has No Effect on Growth of China's PC Market." *EBN,* September 1, 6.

"SARS: The Global Spread Continues." 2003. *Asia Times,* April 1.

Shari, Michael, Frederik Balfour, Bruce Einhorn, and John Carey. 2003. "SARS: The Sequel? Across Asia, Governments and Companies Are Getting Ready." *Business Week,* October 27, 24.

"Taiwan Ponders Suspending Links with China." 2003. *Asia Times,* May 17.

"Travel Brief: EVA Airways." 2003. *The Wall Street Journal,* September 2.

The US-China Business Council. 2003. "Out of Nowhere." The US-China Business Council.

Young, Ian. 2003. "The Long March Continues SARS Dents Growth, but the Outlook Is Healthy." *Chemical Week,* 165 (30):21.

————. 2003. "Sinopec's Chemicals Swing to Profit, Despite Effect of SARS." *Chemical Week,* 165 (30):17.

INDEX

ABOUT THE EDITORS

Anuradha Dayal-Gulati is a clinical associate professor at the Kellogg School of Management and is an affiliate of the Center for International Business and Markets. Prior to joining Kellogg in 2001, she spent seven years at the International Monetary Fund in Washington, D.C. She has published research on policy issues in China and Southeast Asia. She holds a Ph.D. in economics from Brown University, a master's in philosophy in economics and politics from the University of Cambridge, England, and a bachelor's in economics from St. Stephen's College, Delhi University, India.

Angela Y. Lee joined the Kellogg School of Management faculty in 1995 and is currently an associate professor of marketing at the school. Professor Lee's research interests include consumer learning, the effects of advertising on judgment and brand choice, and cross-cultural similarities and differences in information processing. She holds a Ph.D. in marketing from the University of Toronto, a master's in philosophy in economics from the University of Hong Kong, and a B.B.A. in marketing and travel industry management from the University of Hawaii at Manoa.